PRAISE FOR KEN JENNINGS AND
100 PLACES TO SEE AFTER YOU DIE

"Ken Jennings knows about everything. That now includes the afterlife."
—NPR

"Jennings conveys substantial amounts of information in his usual witty style, including lots of facts and zero proselytizing. . . . A lot of fun for trivia buffs and other curious souls."
—*Booklist*

"Jennings's breezy approach and exhaustive knowledge allow him to range from *Twin Peaks* to Dante's *Divine Comedy* with ease, and even casual readers who dip in intermittently will be enlightened. Anyone curious about the great beyond should take a look."
—*Publishers Weekly*, starred review

"Light and irreverent . . . long on knowledge and mercifully short on claims about the grand truth of things."
—*The Washington Post*

"Ken is brilliant and incisive and the kind of guy with so many smarts that it makes you go, 'Man, that guy's really smart.'"
—Michael Ian Black

"Jennings is a very witty, insightful writer."
—Pauline Frommer, travel writer and founding editor of Frommers.com

ALSO BY KEN JENNINGS

Planet Funny: How Comedy Ruined Everything

*Because I Said So!: The Truth Behind the Myths, Tales,
and Warnings Every Generation Passes Down to Its Kids*

Maphead: Charting the Wide, Weird World of Geography Wonks

Ken Jennings's Trivia Almanac: 8,888 Questions in 365 Days

*Brainiac: Adventures in the Curious, Competitive,
Compulsive World of Trivia Buffs*

100 PLACES TO SEE AFTER YOU DIE

A Travel Guide to the Afterlife

KEN JENNINGS

SCRIBNER

New York   London   Toronto   Sydney   New Delhi

Scribner
An Imprint of Simon & Schuster, LLC
1230 Avenue of the Americas
New York, NY 10020

First Scribner trade paperback edition June 2024

SCRIBNER and design are registered trademarks of Simon & Schuster, LLC.

Simon & Schuster: Celebrating 100 Years of Publishing in 2024

For information about special discounts for bulk purchases, please contact Simon & Schuster Special Sales at 1-866-506-1949 or business@simonandschuster.com.

The Simon & Schuster Speakers Bureau can bring authors to your live event. For more information or to book an event, contact the Simon & Schuster Speakers Bureau at 1-866-248-3049 or visit our website at www.simonspeakers.com.

Interior design by Carly Loman

Manufactured in the United States of America

10   9   8   7   6   5   4   3   2   1

Library of Congress Cataloging-in-Publication Data

Names: Jennings, Ken, 1974– author.
Title: 100 places to see after you die : a travel guide to the afterlife / Ken Jennings.
Other titles: One hundred places to see after you die
Description: New York : Scribner, 2023. | Includes index.
Identifiers: LCCN 2022037903 (print) | LCCN 2022037904 (ebook) | ISBN 9781501131585 (hardcover) | ISBN 9781501131615 (ebook)
Subjects: LCSH: Future life in popular culture.
Classification: LCC BL535 .J45 2023 (print) | LCC BL535 (ebook) | DDC 202/.3—dc23/eng20221209
LC record available at https://lccn.loc.gov/2022037903
LC ebook record available at https://lccn.loc.gov/2022037904

ISBN 978-1-5011-3158-5
ISBN 978-1-5011-3159-2 (pbk)
ISBN 978-1-5011-3161-5 (ebook)

Interior images by Adobe Stock.

CONTENTS

INTRODUCTION

When Shakespeare called the afterlife "the undiscovered country, from whose bourn no traveller returns," he was echoing a tradition as old as recorded human history. Death, our stories have always said, isn't a condition. It's a place, a journey.

For the ancients, this was a very literal kind of travel. People from Persia to Ireland to Polynesia speculated on which specific caves or islands in their landscapes might be entrances to the underworld. The Egyptians and Aztecs died with itineraries in mind, maps and guides to help navigate a confusing and high-stakes tour through the world to come. In the Middle Ages, visionaries and poets produced elaborate travelogues of heavens and hells and purgatories. Dante was the "world-building" champ of his day, the medieval equivalent of a George Lucas or George R. R. Martin, and centuries of readers pored over his careful geographies in the same way a modern audience might wander imaginary places like Hogwarts or Hyrule.

Of course, it takes a certain kind of fundamentalism to read Dante's detailed travel notes about a nine-level pit and literally expect to spend eternity there. We live in a time of unprecedented religious skepticism, but the afterlife is as lively a topic as ever—now with new options that Dante never considered, thanks to the West's comparatively recent discovery of reincarnation, astral planes, and ghost hunter reality shows. A 2016 study of religious participation and belief found that, even though the number of Americans who believe in God, pray, or attend religious services has declined steeply since the 1970s, the number of us who believe in the afterlife has actually *risen* slightly over the same time span. Even many die-hard rationalists, it seems, are reluctant to imagine that death is a final ending. All that time and complexity and experience—for nothing? It would seem such a cosmic waste.

When you look at afterlife journeys from stories told over the millennia, from ancient Sumer all the way up to *The Good Place*, the same routes and themes recur over and over. Ghosts are in at least their fifth century of moping around their old houses, moving objects by focusing *very hard* on them, and not even always knowing that they're dead. "Psychopomps," immortal guides, still appear after death to lead the soul away from mortal life. Heavens, whether Miltonian, Hindu, or Capra-esque, are still heavy on music and clouds and wings. Hell hasn't changed much between ancient China or Mesoamerica and *South Park*: still the same turnabout-is-fair-play "ironic" punishments, the same jaw-droppingly long torture sessions, even the same gross bodily fluids. Dim underworlds still lie across rivers. (This trope probably arose from simple geology. Early humans knew that wells were deeper than graves, so buried souls would have to cross a layer of water as they headed downward.)

But afterlife destinations have changed over time in smaller ways, revealing the preoccupations of the living. In early civilization, life was so punishingly hard that paradise was generally just an *absence*: a place without disease, without winter, without crop failures. Later, as we could imagine a more luxurious life, new abundances appeared, feasts and harems and precious gems. The twentieth century saw a rise in benign but bureaucratic heavens that mirrored our efficient new age: lots of sterile waiting rooms, lots of fussy angels with clipboards. More recently, we've downgraded heaven further to fit into our new gig economies (*Dead Like Me*, *Miracle Workers*) or worries about technology (*Black Mirror*, *Upload*).

In this book, you'll get the inside travel scoop on one hundred afterlife destinations, organized alphabetically within seven main categories— a chapter apiece for mythical afterlives, scriptural afterlives, movie afterlives, and so forth. There are even afterlife possibilities gleaned from paintings, video games, Sunday newspaper comics, superhero universes, and theme park rides. They range from the famous to the infamous, the well known to the off the beaten path. Browse them in any order you like, pausing on familiar destinations you'd like to learn more about or adding intriguing new ones to your post–bucket list.

As Hamlet pointed out, no one's ever come back from any of these places, but despite that, I've tried my best to sketch in their regional highlights and most notable attractions. And like any good travel writer, I try to give something more elusive as well: the overall impression of a place, the vibe. A smaller number of prominent afterlives get longer entries, with more detailed information on dining and accommodation and day trips.

There's no way to know for sure where you're going when you die—and it might, of course, be nowhere. But this book isn't just for armchair adventurers. Why not start assembling your own afterlife travel checklist now? If the gloomy Hel of the Vikings appeals to your inner goth, you'll need to start offering sacrifices to the old Norse gods and avoiding—at all costs!—a brave death in battle. If the blissful Pure Land of East Asian Buddhism is more your speed, start chanting the name of Amitabha Buddha to yourself every day, because you'll never understand the dharma without him.

It's never too early to investigate your options and start making travel plans. Eternity is an awfully long time to end up in the wrong place, and you never know when your departure is going to be. So turn the page and begin to discover the "undiscovered country" for yourself. These are trips that billions of people are dying to take!

MYTHOLOGY

ADLIVUN AND QUDLIVUN

The Inuit

Even by the icy standards of the Arctic, the Inuit peoples of Alaska, Canada, and Greenland invented a remarkably chilling vision of the underworld. Your most likely destination on this itinerary is a disturbing house straight out of a modern microbudget horror movie—but at least you'll only have to spend a year there.

According to the Inuit, all living creatures have a soul called a *tarniq*. Your *tarniq* is a tiny version of yourself that lives in an air bubble in your groin, and it floats free at the moment of your death. Have you committed any misdeeds or violence in your life? If so, the news isn't good. You're heading to Adlivun, a land below the sea.

Adlivun is a dark, grim underworld of never-ending storms. When you arrive, follow the trail of clothing you see on the ice, which was discarded by victims of drowning. It will lead you to the door of the Sea Woman. She has many names—Takannaaluk, Nerrivik, Idliragijenget—but most know her as Sedna.

MEET THE LOCALS

In the Inuit creation myth, Sedna was a giant who gave her father no end of grief. She refused to marry and ran off with a hunter who turned out to be a seabird spirit in disguise. Sedna's father later pierced out one of her eyes, threw her overboard in a storm, and chopped off her fingers when she tried to clutch the side of his kayak. Her finger bones sank into the ocean, where they became the first seals, walruses, and whales. Sedna soon followed them into the depths, becoming a goddess of the sea and all its creatures.

Sedna's dwelling, the House of the Wind, might appear to you as a simple igloo or as a grand mansion of stone and whale ribs. Take care as you enter, because Sedna's dog will be stretched across the southern threshold, gnawing on some suspicious-looking bones.

Once inside the dark house, you'll hear the terrible sighing and groaning of the dead, muffled as if by water, as well as the blowing and splashing of sea creatures. On the far side of the room, Sedna will be seated on a bed with her back to a stone lamp. She keeps the souls of sea creatures in the lamp's drip bowl, giving them new life in new bodies. (The exceptions are sharks, which she keeps in her chamber pot. This is why shark meat has that urinelike ammonia taste, in case you ever wondered.)

Sedna's face, with its single pale eye, is covered in filthy, tangled hair. She is almost suffocating on the foul smoke rising upward, clouds of sins from the agonies of the dead. Just as you get your head around this horrifying scene, you'll feel something on your ankle, cold and cracked like a caribou antler. The chill hand of death has reached out from under a bearskin and caught you in its clawlike grip. This is Sedna's father, whom she brought down to Adlivun with her. He's also missing an eye and some fingers, the result of Sedna's ancient revenge. He lies across the room from her, frozen and almost motionless under dirty old skins, waiting to pull you under his blankets and torment you for a year as you lie by his side, suffering for all your sins.

After your time with the creepy bearskin dad is over, you might be reincarnated as one of Sedna's sea creatures, but most of the dead are released to the Qimiujarmiut, the "people of the narrow land" in the midst of a subterranean sea. There you can live and hunt abundant game in the Land of the Dead forever.

A small group of people avoid the terrors of Adlivun altogether. If you lived a virtuous life, or died by violence (including at your own hand, which could explain why suicide wasn't historically uncommon in some Inuit cultures), you can follow the rainbow upward toward the dawn to Qudlivun, the land of the moon spirit.

The moon spirit was once Igaluk, a blind boy who was given supernatural "second sight" by a loon who lured him out to sea in a kayak. After he and his sister Malina ascended to heaven, they chased each other across the sky as the sun and moon. The moon at night is Igaluk crossing the heavens on his dog sledge, over the ice of the sky and the snowdrifts of the clouds. He's a mighty hunter and kindly protector of his vaulted heavenly realm, which revolves around the mountains of the north.

Qudlivun is an outdoor paradise second to none. There the "people of day" live in a land where there's never ice or snow, and they can hunt all the deer they like. You will laugh in the never-ending warmth, playing games with a walrus head for a ball. Your athletic prowess will be appreciated back on earth as well, because immortals kicking around a walrus head in the sky is actually what produces the Northern Lights. Who knew?

DIYU

China

To the Chinese, we currently live in the "yang world," but that's only half the story. Our ancestors have gone on to the "yin world," a realm of spirits who spend their days much as we do, with all the daily pleasures and headaches—right down to the endless layers of bureaucratic red tape.

In the hot pot of Confucianism, Taoism, and Buddhism that forms Chinese religion, heaven is Tian, the supreme power that keeps the cosmos running. As an afterlife destination, it lies beyond the hazy Kunlun Mountains of the far west. You need to climb Cool Wind Mountain, which will confer immortality, then scale another peak twice as tall: Hanging Garden Mountain. This feat will grant you the power to control the weather. You can then tackle another mountain that is *again* twice as tall, which will elevate you to heaven.

The nine gates of heaven are a sight not to be missed. Each is a set of two great pillars with a phoenix resting on each, sometimes flanked by auspicious animals like dragons and tigers. The music of bells is always in the air, and the gods dwell within, as well as the sun and moon. (Look for an enormous mulberry tree. That's where nine of the ten solar orbs rest while the on-duty one is taking its turn crossing the sky.) A Master of Cloud will guide you through the Bright Walls to the Palace of Mystery, where the Thearch on High reigns, just as the emperor does on earth below.

But most souls aren't ready for Tian on their current spin through the wheel of reincarnation. You're much more likely to be headed to the underworld of Diyu: the Dark City, the Yellow Springs. This is a purgatorial world of ten tribunals, each the jurisdiction of a legendary judge-king. You'll see that each level of this hell is more like a county courthouse or DMV than a Dantean inferno: each lord rules not from a throne but from a desk strewn with scrolls and paperwork, surrounded by a complex apparatus of clerks and bureaucrats with titles like "minister of grave mounds" or "warden of gates" or "assistant magistrate of the underworld." (Assistant *to* the magistrate of the underworld?) See, these afterlife myths developed during the Qin dynasty, at the same time China was building out its own massive civil service. Back then, the dead would often be buried with documents addressed to afterlife registrars, certifying their possessions, legal status, tax exemptions, and so forth. Make sure your paperwork is up to date before your departure date arrives!

The ten courts of Diyu form a great ring on the underside of the world. As you advance counterclockwise through its procedures, beginning in the south, each honorable king and his courtiers will painstakingly pore through records of your life, noting all your misdeeds and even wrong thoughts. In the first court, gaze into the Mirror of Karma for a complete rundown of your Confucian virtues, or lack thereof. Then in the following courts, ghoulish bureaucrats like Horse-Face and Ox-Head will administer punishments to expiate all of your sins in turn. Each court is divided into sixteen wards, and each ward includes punishments for eight different sins, so many of the offenses addressed here are charmingly specific: people who complained about the weather, people who threw broken pottery shards over the fence (Han dynasty litterbugs!), people who borrowed books and didn't return them.

The accounting may be thorough, but the penalties are brutal. You might be sawed in half, drowned in a pool of blood, pounded to meat jelly in a giant mortar, boiled in hot oil. The lustful are placed next to a superheated brass pillar, which they will repeatedly throw their arms around, mistaking it for their beloved. Arsonists are fed through a rice-husking machine, and committers of infanticide get iron snakes slithering in and out of their eyes and ears and mouth.

But the most diabolical torture of all is a simple tower called the Terrace for Viewing One's Own Village. Climb up and take a clear-eyed look at your earthly hometown. Surprise! You've been completely forgotten!

Nobody is praying for you, your last wishes have been disregarded, your partner has remarried, and your heirs are squandering your hard-earned possessions.

After a few years of purgatory, the Wheel of Fate in the tenth court will take you to reincarnation in one of six realms. But if you want to spend a few decades relaxing here in the yin world first, that's fine. Now you're one of the venerated ancestors, free to bling yourself out via the prayers and offerings of the living. If they burn some little yellow circles of cardboard, for example, you'll receive a corresponding number of gold coins in the afterlife. If they burn paper dolls for you, you get servants. The same goes for magazine clippings of a fancy house or a flat-screen TV.

WHEN TO GO

The full moon of the seventh month each year is the Ghost Festival, when the gates of Diyu open and you can wander the living world unseen. The living will lay out incense and fresh fruit for you, and the front row will be left open at public performances if you want to enjoy some Chinese opera or burlesque. Two weeks later, look for a trail of lotus-shaped lanterns and follow them back to the underworld.

When you're tired of ghost life and ready for reincarnation, head for Grandma Meng's bridge and have the old crone pour you a cup of her famous tea of forgetfulness. Then wade across Wangchuan, the river of oblivion, as memories of your past life slip away. The only way to retain any of your old self is to carve a message to yourself in the Rock of Three Lives, which sits midway across the river. This rock can hold information about your current life, your past one, and your next one. If you don't use it, you'll have to start completely from scratch on your next pass through the yang world.

> Let there be prepared for me a seat in the boat of
> the Sun on the day whereon the god saileth.
>
> —*The Book of the Dead*

DUAT

Ancient Egypt

Thanks to the artifacts left behind from their elaborate rituals, we know more about how the ancient Egyptians died than how they lived. Five thousand years ago, embalmers would spend *months* preparing each corpse for its journey to the next world. Their preparations ranged from the brutal (like jabbing a metal hook up the deceased's nostrils to puree and then drain their brain) to the sublime (postmortem manicures and nose jobs). All bodily organs except the heart were removed and placed in ceremonial jars.

Mummification was a big deal in Egypt because it was believed that death split the soul up into five components, like Voltron. There was your *ka* (life force), *ba* (personality), *ib* (heart), *ren* (name), and *sheut* (shadow). The tomb represented a nexus between this world and the next, and the *ka* and *ba* would be left homeless if there were no body there to return to. Only a good, decent person could pass the final trial of their heart and have their *ka* and *ba* reunited as an immortal spirit called the *akh*.

Duat, the underworld, was full of obstacles, which could only be navigated successfully with the protective spells found in the Egyptians' famous *Book of the Dead*. Those obstacles comprise a full Indiana Jones temple of doom: there's a lake of fire, crocodiles, bugs, decay, torture chambers, and even booby traps like decapitation blades and a giant net strung between heaven and earth. The spells are like video game cheat codes, instructing the dead on what to do when faced with the dangers of Duat.

For the adventurous traveler, the iron walls and turquoise trees of Duat make for an afterlife unlike any other. Just don't forget to study your scroll of magic spells.

TRAVEL TRIVIA

Of the 189 spells in *The Book of the Dead*, the very last one protects travelers from a seemingly unlikely misfortune in the world to come: having to eat and drink their own poop and pee.

TOP ATTRACTIONS

THE MYSTERIOUS PORTALS OF THE HOUSE OF OSIRIS—A ring of twenty-one gates surrounds Osiris, the god of the underworld, along with a series of mounds and caverns. Each portal, mound, or cave is guarded by an animal-headed god squatting before you holding enormous knives. You'll only be allowed to pass if you can name the god and his gate. Try not to worry that most of the guardians have ominous names like He Who Lives on Snakes, He Who Dances in Blood, and He Who Hacks Up the Dead.

THE HALL OF THE TWO TRUTHS—A can't-miss. Get an early start, because you'll want to arrive washed, anointed in myrrh, and wearing fresh clothes and white sandals. Final judgment in Duat takes place in this long, columned chamber, where Osiris and the other Egyptian gods sit enthroned under a canopy. Make sure you've studied up on the cryptic answers to their questions. For example, if they ask "Where have you passed?," they're not just making small talk. You need to have a very specific answer ready: "I have gone past the place to the north of the thicket." The ibis-headed figure you see will be Thoth, the god of science and magic. He'll watch carefully as Anubis, the jackal-headed judge of the dead, weighs your heart against an ostrich feather, a symbol of order and morality. (The Egyptians believed the heart was the seat of consciousness and memory, while the brain was only good for secreting mucus.) If the scales balance exactly, you'll walk through the gate flanked by two giant statues of Ma'at, the goddess of balance, and Osiris will welcome you into the afterlife.

MEET THE LOCALS

The forty-two judges who assess you in the Hall of the Two Truths represent the forty-two nomes, or territories, of ancient Egypt. So no matter what part of Egypt you're from, you'll see a friendly face from your hometown!

THE SUN BARQUE OF RA—Every day, the god Ra travels across the sky in his gleaming solar boat. But at night, when the sun sinks beneath the horizon, he enters the underworld and spends the night in endless battle with the serpent Apep. As a denizen of Duat, you'll get the chance to hop aboard and help Ra navigate one of his nightly duels!

DAY TRIPS

COMING FORTH BY DAY—Even after death, your *ba*, or personality, is allowed to leave the rest of the soul and wander back on earth. Different spells will allow it to take different forms: a falcon, a snake, a lotus flower, or even a god. Splurge on a sarcophagus shaped like a house or palace, so your *ba* has someplace to stay. A ceremonial "false door" on your coffin will let your *ba* get out and stretch its legs. (Unless it's a snake at the time.)

WHERE TO STAY

AARU, THE FIELD OF REEDS—If your heart gets the okay from Anubis, you move on to Aaru, located in the east where the sun rises. Aaru is a

Nile-like delta of waterways that flow past abundant crops. The barley grows five cubits high here, and hunting and fishing are plentiful. The Field of Reeds has all the comforts of home: good food, good harvests, good sex. Live here with the gods in happiness and peace.

THE DEVOURER OF THE WEST—If, on the other hand, you are judged unworthy of Aaru, your soul will be delivered to Ammit the Devourer, a fearsome creature with the head of a crocodile, the body and claws of a lion, and the hind parts of a hippopotamus. Ammit feeds on souls, and those whom she slaughters die a (permanent) second death. Not recommended.

GETTING AROUND

Navigators through Duat should make sure they know the names of the four rudders of heaven: there's Good Power in the northern sky, Wanderer in the west, Shining One in the east, and Preeminent in the south. And catching a ferryboat here isn't as simple as buying a ticket. You'll have to know the names of the oars ("the fingers of Horus"), the hull beam ("she who presides over gardens"), the wind, the riverbank, and so on. Then they'll know you're a powerful magician and take you where you want to go.

EATING AND DRINKING

THE CELESTIAL HERD—If you know the names of the seven cows of the celestial bull, they'll provide daily portions of bread and beer.

THE SYCAMORE FIG—The sky goddess Nut dwells in a sycamore fig tree, which was often depicted in Egyptian tombs as a source of food and drink for the wandering spirit.

THE HERON OF PLENTY—Perched on his pyramid, this god guards heaps of grain that feed the spirits in Aaru.

IN-ROOM DINING—You may want to do as the pharaohs did and arrange to be buried with an afterlifetime supply of mummified eats. King Tut, for example, packed along forty boxes of jerky, which archaeologists say still looks edible today.

WHAT TO PACK

Good news: you *can* take it with you. Egyptian VIPs were buried with all kinds of crazy stuff, from chariots to toilets to mummified pets. Little figurines called *ushabti* can serve as your laborers in Aaru if you feel like kicking back. In fact, the lazier Egyptians even packed along 365 of them, so they'd never have to work a single day of the year. Some kings didn't mess around with *ushabti*—they just ordered their household servants killed and buried with them! It's so hard to find good help these days.

THE GHOST ROAD

Native Americans

The popular notion of Native American belief in a "happy hunting ground" afterlife is, like a lot of nominally "Indian" lore, largely an invention of European settlers. As far as we know, no Indigenous person ever used the phrase "happy hunting ground" before James Fenimore Cooper had his Mohican character Chingachgook speak it in his 1823 novel *The Pioneers*. Soon it caught on with other white chroniclers of the frontier, from Washington Irving to Mark Twain.

There are hundreds of different Native peoples with hundreds of different afterlife traditions, and many have told stories about a resting place of peace and abundance. But from the woodlands of the Northeast to the Great Plains to the Southwestern desert, the most common element in Native American belief about the next world is the road one takes to get there: the largest object in the heavens, the Milky Way.

Today, the hazy band in the plane of our spiral galaxy can be easy to miss at night, but in a time of outdoor living, celestial navigation, and darker skies, the Milky Way was something to behold. On a moonless night away from urban glow, the Milky Way is an eye-popping phosphorescent river, bright enough to cast faint shadows. Whether they called it the Hanging Road, the Wolf Trail, or the Bridge of Souls, dozens of Native cultures agreed that this was the path to the spirit world.

Death is a one-way trail, so the Cheyenne, among other tribes, advise that the newly deceased first examine the ground at their feet. Look for a path where all the footprints face the same direction. It'll lead you to the great Road of the Departed in the sky. The Shoshone had a shortcut: they would simply rise through the air and land on the heavenly road.

There have been many different traditions to explain why this "ghost pathway of departed warriors" should glow so brightly. The Pawnee called the light "buffalo dust" from an ancient race between a buffalo and a ghost horse, while the Shoshone saw snow shaken off by the great grizzly bear that first marked this path to the Land of Souls. The Seneca believed the countless points of light were the footprints of the dead; the Sioux described them as campfires along the route. To the Cherokee, they were grains of cornmeal dropped by a thieving dog spirit as it made its getaway.

Perhaps you'll learn the truth as you walk across the sky, arcing upward and south from the northeast horizon. The Apache traditionally described this as a four-day march. You'll be able to see the true character of the stars as you pass: Cygnus is a great eagle or turkey vulture; Canopus is the god of tornadoes whose wind drives you along the trail; Orion is a great severed hand with an eye in the center of its palm, through which the road will pass like a tunnel. Don't worry if your faithful hunting dog isn't with you on this path. The Huron said there was a separate canine route through the heavens, the Way of the Dogs.

> **TRAVELER BEWARE!**
> There's a dark patch in the Milky Way that astronomers call "the Great Rift," a thick cloud of stellar dust. Up close, you'll see it as a deep, swift river. The Ojibway warn you to be careful of the big tree stump bridging the gap: it's actually a serpent! Leap over the head and continue on your way, because the other path peters out shortly ahead, consigning you to reincarnation or oblivion.

Many Indigenous cultures have no tradition of judgment in the afterlife at all. It stands to reason that the spirits didn't reward or punish everyone perfectly in this life, so why should they start now? The Lakota, however, warn that you'll have to face an old crone called Hihankara, the Owl Maker, to reach your reward. She'll examine your wrist, forehead, and chin for the correct tattoos, and push you off the trail if you're missing them. Only travelers with the right markings will make it to their final destination.

And what is that destination? The Shoshone imagined the Milky Way ending at a lake with a conical rock in the middle, and a passage on that island leading to a beautiful world of grass and flowers. It's a camp not unlike those of the living, but here all your ancestors await you. There's no disease or death in the Land of Many Lodges, game is plentiful, and the storehouses are full of corn, beans, and squash. But that still doesn't mean it's the "happy hunting ground"!

> Beach your vessel hard by the Ocean's churning shore
> and make your own way down to the moldering House of Death.
>
> —*Homer*

HADES

Ancient Greece

The Greek god of death was named Hades, meaning "the unseen one." It's true that death comes upon us unawares, and the Greeks chalked this up to magical headwear. Hades, they said, possesses a cap that renders him invisible by surrounding him in the "awful gloom of night." It's appropriate that Hades's name was later applied to his whole underworld realm. It is, for the most part, an awful and gloomy place.

Virgil described Hades as a bodiless realm of empty dwellings, all dim and colorless, the way a forest might look on a faintly moonlit night. The inhabitants here are insubstantial shades, a largely unhappy lot who still bear the marks of their deaths. Three great earthly kings—Minos, his brother Rhadamanthus, and the just Aeacus—lay down the law here, assembling juries by lot and judging each silent shade in turn, sending them either to punishment in Tartarus or relative ease in Elysium.

You will approach Hades through the dismal plains of Erebus, where Persephone's groves of poplar and willow grow. She is the queen of the dead, the white-armed fertility goddess famously abducted by Hades when his golden chariot emerged from a fissure in the ground one day while she was picking crocus and hyacinth flowers. Now she spends four months every year in Hades while crops wither and die above, all because she ate a few subterranean pomegranate seeds.

Follow the dark, roaring Cocytus river to where it flows into the muddy Acheron. Here you'll find the gates of hell surrounded by terrible creatures, personifications of grief, sorrow, sickness, age, fear, hunger, want, death, suffering, and sleep. Violent War is there as well, and mad Discord with bloody ribbons holding back her serpent hair. Wander over to the nearby stables to visit the shades of slain beasts: centaurs, Gorgons, Harpies, and even big-name creatures like the fire-breathing Chimera and the three-bodied giant Geryon. A dark and ancient elm tree by the gate holds empty dreams under every leaf, to underscore the bleakness of your future once you walk inside.

TOP ATTRACTIONS

CERBERUS—The iconic mascot of the Greek underworld is a savage three-headed hound, each of his necks bristling with snakes. Mythology is full of stories of Cerberus getting his butt handed to him: lulled to sleep by Orpheus, distracted by Psyche, wrestled by Heracles, drugged by Aeneas. But remember: those were all living souls venturing into Hades. For you, the dead, he will be a meek little puppy dog as you *enter* hell but will pursue you relentlessly and not hesitate to devour you should you ever try to *exit*. Get your cuddles in the first time you pass Cerberus, because hopefully you'll never meet him again.

TARTARUS—When the Greek gods rose to power, Zeus cast their predecessors, the Titans, down into the earth's deepest pit, surrounded by Poseidon's bronze fence and a triple barrier of gloomy night. Today, this abyss is where evil souls go after death, twice as far under the ground as Mount Olympus is high. The entrance to Tartarus is a cliffside fortress of adamantine pillars surrounded by the Phlegethon, a raging river of fire and boulders. Tisiphone and the other Furies keep watch in blood-soaked cloaks from an iron tower. Linger on the riverbank—maybe you'll get lucky and the gates will open. Then you'll hear moans and lashes and clanking chains, and maybe even glimpse a five-headed Hydra, the Furies flailing the damned with serpents, or Rhadamanthus extracting confessions. That's as close to Tartarus as you're going to want to get.

TITYUS—The Tartarus tourist trail centers around longtime fixtures like Sisyphus, always pushing his boulder not quite up to the crest of a hill, and Ixion, bound to his famous fiery wheel. But the real eye-popping attraction here is Tityus, a giant who was cast down for trying to rape the mother of Apollo and Artemis. His shade in the underworld is the same size as his earthly body, so it covers *nine acres* of ground. Chained to the rock, he futilely tries to fight off the pair of vultures chewing on his liver.

OTHER MUST-DOS

THE BUTT OF THESEUS—The heroes Theseus and Pirithous once came up with a harebrained scheme to infiltrate Hades and kidnap (again!) poor Persephone. Presumably they'd been drinking. But when they stopped on a stone bench in the underworld to rest, the stone fused to their skin, trapping them there. Years later, when Heracles was in Hades to steal Cerberus, he came upon the pair and successfully pulled Theseus up—but left his buttocks behind on the seat, where you can still see them today, stuck fast next to the shade of Pirithous. For the rest of his life, the hero was known as Theseus Hypolispos, meaning Theseus Smooth-Butt.

FIELDS OF MOURNING—The most romantic spot in Hades, home to the shades of all those who died for love. These mopey souls wander and wail and hide in myrtle thickets, just like they probably did during their emo lives.

ASPHODEL MEADOWS—Despite the fields of asphodel here—a flower the Greeks associated with death because it grew on tombs—this is, like most of Hades, a dreary and chilly dominion. But it's worth a stop for the celeb-spotting. Odysseus saw his Trojan War compatriots Achilles and Ajax in the meadow, and the legendary Orion is known to walk here as well, hunting phantom beasts with his mighty bronze club.

WHERE TO STAY

THE ELYSIAN FIELDS—Try to reserve a spot here in the Blessed Groves of Elysium, at the far end of the world. This is where virtuous souls go to live the good nonlife: There's never rain or snow in these rolling meadows, and an invigorating west wind sings softly from the sea. Great warriors take off their armor, graze their horses, and, except for the occasional tournament or wrestling match on the greensward, just chill. Poets and priests sing in the scented laurel groves by the stream Eridanus. Just as Tartarus cleanses life's stains from evil souls, so the good are purified here. But after a thousand years, you may find you miss the sky. (Elysium has its own sun and stars, but they're not the same.) Walk down through the valley to the banks of the river Lethe, and let its waters wash your memory clean so you can return to a new life in the world above.

ISLES OF THE BLESSED—If you return to the underworld three times with a pure soul, you are judged worthy of even ritzier accommodations: the Fortunate Isles in the west, a perfect paradise beneath the tower of Cronus. Flowers of gold blaze there, both in the waves and in the boughs of the trees on shore. You can spend your days weaving them into garlands and wreaths, if that's what you're into.

GETTING AROUND

The river Styx, so sacred to the Greeks that the gods themselves would swear oaths on its name, winds in nine coils around Hades's kingdom. The only way across is by grabbing a bench on the patched-up vessel of Charon, ferryman of the dead. Charon is a cranky old man with a bristly white beard, flaming eyes, and grubby robes. Thousands of would-be passengers mill about for centuries on the riverbank, but only those who have received an honorable burial are eligible to board. If a coin was placed in your mouth after death, make Charon take it out of your mouth himself.

> **TRAVELER BEWARE!**
> On the ferry, you might be tempted to help out the rotting corpses who reach up to you out of the marshes, or the old women on the other side who claim they need help with their loom. Resist the temptation. These are traps!

EATING AND DRINKING

TANTALUS'S POOL—The most famous meal in Hades is one that never begins. Tantalus cooked up his own son Pelops to serve to the gods at a banquet, and as punishment he stands forever in a lake in Tartarus with the water up to his chin. He's parched with thirst, but if he leans forward to drink, the water recedes to dry ground. The branches above him are full of pears, pomegranates, apples, figs, and juicy olives, but the wind pushes them up out of reach when he grabs for them.

> **TRAVEL TRIVIA**
> Tantalus's mythological torment is where we get our modern English word "tantalize."

THE FEAST OF THE FURIES—At this royal banquet in Tartarus, an elaborate feast is spread on a huge table, and diners recline on golden-legged couches. Unfortunately, yes, this one is a con as well. If you even reach for a salad fork, the leader of the Furies will rise from her seat, waving a torch and shrieking at you.

HEL

The Norse

Thanks to Marvel movies, the History channel, and some of the weirder kinds of heavy metal, Norse mythology is hotter right now than it's been in almost a thousand years. And Viking warriors always had a pretty appealing afterlife, as you'll see when we tour Valhalla on page 35.

But the vast majority of mortals do not die a valiant death. By the numbers, your odds of getting past the velvet rope at a fancy spot like Valhalla or Folkvangr are slim. Most of the Norse dead wind up underground in Hel, beneath the roots of Yggdrasil, the world-tree. Odin gave this part of Niflheim, an icy realm of mists, to Loki's daughter Hel. This is where the unrighteous go, and the truly wicked will experience *another* death there, dropping them farther to an even darker hell below.

There are many roads that lead to Hel's dominion. One path is nine days' ride through valleys so deep that you'll be in utter darkness. You may have to brave the fangs of Garm, the baying hellhound chained at the entrance of the Gnipa cave, or you may cross sunny fields where hemlocks grow. (It's summer in Hel while it's winter above, and vice versa.) The underworld river Gjoll has weapons swirling in the eddies and rapids of its blue-black waters, and two armies fight nearby in everlasting combat. Cross the shining gold bridge and then ride north to the immense gates of Hel, set into high walls.

Hel is the grim, cruel mistress of the hall of Eljudnir (meaning "damp with sleet," a weird thing to brag about). She rides a pale three-legged horse and her visage is half black, half white—but if you look in a mirror, you'll see that you don't have much of a rosy glow down here either. Her dish is Hungr ("hunger"), her knife is Sultr ("famine"), her bed is called Kor ("sickbed") and its curtains are Blikjandabol ("gleaming disaster"). In short, she runs the world's worst Ikea.

Step carefully as you enter Eljudnir; the threshold is a trap called Fallandaforad, and Hel's lazy servants Ganglot and Ganglati will be no help. This ain't Valhalla, so don't expect any noisy feasting here. The only big name in the VIP area will be Balder, doomed to the underworld centuries ago by the trickery of Loki. Balder was once a proud god of light and purity, but at this point, slumped in his seat of honor, he'll probably look, well, like he's been through Hel.

BEST TO AVOID

The worst part of this netherworld is Nastrond, the shore of corpses. This dark, drowned hall is built from the skeletons of great serpents, and their venom still drips onto the murderers, adulterers, and oath breakers within. The good news is you probably won't notice the venom. The bad news is that's because the winged dragon Nidhogg will be gnawing at your body for eternity.

KUR

Ancient Mesopotamia

In the Bronze Age poem *The Epic of Gilgamesh*, Gilgamesh's loyal friend Enkidu has a terrifying vision of the afterlife, in the dismal subterranean realm of the queen of darkness. Over the next two thousand years, the people of Mesopotamia had various names for this house of dust. But no matter what they called it—Kur, Arali, Kukku, Irkalla, or Ersetu—the Sumerians, the Akkadians, and the Babylonians all ended their days in this "house from which none who enters ever returns, down the road from which there is no coming back." That was the one thing the world's oldest civilization had figured out about death: that it was extremely permanent.

The Mesopotamian afterlife is only available to travelers who were buried with all the correct rites, so the first step is arranging to not get dragged off into the desert by wild dogs or something. Your ghost (*gidim* to the Sumerians, *etemmu* to the Akkadians) will leave this vessel of clay as soon as your blood stops flowing and your breath ceases. Then there's a long journey ahead of you across demon-infested plains to the Hubur river. You'll recognize the ferryman there because he has the head of a bird, four hands, and four feet. Luckily, his name, Khumut-Tabal, means "Take me there quickly!" in Babylonian, so just greeting him should get you across the river to the Gate of Captives.

> **TIME-SAVER!**
> For a quicker journey, or if you're prone to getting sick in boats, descend to Kur via Simmelat Ganzer, the "stairway of the underworld." This shortcut will drop you straight at the gates, bypassing Apsu—the waters beneath the earth—altogether.

The Gate of Captives is the first of the seven gates of Kur, and it's guarded by Bidu, who has the head of a lion, human hands, and the feet of a bird. Luckily "Bidu" means "Open up!" so once again you can just call his name. Each time you pass one of his gates, you'll lose an article of clothing, and Namtar, the vizier of the Lowest Earth, will hand you off to the *gallu* demons while Bidu locks the dusty bolt behind you. Finally Ningishzida the throne bearer will lead you on naked to the Anunnaki for judgment.

The Anunnaki are six hundred old gods imprisoned here by Marduk, and they now form a kind of underworld tenants' council. They'll descend from their temple tower and, assisted by their scribe Berit-Seri, assign you a new afterlife. But this is more of a clerical decision than a judicial one, because no one is really rewarded or punished for their deeds here. Kur is a dark underground cavern built from the stone corpse of the primordial demon Asakku and later given to Ereshkigal, the mistress of the great earth, as a gift. She and her consort, the warrior-god Nergal, rule this land from the palace of Ganzer. It's a strange, shadowy place, like the living world but somehow not. There are rivers that carry no water, fields that grow no grain, sheep that have no wool. It's deathly silent, so quiet that Gilgamesh had to take off his sandals to sneak around. No stars shine in Kur and no fires can be lit, so it's utterly dark unless the sun god Shamash is making his nightly visit as he passes from west to east.

Now you'll dress in feathery, birdlike garments and spend your days sightseeing at underworld highlights like the courtyard of Ereshkigal or the roots of the cosmic *mesu* tree that holds up the universe. You get to spend time with your relatives who moved here before you, kind of like Florida, but you don't retain much of your personality. Rulers and great heroes have their own shrines, like the underworld gods do, but most "sleepers" lead fairly ordinary existences. The only status comes from your next of kin. If they keep up your grave nicely and bring yummy offerings, you'll have food and drink here, and even a nice couch for reclining on or inviting company over. But if no one visits your resting place, bad news—the bread here is dust and the water brackish. You'll be begging for scraps in the streets of Kur.

If you were unburied or are forgotten, eventually you'll become a vicious demon! Then you can return to the surface through cracks and fissures in the ground, and spend your days haunting and pummeling the living or entering through their ears to possess them. But if you'd prefer slightly upgraded food and beverage service, start laying the groundwork now. Have as many offspring as possible, dote on your grandkids, and hope they bring flowers to your grave.

MICTLAN

The Aztecs

Life could be brutal and short in ancient Mesoamerica, so death was always present for the Aztecs. Childbirth rituals informed every Aztec newborn that their life would be painful and violent, and might very well end in battle or by human sacrifice. So much for a "bundle of joy."

As a silver lining, many of the violent ends you could meet in ancient Mexico did lead to paradise. Brave "eagle-jaguars"—warriors killed in combat—would head to Ilhuicatl-Tonatiuh, one of the thirteen levels of heaven. On this arid, cactus-covered battlefield, they clash their shields every morning to make the sun rise, and return to earth in the afternoon as birds and butterflies, peacefully sipping nectar from the flowers. Women who died in childbirth were worthy of the same reward and escort the sun into the sky every day in a litter of green quetzal plumes.

Those who died in infancy enjoy the orchard of Chichihuacuahco, where they are suckled by the "nursemaid tree"—literally a tree with udders hanging from its branches. Those who died by drowning or storms wind up in Tlalocan to attend the rain god Tlaloc. In his lush domain, delicious squash, corn, and peppers grow wild year-round.

But most dead Aztecs, noble and commoner alike, headed north to Mictlan. Mictlan is the realm of Mictlantecutli, the king of the dead. It's a realm of cold, darkness, rot, and despair—"the Place of the Fleshless." And as if that's not bad enough, its nine levels each hold a terrifying torture or obstacle.

At least you'll have a guide. Find a yellow dog and follow it across the nine rivers of Mictlan—and it must be a *yellow* dog. The white dogs you encounter will tell you they can't ferry you across the river because they've just washed; the black dogs will tell you that the river would wash off their black stain. After a death, Aztec families would sometimes sacrifice a yellow dog, the breed we call Mexican hairless today, and bury it with the deceased. That way they knew their loved one wouldn't have to brave the abyss alone.

Whatever else you can say about Mictlan, it's certainly not a foodie destination. The Lord of the Dead and his hideous consort drink a gruel of pus from human skulls. Your own meals will be a terrible parody of delicious cantina fare: tamales full of beetles, bloody hearts instead of frijoles, garnishes of poison herbs and prickly poppies.

All the while, you'll be crossing burning deserts, freezing gorges, and valleys swept by spinning knives and gale-force winds. You'll shred your dead hands on Itztepetl, a mountain of razor-sharp obsidian shards, and brave a terrible blue lizard. Arrows will fly at you and a jaguar will eat your heart. Two great cliffs will clash together in your path with the fury of one hundred earthquakes, so your timing will need to be impeccable.

After four long years, what does all your suffering lead to? You arrive at the foot of Mictlantecutli's throne . . . and are immediately dissolved into nothingness. Oh, well. They say life is all about the journey. Maybe death is too.

THE OTHERWORLD

The Celts

Before Christianity arrived in Britain and Ireland, the druids believed in a cycle of reincarnation: death and rebirth, just as the stag loses his antlers or the snake sheds its skin or the oak grows new leaves in the spring. But if you're planning a Celtic afterlife, there's a lot to see in the next world before your feet return to the auld sod.

Your first stop on your journey to the Celtic Otherworld is Tech Duinn, the house of the dead. This is the dwelling place of Donn, the toothless king of the underworld.

MEET THE LOCALS

Donn was the first of the Tuatha De Danann, the old gods, to arrive on Irish shores, but when the goddess Eriu prophesied his victory, he insulted her, and she used her powers to drown him in the sea off the southwest coast of Ireland.

A cairn was raised to Donn's memory after his defeat, and you can still see it today: Bull Rock, a tiny islet off the Beara Peninsula with a natural tunnel running straight through it. The ancient Celts saw this passage, through which the setting sun sometimes shone, as the gateway to the land of the dead.

Donn's last words were "To me, to my house, you shall all come after your deaths!" and so you'll begin your journey by assembling with other spirits in his dark realm. Donn, also called Da Derga, may send out three red riders on red horses to meet you, or on a stormy night he may ride out himself on his white phantom steed. In his house, you might glimpse the Badb, a goddess of destruction, in her guise as a carrion crow or as a trio of ugly crones, bleeding and with ropes around their necks.

But from Tech Duinn, you can move on to other, more pleasant fields. The Otherworld is actually a series of worlds, like an archipelago of islands in the western sea or a network of *sidhe* (fairy mounds) in the earth. Whether they called it Mag Mell ("the Plain of Delights"), Tir Na Nog ("the Land of the Forever Young"), or the Welsh Annwfn ("Land Without Enough Vowels"), the Iron Age Celts agreed that the dead enjoyed a beautiful land of promise without sadness, death, or decay. You can look forward to meadows of grass and clover bedewed with honey, scored with the music of bees and purple-headed birds, as well as forests of leafy oaks, hazel trees yellow with clusters of nuts, and fruit-laden apple trees. Grab a fragrant golden apple and take all the bites you want. The fruit will never diminish.

The houses here are made of white silver and thatched with the feathers of birds. The warrior kings of old, now clad in green, live in great fortresses of marble, silver, and gold. Plan a visit to the Fountain of Knowledge, a bubbling spring of five streams (each representing one of the five senses) shaded by the nine purple hazels of Buan. Nuts falling from the trees feed the salmon who live there. Fishing isn't allowed, but do take a long, refreshing draft of the wisdom-bestowing water there—the ultimate "smart drink."

The Otherworld is a place of perpetual feasting, each realm with its own cauldron of plenty. Every feast is presided over by the lord of that particular *sidhe*, who will appear as a hunter with a boar slung over his shoulder. The drink is endless, and the game is resurrected each night for the following day's hunt.

All the dead souls enjoy mock battles and the company of fair lads and colleens. At his feast, Goihbniu the blacksmith-god brews a special ale that confers immortality. Other *sidhe* field fifteen-player teams to challenge each other at the ancient Gaelic sport of hurling, a ruthlessly fast hybrid of lacrosse and field hockey.

> **SAVVY TRAVELER TIP**
> If you're serious about winning this heavenly rec league, you might need a "ringer." The trickier gods sometimes recruit star athletes from the living world to fill out their rosters.

It's all eternal good *craic*, a Pogues song that lasts forever. Just remember to respect your hosts. When the Celtic world was Christianized, the old supernatural beings were demoted from godhood and reimagined as the magical Fae. When you wander their lands, call them the Fair Folk, the Hidden People, the Good Neighbors—whatever you like. Just remember, they may be offended if you call them fairies!

RAROHENGA

The Maori

The journey to the next life is always a leap into the unknown, but never more literally than for the Maori people of New Zealand. This is your only afterlife option that begins with a thrilling cliff dive.

Traditional Maori belief is stamped by the cultural memory of their first arrival in New Zealand, as Polynesian explorers rowing open canoes across the Pacific around seven hundred years ago. When you die, your soul's itinerary begins with a return to Hawaiki, the ancestral homeland of the Maori.

So, as death approaches, swallow the *o matenga*, the final bite of food, and the *wai o Tane-pi*, the final sip of water. Your *wairua*, or soul, will leave your nostrils and flutter about your lips as your body dies. But then it's off, traveling north toward Te Rerenga Wairua, the leaping-off place of spirits, at the northwesternmost tip of New Zealand's North Island.

First you'll pause on the hill of Waihokimai. There your spirit can let it all out, wailing and lamenting the end of your earthly life. You'll remove your clothing and use sharp stones from the hilltop to gash and batter your limbs. Feel better? Then it's on to the nearby hill of Waiotioti, where you'll permanently turn your back on the living. There is no reviving your body now.

Your final stop is the headland now called Cape Reinga, where the currents of the Pacific Ocean meet those of the Tasman Sea, clashing and roiling at the base of the cliff. Stand by the gnarled old pohutukawa tree and watch the seaweed swirl below you. The second the waters subside and you see a break in the seaweed, dive off the cliff. You're headed home.

SAVVY TRAVELER TIP

If your *wairua* is of the less thrill-seeking variety, try shimmying down the dangling tree roots rather than diving into the waves.

You can make one last stop on the tiny island of Manawatawhi to turn back and bid New Zealand farewell, but then it's off to Hawaiki, where you'll undergo the ritual called *pure* to prepare you to ascend to the summit of the great mountain Irihia and enter the *tapu* edifice of Hawaiki-nui. This large house is a crossroads for the *wairua*, with four fire pits and corresponding passageways leading out in all four cardinal directions. Follow your intuition. The eastern path leads to the highest of the twelve heavens, where the forest god Tane first found the three baskets of knowledge and delivered them to humankind. You will be blown upward on the stormy *ara tiatia*, the whirlwind path, and then climb the *toi huarewa*, the web that hangs downward from heaven.

The westward passage, into the setting sun, is the path to Rarohenga, or Po: the underworld. The uppermost level of Rarohenga is relatively pleasant: a sunny realm on the shores of a lake, surrounded by hills. There you and the other departed will resume something like the patterns of your earthly lives. You will build homes, play games, give each other tattoos, and harvest crops—sweet potatoes and taro that grow more abundantly than they ever did above.

Unfortunately, the lower levels of the underworld are not so pleasant. There the dead dine on flies and their own excrement—so even if you're not a big fan of sweet potatoes and poi every night, you'll be missing them soon. This is a fiery region (the Polynesians were well aware of the red-hot molten stone the earth contained) ruled by Whiro, the lord of darkness and enemy of man. He'll try to devour your soul, but you may be protected by the giant goddess Hine-nui-te-po. She was once Hine-titama, maid of the dawn, but when she realized the father of her children was in reality her own father Tane, she descended to the underworld in shame.

Eventually you'll descend so low that you may be reborn on earth as the basest of creatures, a worm or a moth, and your second death there will be a final extinction. But throughout your time in Rarohenga, you may be able to contact the living. The Maori believed that night noises in the forest were *parangeki*, messengers from the underworld whispering their secrets. As the old Maori saying goes, the barrier between life and death is like the leaf of the wharangi tree: opaque, but very, very thin.

VALHALLA

The Norse

Hel being pretty damp and unpleasant, the preferred afterlife of Viking warriors was one of the rowdy house parties of the other gods. When you "come from a land of ice and snow," it makes sense that you'd imagine the next world as a sunny, never-ending spring break!

The key to the Norse afterlife is to die in some noble, valiant way, and that's a little harder today than it was in the tenth century. (Does a brave battle with cancer qualify? An epic skateboarding fail?) But if you manage it, you'll land on the short list of the Norse gods Odin and Freyja, who divvy up the honored dead fifty-fifty between them. You can't go wrong here. Freyja is a beautiful fertility goddess with a magic necklace, a feathered cloak that allows her to fly, and a chariot pulled by harnessed cats—basically a pre-modern pop diva. The pleasures of her beautiful meadow, Folkvangr, are endless.

But the hottest ticket in Asgard is Odin's hall of the slain, Valhalla. You'll know you've been selected for Valhalla if, after your demise, you see flashes of lightning and flocks of ravens surround you. That means Odin, the wise all-father, has sent the Valkyries, his death maidens, to give you a lift. They'll be riding winged steeds with blazing spears and helmets, wearing armor dripping with blood.

But (in a sexist twist) the Valkyries also moonlight as barmaids, bringing ale and cups to the carousing warriors in Valhalla. Valhalla is a gleaming golden hall in the realm of Gladsheim, beyond the red-gold grove of Glasir, the most beautiful forest in the Nine Worlds. Its roof is so high you can barely see over it, but if you crane your neck you might glimpse the great tree Laeradr rising above its spires, its leaves feeding the goat Heidrun and the stag Eikthyrnir, from whose antlers a great river cascades.

This sacred sanctuary boasts 540 doors, each broad enough that 800 men can enter abreast, but you should make a beeline for Valgrind, the main gate, and check out its famed cunning lock. In some of Valhalla's multitude of chambers, the fallen will be playing at games of chance. In other rooms, you can practice your sword fighting.

LEARN THE LANGUAGE
The guests of Valhalla are called the *einherjar*, "those who fight alone." This is confusing, since there are no myths about them actually fighting alone.

The main hall is for feasting and drinking. You've been adopted by one-eyed Odin as a result of your merit in battle, and so the décor here is pure warrior chic: spears for rafters, shields for roof tiles, a wolf's head mounted west of the doors, benches upholstered with chain mail. Every dawn you'll be woken by Gullenkambi, the golden-combed heavenly rooster, for another day of hard Scandinavian partying. The flagons of mead, made from the alcoholic milk of Heidrun, flow freely, and the cook Andhrimnir will serve up all the delicious wild boar you can hunt and eat. (That's because Saehrimnir, the great sooty beast of Asgard, gets reborn every night after getting cooked up every day in Valhalla's kitchen cauldrons.) You'll even have access to all your earthly possessions—as long as you buried them in the earth toward the end of your life, or instructed survivors to throw them onto your funeral pyre.

If you're into afterlife celeb-watching, it's not unusual to spy gods like Thor at the next table, and Odin himself will often sit up front with a flagon of wine, tossing meat to his hounds Geri and Freki or listening to his ravens, who bring him the latest news from all over creation. Sometimes, for reasons that remain unclear, Odin chooses to reign over Valhalla in the form of three mysterious chieftains. These three lords sit on three thrones, each of which is taller than the two others. (Try not to let the physics of Valhalla get to you. After all, you're eating reincarnated pork every day.)

But like all parties, this one doesn't last forever. Odin knows that the great battle of Ragnarok, the twilight of the gods, is coming. On that day, you and the rest of the *einherjar* will march out the great wide doors of Valhalla to battle the wolf Fenrir and Odin's other enemies. Maybe this sounds like fun after centuries of drunken mock combat in Valhalla, but make no mistake: You are going to die. Again. Then you'll earn a *permanent* military discharge and retire to the gold-thatched hall of Gimle at the southern reaches of heaven—a third heaven, Vidblain, where only the light-elves live today. There the party will continue!

XIBALBA

The Mayans

To the ancient Mayan people, the axis of the universe was Yaxche, an enormous ceiba (or kapok) tree like the ones whose canopies spread over the rain forests of Mesoamerica. The blessed dead would go to their eternal rest in a paradise shaded by the sacred leaves of this giant tree. But to get to heaven, you had to pass through one hell of an ordeal first: Xibalba, the Mayan underworld, the "Place of Fear."

The Mayan civilization collapsed more than five centuries before Europeans showed up in Mexico with gifts like Catholicism and measles, so our modern knowledge of Mayan cosmology comes from just a few fragmentary accounts. Most of what we know of Xibalba comes from a text called the *Popol Vuh*, which is mostly stories about *living* heroes venturing into the afterlife. But if your experience is anything like theirs, you're in for a bad time.

The journey to death begins at a literal crossroads, where four colored paths stretch to the four corners of the earth. Follow the Black Road west past flocks of gathering hawks. You'll cross Rustling Canyon, Gurgling Canyon, Scorpion Rapids, the River of Blood, and the River of Pus—all exactly as nauseating as they sound.

Finally you'll plunge through caves into the nine-level underworld ruled by the Lords of Xibalba. The original rulers of Xibalba were two death gods called "One Death" and "Seven Death," but they were overthrown by two brave hero twins in the *Popol Vuh*. Now you'll be facing a grisly pantheon of ten midlevel gods who all sound like titles of Cannibal Corpse songs and who all represent different varieties of death. Their names will give you power over them, so pay attention: there are Scab Stripper and Blood Gatherer (death by bleeding), the Demon of Pus and Demon of Jaundice (death by illness), Bone Scepter and Skull Scepter (death by wasting away), the Demon of Filth and Demon of Woe (death by grief and grime), and Wing and Packstrap (death during travel). Their messengers to the surface world are monstrous owls.

These Lords of Xibalba are brutal pranksters. When you see their thrones, make sure you're actually addressing the lords themselves and not carved wooden mannequins. They love that classic joke! Don't sit on the stone bench they offer; it will be hot enough to scald your rear end. Then they'll invite you into five houses, each more perilous than the last. The Dark House is pitch-black, and the Razor House is full of sharp stone blades constantly roving around like Roombas, looking for someone to cut. The Rattling House is a freezer, swept by icy drafts and showers of hailstones. The Jaguar House is packed with hungry jungle cats, and the Bat House holds a swarm of shrieking bats with snouts like knives, looking to swoop down and decapitate you if you peek out from under cover for even a second.

SAVVY TRAVELER TIP

Take heart! The hero twins managed to outwit all these traps, and you can too. Follow their lead: send a mosquito on ahead to spy on the lords' plans for you. Use fireflies in the Dark House; throw bones to the jaguars. If you survive, you'll be led to your final confrontation with the Lords of Xibalba.

The word "Xibalba" sounds like a great Scrabble play, but in fact the game of choice in the Mayan underworld is the same brutal ball game that Mesoamericans played on their outdoor courts in life. At the Place of Ball Game Sacrifice, the lords will try to replace the regulation rubber ball with one of their own, but don't fall for it! Theirs is the ultimate spitball: it conceals a white dagger they want to use on your flesh. If they win, they'll cast your body into the stone oven where they brew their booze.

Thanks to the heroic twins of the *Popol Vuh*, the Lords of Xibalba no longer have power over all humankind. Only the guilty and violent and wretched are now subject to their mean pranks and jaguar-infested caves. Everyone else can just, as the saying goes, refuse to play ball.

Creepy-Crawlies

YOMI
Shintoism

The Japanese traditions of Shinto are centered firmly in the present. The living world is full of eight million godlike spirits called *kami*, and the aim of life is harmony with nature and these deities—not fitness for some other supernatural world to come. But there is also a world of the dead in Shinto, described in some of its earliest and most important legends. And the legends agree: the underworld is gross.

The Shinto afterlife is called Yomi, short for Yomi-tsu-kuni, the Land of Darkness. When you join the rest of the dead there in the Hollow Land, the Land of Roots, you won't be in paradise or hellfire. It's a dark world analogous to ours, with dwellings and communities and things to eat and wear. If you suffer, it will only be because of your separation from the living. Your life energy will continue, and you may even be remembered by the living as one of the *kami* yourself—either venerated as a great soul or appeased as an angry, vengeful *goryo*.

But followers of Shinto are concerned above almost all else with avoiding *kegare*, impurity or pollution, and nothing is considered more impure or polluted than death. To this day, cemeteries are never built near Shinto shrines, and funeral planners pass out small bags of salt that guests can scatter at home afterward to purify themselves—a little hand sanitizer for the soul. As you would expect, Yomi is always described as a place of filth and defilement, full of unclean spirits.

In early Shinto myths, the creator god Izanagi descended to Yomi after the death of his sister-wife Izanami. She told him that she'd already eaten food cooked in the underworld (like Persephone!), which might make it impossible for her to return to the land of the living, but she'd take it up with the deities of Yomi. Izanagi was commanded not to look at her, but he couldn't take the suspense (like Orpheus!) and finally lit a fire. In that moment, his beloved was revealed to be a rotting corpse swarming with maggots, and her body was possessed by eight thunder *kami*. Izanagi fled, and Izanami sent the thunder *kami*, an ugly hag, and five hundred warriors of Yomi in pursuit of him. At the entrance to the underworld, he picked three peaches from a tree and threw them at his pursuers, and when his corpse bride followed he blocked the pass with an enormous boulder, which can still be seen near Izumo, Japan.

The impurities of Yomi also appear in a legend about Susanoo, the storm god. Susanoo couldn't get over the death of his mother, Izanami, so Izanagi banished him to the underworld, where he and his mother reigned from a palace near the entrance. When the god Onamuji sought refuge in Yomi, he fell in love with Susanoo's daughter. In true "creepy dad" fashion, Susanoo put Onamuji through the literal courtship from hell, filling his bedchamber with snakes, centipedes, and bees that ended up crawling through Onamuji's hair. With his beloved's help Onamuji made it through all the gross trials unscathed and they escaped Yomi together.

As you can see, Yomi is only recommended for the adventurous afterlife traveler. One who doesn't mind maggots beneath their skin and centipedes in their hair.

RELIGION

AERIAL TOLLHOUSES
Eastern Orthodoxy

Almost all posthumous itineraries agree on one geographic fact: the damned are sent downward. Hell is underground. But Eastern Orthodox Christianity prepares sinners for a journey *upward*, in which souls are tormented in the air. Or rather, at a series of floating stations in the air. As in a long earthly journey, you can't enter the afterlife without "clearing customs" first.

The tradition derives from Paul's letter to the Ephesians, which refers to "spirits of wickedness" who live "under the heavens" and calls Satan "the prince of powers of the air." The idea that the prince of darkness hounds the dead in an aerial realm between earth and heaven is so common in the patristic texts of Eastern Orthodoxy that it's made its way into the prayers and hymns of the church's liturgy—even though the theology is somewhat controversial. Some scholars consider the idea of these demon-staffed way stations to be heretical, but the belief became more popular in the twentieth century when it was propagated by an influential California monk called Seraphim Rose.

Father Rose drew from the work of a tenth-century Byzantine saint, Basil the Younger, who once had a vision of the death of an enslaved woman named Theodora. According to St. Basil, the dying are visited by three parties. First, you'll see demons with glowing red eyes and sooty black faces. (The implied racism here is even less subtle in the original text, where Basil calls the demons "Egyptians.") They'll snarl and snap at you, but they'll also be unrolling scrolls and preparing charts, like execs before a big presentation. Then radiant angels will descend with hair like snow, dressed in gold and lightning. Finally Death itself will appear, a skeletal figure roaring like a lion and wielding a whole kit of terrible torture instruments: swords, scythes, arrows, spears, saws, and some you won't even recognize. Death will take out a small axe and hack away at your limbs and head, separating each part of your spirit from the body. Finally, it will administer to you a cup of bitter poison, and you will die.

At that point, the demons will pounce. God appointed you a guardian angel during your life, but the powers of hell also assigned you a guardian *devil*, to keep track of all your evil thoughts and misdeeds. Now they have a full accounting, and they're going to make you pay. The angels will attempt to carry you upward, but to get to heaven, you'll need to pass a series of *telonia* ("tollhouses" or "customhouses") floating in the azure expanse of the sky.

Each of the twenty tollhouses is devoted to punishing a particular kind of wickedness. In order, the twenty sins examined will be idle speech, lying, slander and gossip, gluttony, sloth, theft, greed, usury, injustice, envy, pride, anger, bearing grudges, murder and other violence, sorcery, lust and fornication, adultery and rape, sodomy, heresy, and lack of mercy. At each booth, your demonic tax collector (tollbooth phantom?) will try to extract spiritual payment from you for every single unconfessed sin on your record, in amazing and humiliating detail.

MEET THE LOCALS

You'll find the demons on staff here to be a motley crew. The persecutors of gluttony look like pigs and drunkards; the sorcery specialists are serpents and toads. The anger tollhouse is run by a furious figure on a throne surrounded by underlings who lick their chops like hungry dogs, while the demons of sodomy ooze with pus and a terrible stench.

Luckily, the angels accompanying you can help pay those tolls using your good deeds and piety as currency. (Heaven was keeping its own tally.) They can anoint you with oil and myrrh to withstand the terrible ordeal, and when your own good deeds fall short of your sins, they may even be able to cover your debt using the prayers of others made on your behalf.

If at any point you go bust, the demons will gleefully cast you into hell. But if you can make it past all the invisible dignitaries and powers of the air, you'll enter through the crystal gates of heaven. The waters above the earth will part, allowing you to pass through clouds to kneel at the throne of the unseen God.

Then it's an eternity in golden palaces that glisten like stars, walking in gardens of sweet-smelling trees, and enjoying banquets where the food replenishes itself endlessly. If you're ever bored, stop in at the abode of father Abraham and play with all the cute Christian babies. Wherever you go, your fellow saints, clad in fiery garments, will pause in their divine song to receive you with joy, genuinely stoked that you made it through the same tollbooth gauntlet they did.

THE BARDO

The Tibetan Book of the Dead

Travel isn't always predictable, and that's doubly true for afterlife travel. Sometimes things go wrong; you just have to roll with the punches and improvise. And nobody's better prepared for postmortal hitches and glitches than a Tibetan Buddhist.

Around the year 1340, as the story goes, an unusually spiritual Tibetan teen climbed a holy mountain called Gampodar and uncovered a hidden treasure trove of ancient manuscripts. One text, the Bardo Thodol ("Liberation Through Hearing During the Intermediate State"), was eventually published in the West as *The Tibetan Book of the Dead*. It became massively popular during the 1960s, when psychedelic experimenters like Aldous Huxley and Timothy Leary decided its teachings also worked as a guide to LSD trips.

"Bardo" is Tibetan for a boundary state between death and rebirth, and the *Book of the Dead* actually describes three different bardos. The first is the Chikhai Bardo. At the moment of death, you will get a glimpse of the Radiance of the Fundamental Clear Light of Pure Reality, like a mirage moving across a landscape in spring, with the sound of a thousand thunders. For the very enlightened, that may be enough to embark on the Great Straight-Upward Path and achieve Buddhahood immediately!

But if not, don't despair. Your consciousness principle will leave your body, and you will see the living around you, grieving. You may not know you're dead. In your new, shining illusory body, you'll hover around places you knew in life for a few days. Don't try to reenter your body—it will feel like you're trying to squeeze into the cracks in rocks.

Soon you'll be ready to come out of your postdeath swoon and tackle Plan B: the Chonyid Bardo, which may last up to two weeks. On each day, you'll see a new set of Peaceful and Wrathful Deities, but just keep chanting to yourself: These visions aren't real. They're reflections of your own consciousness.

On each day of the first week, you'll see a different Buddha of Wisdom seated on a throne. On day one, for example, you'll bask in the blue light of Vairochana, sitting on a lion throne and holding an eight-spoked wheel as the Mother of Heaven embraces him. It's normal to be afraid of his radiance—that's your bad karma talking. Focus on the bright blue light you see, not the dull white light next to it. Each of these days is a chance to end the bardo by embracing the light and merging into the heart of Buddha. But if you flee, there's always a backup plan. Different deities will appear tomorrow.

BEST TO AVOID

Whatever you do, never embrace the dimmer lights! You'll just be whirled around in Sangsara, the Ocean of Misery, and might wind up in hell, or the land of hungry ghosts. There are worse planes to be on than the bardo.

In your second week of Chonyid Bardo, the wise, placid deities will be replaced by wrathful ones, wrapped in halos of flame and drinking blood. Some have animal heads; others will be chewing on corpses or licking bloody intestines. Even the medium-sized ones are as big as Mount Meru. Don't freak out! The second you realize that these monsters are just Buddhas in disguise, you'll be liberated from the bardo.

Hopefully by this point you've achieved Buddhahood, but that all depends on your karma. If you're still in the bardo at the end of week two, we go to Plan C: the Sidpa Bardo, where you might stay as long as five more weeks. This stage begins with tumultuous visions of storms, crowds, avalanches, stampeding beasts . . . but if you try to escape, you'll be stopped by three cliffs, respectively colored white, black, and red. They represent anger, lust, and stupidity. The Lord of Death will look into his Mirror of Karma to see your life, and his spirits will count out pebbles as they watch: a white pebble for each good deed, and a black one for each evil deed. As long as the black pebbles keep coming, furies will torture you.

Next you'll come to the womb doors. These are entrances to a new life, and ideally you want to close them all to end the cycle of rebirth. Meditate on how they are all illusions, like a reflection of the moon in water. If that doesn't work, the best rebirth you can hope for is "supernormal birth," reincarnation in a paradise realm. Look for the door through which you can glimpse a gold temple—that's the heaven of the godlike devas. Stay away from the other doors! A vision of a cavern means you'll come back as an animal. A vision of black roads accompanied by songs of wailing means you're headed to hell.

But if your karma doesn't merit advancement, you'll be returning through one of the womb doors that lead back to the human world. You might see glimpses of men and women in, um, "union." Those are your future parents getting it on!

SAVVY TRAVELER TIP
In an alarmingly Freudian twist, you may be able to sense your next gender by noting which parent you feel angry about and which one you feel a little attracted to.

It's important to set aside your feelings of attraction and revulsion toward any particular womb doors and instead focus on your ultimate goal. Emit mental gift-waves of grace, and your next life might become a celestial mansion. Dress, in other words, for the womb you want and not the womb you have. But wherever you get reborn, you can be sure you'll be back in the bardo sooner or later. On your next visit, you can choose a different adventure.

THE EIGHTEEN HELLS

Buddhism

In many world religions, the fires of hell aren't eternal like they are in Christianity—but for Buddhists, they might as well be. If you didn't devote yourself to the practice of the pure dharma in life, you will certainly suffer for it in the world to come. Samsara, the cycle of birth and death, means that each afterlife is not only an ending but also a beginning, and eventually you'll be reincarnated out of hell to this life or another. *Eventually.*

The earliest Sanskrit and Pali writings on Buddhist perdition agree that there are eight fiery hells staked under the earth. Each is a square fortress about eight hundred miles on each side, walled by iron plates and vaulted with an iron roof eight hundred miles above. The floor of these prisons is hot iron, and the flames rising from them spread for miles in all directions.

Each hell is divided into sixteen sections called *utsada*s, each with its own specific punishments. There's lots of the boiling and scorching and spit-roasting you'd expect, and you shouldn't be surprised to have five glowing stakes driven through your limbs and belly, or be forced to swallow red-hot metal balls that pass excruciatingly through you, pulling out your intestines as they leave. As an occasional break from these heat-related tortures, you may be smashed between two mountains; tossed into the Vaitarani, a river of caustic blood; or driven into a thicket where thorns and razor-sharp leaves slice off your ears and nose and fingers and toes. There is little emphasis in Buddhism on who exactly is tormenting you, but the implacable wardens of hell, whoever they are, do employ some terrifying servants: ravens with iron beaks, fire-breathing donkeys, and needle-mouthed creatures who bore straight into your bones to eat the marrow.

Between vivisections and drinks of molten copper, you might get a taste of some subtler punishments: familiar earthly weaknesses like blindness, leprosy, insanity, ugliness, or lonely childlessness. Other maladies are a little more specific. You may suffer for a time with bad breath, worn clothes, crooked teeth, or even, according to one sutra, "a scrotum [that] is very big; in walking, standing, sitting, or lying down it is extremely cumbersome."

If you find the eight fiery hells to be a little warm for you, later texts add ten "cold" hells on a dark faraway mountain located at the end of the sky. They are karmic punishment for those who never shared warmth with the cold and needy in life.

LEARN THE LANGUAGE

Some of these icy hells are named for the sounds you will scream as bitter winds blast you, stripping off skin and snapping tendons: "Atata!" "Hahava!" Others are named for the shapes of the red and blue sores that will appear on your frostbitten extremities.

How long do you need to withstand these tortures before karma is satisfied and you can be reborn? Well, there's the rub. The *Sutra on the Eighteen Hells*, from the second century BC, is very specific about the duration of each hell. Samjiva, the hell of fighting, lasts a mere 135 billion years, while you'll spend 17 *trillion* years in Pratapana, the hell of roasting.

The cold hells carry even longer sentences, so mind-bogglingly interminable that the Buddha had to resort to story problems to explain them. Imagine a cartload of mustard seeds, a pile taller than a man. Once every century, you remove a single seed from the cart and carry it away. When the cart is finally empty, *you will still be shivering in Arbuda, the first cold hell.*

For each subsequent hell, the pile of mustard seeds doubles in size. Bring a scarf.

GEHENNA AND GAN EDEN

Judaism

Jewish theology is famously focused on this life—how to live right in the here and now. But that doesn't mean there's no rich tradition of eschatology in Judaism. It just means that *olam ha-ba* ("the world to come," as it's called in rabbinic literature) is so distant and unknowable that we apprehend it through analogy only.

In the Hebrew Bible, the afterlife is just "Sheol," the land of the shadow of death. Here we picture a gloomy, dusty subterranean cavern through which ghostly shades shamble aimlessly. These are both the wicked and the righteous, awaiting a judgment or resurrection that may never come.

But later rabbis, from the medieval period on, described much more colorful visions of the Jewish afterlife. Sheol was replaced by Gehenna, a Dante-like hell supposedly named for the valley outside Jerusalem that became a putrid, smoldering pit when the city began to dump its garbage there.

Your journey to Gehenna will begin with a visit from the Angel of Death, a hideous messenger said to be "full of eyes." He will draw his sword and use it to drip bitter gall into your mouth. You'll be surrounded by an indistinct roaring sound that no one else can hear, and then your life will be over.

Gehenna will open its jaws and swallow you into a dark abyss. Its gates are guarded by huge serpents with flaming eyes, long fangs, and faces "like lamps that have been extinguished," whatever that means. You will now have the body of an eagle and a face that's colored green or black, depending on how wicked you were in life.

This is a hell of contrasts: murky fire, but also frost and ice. You'll be tormented by rivers of hot pitch, open pits full of lions, hideous black worms, terrible itching, and angels of destruction bashing your teeth in with rocks. Plan to spend much of the day hanging on a hook from the specific part of your body that offended HaShem: the proud dangle from their eyes, liars from their tongues, thieves from their hands. You really have to feel bad for the adulterers.

MAPPING YOUR JOURNEY

At least there's no shortage of room in Gehenna for new arrivals! It's a hell of seven levels, each with seven thousand rooms. Each room has seven thousand windows, and each windowsill has seven thousand vessels of poison—that's almost two and a half trillion poisons, if you're keeping score at home. Also, each chamber has seven thousand crevices, each filled with seven thousand scorpions. You'd better hope some of your copious poison vials work on bugs!

But after a year of this purification, the next leg of your journey will be a huge upgrade. You'll pass through seven heavenly walls (of glass, cedar, silver, gold, olive, onyx, and crystal) and two gates of ruby to enter the garden of the righteous, Gan Eden. The archangel Michael will grill up a sacrifice on his altar to welcome you. Enjoy your new white robes made from the clouds of glory and your complimentary set of not one but *two* heavenly crowns! Then check into your fancy new chamber, lit by a pearly, glowing vine.

All the fruits and flowers in Gan Eden are always in full bloom, and the sapphire sky is supported by a revolving pillar. Two springs flow through the garden, one of milk and honey and the other of oil and wine. Each level boasts its own canopied palace with a fancy name like "the Palace of Splendor" or "the Bird's Nest." That second one is where the Messiah lives, emerging every so often to roar like a lion in praise of righteous Jewish martyrs.

There's so much plenty here compared to earth that even a single grape, when brought to you, will refill your flagon with wine thirty times.

Each day you'll pass through the four ages of life—child to youth to adult to elder—enjoying the pleasures of each in turn. You'll sit in the center of the garden under the crimson Tree of Life with its half million varieties of fruit, studying the Torah. But this is a very special shul, because you'll be studying alongside the very patriarchs and righteous women described in the text.

OFF THE BEATEN PATH

Some of the best sights here are the ones that descend through the clouds toward earth. Keep your eye on the ground and you might spot the mills where God grinds manna for the righteous—or even the top of Jacob's Ladder.

At some point, you'll probably want to head back to earth in time for the resurrection. Luckily, your earthly body had a special bone called the *luz* at the top of your spine. The *luz* never decomposes, so God can use it to bring you back to life. Your soul will have to journey through underground passages to get back to your burial place—and that's why, to this day, some Diaspora Jews are buried with a little stick or fork, to help them dig back to Israel for the resurrection.

THE HOUSE OF SONG

Zoroastrianism

Zoroastrianism is the oldest of the world's monotheistic religions. It was the state religion of the great Persian empires five hundred years before Julius Caesar, and it's still hanging in there, practiced today by about one hundred thousand followers, most of them in India and Iran. For over twenty-five hundred years, these believers have been looking forward to a final cosmic battle, when the creator god Ahura Mazda will finally defeat his adversary Ahriman and cleanse the universe of corruption.

Ancient Zoroastrian priests rubbed the dead with consecrated cow urine, then dragged the body up to a mountaintop for birds and wild dogs to eat as carrion. Whether that's your funerary fate or not, your *urvan*, the part of your soul that travels on, will linger near your body for three days. At dawn on the fourth day you'll arrive at Chinvat Peretu, "the Bridge of the Separator," a rainbow arcing between this life and the next.

Chinvat is nine spears wide for the righteous but narrow as a razor for the wicked. You'll get a first clue of which fate awaits you by following your nose. Good souls will sniff a balmy, fragrant breeze from the south and see a beautiful maiden walking toward them accompanied by the four-eyed dogs that guard the bridge. She will be noble, athletic, and "thick-breasted." This busty vision is a manifestation of your own *daena*, or religious insight. She will usher you over the bridge to the ramparts of the *yazata*s, three angels of judgment.

If, on the other hand, you lived an impure life, the wind on the bridge will be a foul-smelling and cold one from the north. Your *daena* will take the form of an ugly old hag who will recite your offenses and offer you no protection from the demons trying to drag you down to hell.

On the other side of the bridge (fingers crossed!) you'll face an angelic tribunal made up of all-seeing Mithra, who dwells above the mountains; just Rashnu, who weighs your virtue on his scales; and gentle Sraosha, who accompanies you onward. They will judge you on your thoughts, words, and deeds but take no account of your wealth or status.

As a consequence, your *urvan* will become a guest in either of two houses. The House of Song is a paradise of endless light, where you'll see Ahura Mazda and seven lesser deities, the *amesha spenta*s. One of them, Vohu Mana, will rise from his golden throne to welcome you. He'll be so impressed! "Righteous one," he will marvel, "how have you come from the perilous world to this place without peril?" This garden of fruit and fertility is a place of superlatives: the best thoughts, the best blessings. In fact, the Middle Persian word for heaven is "*vahisht*," meaning "best." This is a real improvement over the other place, the House of Lies, home to the worst thoughts and the worst smells and the worst company (*daeva*s, the false gods of Zoroastrianism). The House of Lies is crowded with humanity, but it's such a dark and silent place that you'll feel perfectly alone.

But these two houses aren't permanent residences. At the end of time, three great *saoshyant*s, or "benefactors," will arise to lead the armies of light. The slaughter from this final battle will be so great that blood will rise to the girths of the horses. But once the universe is purified, the dead will all be resurrected. Your soul will have bones again. (If your bones are unavailable, Ahura Mazda will have no problem creating a new body for you out of earth and water, the way he did the first time.)

Then every single person who has ever lived undergoes one final ordeal: wading through a stream of molten metal. To truthful worshippers, this will feel like a bath of warm milk, but the deceitful will be scalded. In some accounts, the molten metal annihilates them, but in others, it's a cleansing fire that entitles even these sinners to live in a new, purified universe, where the earth is flat as a disc and everyone shares one language and government. Your new resurrected body is fifteen years old forever, which seems like an odd view of perfection. Hope you enjoyed ninth grade!

JAHANNAM

Islam

"Believers, be careful of your duty to Allah and speak righteous words!" says the Quran. This is good advice, because if you don't, Islam promises some of the worst afterlife suffering ever conceived—and it begins before you even get to hell!

Until God raises everyone up on Yawm al-Din, the Day of Judgment, you will spend your time in Barzakh, a limbo-like state of separation from life. Don't be alarmed when two blue-black beings with red eyes and terrifying tusks appear to you in the grave. These are the angels Munkar and Nakir, and they've come to ask you three questions: "Who is your God?," "What is your religion?," and "Who is your prophet?" We recommend going with "Allah," "Islam," and "Muhammad" as your answers here. The hadith (oral traditions of Muhammad's teachings) say that if you ace Munkar and Nakir's test, they will give your resting place a complimentary upgrade, widening your grave and even installing silks, candles, perfumes, and furnishings for your comfort. But if you fail the quiz, there are no lovely parting gifts. The angels will command the earth to squeeze you so tightly that your rib cage will interlock, and ninety-nine serpents will slither into your grave and chew your flesh.

All this will continue until the final trumpet blows. On that day of resurrection, you'll be driven naked along with the rest of the human race to the Land of the Concourse, a vast and empty white plain. Some will be raised up in forms imprinted by their earthly sins: liars will be monkeys, the prideful will be smeared in tar, the selfish will smell like rotten meat. As you stand there waiting, the heavens will wheel overhead. When the sun rises, it will hang so near you that you'll sweat uncontrollably. Don't worry, this day only lasts for fifty thousand years.

When it's finally your turn, angels will call you up to the Place of Presentation, where God has books and scrolls listing your good and bad deeds, which His angels will hang around your neck. Then a giant set of scales is brought out, and your records will fly into the air, landing in the pans of the scales. How they balance will determine whether you will spend eternity in paradise, or in hell: Jahannam.

Jahannam is a series of vast rings of torture set into a crater on the underside of the world. The Quran usually calls it al-Nar, or "the Fire," but in fact there are seven different layers of torture, called Inferno, Blaze, Flame, Furnace, Fire, Hellfire, and Abyss. (Arabic apparently has as many words for fire as the Eskimo proverbially have for snow.)

This pitch-black realm is unimaginably vast. There are seventy thousand craggy valleys there, each with seventy thousand ravines, each with seventy thousand serpents and scorpions. The snakes are the size of elephants, while the scorpions have fangs the size of palm trunks. Entire oceans are filled with bubbling water, blood, and pus. All told, it would take you five hundred years to travel from one circle of hell to the next.

TRAVEL TRIVIA

If, amid your torment, you ever hear the sound of something clattering near you, here's a fun fact: it's probably just a rock that fell into the pit of Jahannam . . . seventy years ago.

The first level of Jahannam is a place of purgation for not-so-pious Muslims—it's hot, but more of a Turkish-bath hot, and the inhabitants eventually get to ascend out of hell. The seventh level, the lowest abyss, is a pit of freezing cold. But all five of the other circles are largely indistinguishable realms of fire. The heat-related tortures seem to be unending. You'll wear rags and sandals of fire. Ask for water and you'll be made to drink a swallow of molten brass. Everyone eats from the cursed tree of Zaqqum, whose fruit is shaped like a devil's head and is so poisonous that a single drop would pollute all the oceans of earth. Every bite will churn in your belly, ripping your insides apart and releasing terrible fluids. This will come as a painful shock to you, unless you've ever been to Taco Bell.

Aside from the usual torments of the damned (whips, flies, chains, nails, stoning, drowning), there are said to be an awful lot of baroque facial tortures in Jahannam. Look forward to getting the corners of your mouth slit around to the back of your neck, your tongue trampled, your brain liquefied out your nostrils, or your cheeks blackened like charcoal with hellfire. If you're dragged face-first into the flames, your upper lip will roll up to the top of your head like one of those window shades, while your lower lip hangs down and bumps against your belly button.

All these tortures are administered by the nineteen black-robed guardian angels with hooked iron rods who guard the gates of Jahannam. Their leader is Malik, whom Allah has made repulsive to represent His fearsome judgment on sinners. Malik has eyes like lightning and *terrible* breath. He's also said to have billions of fingers, one for every sinner. That way he can sit in the dead center of hell and personally torture everyone at once—not just humans like you, but also the devil Iblis and all his jinn.

A quick note to male travelers: There's a Muslim teaching attributed to Muhammad himself that most of the damned in Jahannam are women. Today this seems like an unfortunate patriarchal tradition, and it's quite possible that hell's gender imbalance has been addressed over the past centuries. Inshallah.

JANNAH

Islam

The abyss of Jahannam is spanned by the as-Sirat bridge, the "Traverse of the Blaze." All the dead must cross it, and for infidels and offenders, it's as narrow as a hair and sharp as a sword. Only the righteous can make it across, and as you go, you'll see your fellow travelers toppling headfirst into hell, as the guardians of Jahannam trip them up with hooks and grapples.

But if you get to the other side, you have much more pleasant accommodations in store. Paradise in Islam is the lush, verdant Jannah, meaning "garden" in Arabic. Enter through one of the eight gates, each admitting Muslims of a different virtue: the Gate of Prayer, the Gate of Fasting, the Gate of Jihad. Two springs emerge from a tree on the other side; take a long, deep drink and bathe in the pool. Your earthly cares will disappear— and so will all bodily functions. You'll never sleep, blow your nose, poop, or menstruate again. Around this time you'll be served the traditional first *amuse-bouche* from Jannah's bottomless buffet: a tiny bite of fish liver.

You and your fellow dwellers in paradise will all be pale and hairless and wear a constant look of delight and serenity on your faces, since you'll no longer have to worry about hellfire. In a tribute to the great prophets of old, everyone here has the height of Adam, the age of Jesus (thirty-three at the time of the Crucifixion), the good looks of Joseph, and the Arabic fluency of Muhammad. But there's no idle chatter or small talk anymore; you'll all greet one another with a simple "Peace."

As you stroll through Jannah, you'll see that it isn't a single garden, but rather a dominion of *seven* terraced gardens located above the canopy of the sky. Depending on your degree of faithfulness, you'll rest in the Abode of Glory, the Abode of Peace, the Abode of Eternity, the Garden of Eden, the Garden of the Refuge, the Garden of Bliss, or the Garden of Firdaws. This last garden is so near to God's throne that you can hear the creaking when He sits!

WHEN TO GO

Every Friday in Jannah is the Day of Surplus, when Allah throws a big bash: first a live concert by the psalmist David, then an elaborate banquet at which God actually lowers His veils and reveals His face to the chosen.

But even the lowest of the gardens here is mind-bogglingly beautiful, with four rivers of milk and honey that flow over beds of pearls. The soil under your feet is ambergris specked with rubies, and the grass in the meadows is saffron. Every variety of tree is here: palms and pomegranates and acacias. When someone asked Muhammad how heaven could have every single tree, even thorn trees, the Prophet outwitted them by replying that the thorn trees in heaven have fruit in place of thorns.

The landscaping in Jannah is a dream come true for a desert people. Most traditional heavens are bright and sunny, but here there are aromatic rains of rosewater, while all the cooling water you can drink bubbles up from springs smelling of camphor and ginger. The heavenly Tuba tree is so large and shady that you could journey on horseback under its canopy for five hundred years and never emerge into the sunlight.

The Quran is quite clear on what the blessed will do in the shade: relax and enjoy sensual pleasures! When the philosopher al-Tawhidi was told that Christian heaven had no food, drink, or sex, he famously exclaimed, "What a sad affair." So live it up! You now reside in an opulent palace of gold and silver bricks, with musk incense for mortar. Put on your gold bracelets and green silk robes, and lounge under your domed tent, a hollow pearl sixty miles high. Thousands of servants will attend you. The branches of the trees will lower to your brocaded couches so you can grab clusters of dates, bananas, figs, pomegranates the size of water skins—whatever you

desire. If you want meat, quail will descend to golden trays . . . and magically replenish the skies when you're done with dinner. If you want to go
for a spin, a camel or winged ruby horse will appear, and you can journey
to visit a neighbor in the blink of an eye. If you want a child, one will appear and grow up to a fun age in less than an hour. Talk about service!

The most celebrated luxury of Muslim paradise is, of course, the presence of the fabled "seventy-two virgins" whose favors await the righteous.
The number may vary, but commentators generally agree that the Quran
is clear on this point: heaven does promise more virgins than a College
Libertarians meeting. These aren't human women, though. These are the
houris, spirits created by God from clay just for pleasure. They're described
as dark-eyed maidens with perky breasts, untouched by man or jinn. Their
faces shine like the moon, and their hair is longer than eagles' wings.
(Some scholars suggest there are male companions as well, for women or
anyone else who prefers that.) All this nonstop eating and sex would normally take it out of you, but luckily God grants you a superhuman appetite
for pleasure every morning in Jannah, seventy times your earthly stamina.

A few scholars have recently advanced the theory that the "seventy-
two virgins" belief actually arises from a scriptural misinterpretation, and
that the "doe-eyed ones" described in the Quran should actually be trans-
lated as "crystal-white grapes." So you might be getting a harem of sexual
playthings, or you might be getting a nutritious snack. It's win-win.

LAN GUINÉE

Haitian Vodou

The vodou (or "voodoo") traditions still practiced in the Caribbean today are a blend of the Dahomeyan religions of West Africa and the Roman Catholicism of the New World. And nowhere is that more apparent than in the vodou afterlife, which is a literal journey back in time to the Mother Continent.

According to vodou, at the moment of your death, two different aspects of your soul will leave your *corps cadavre*. The *gros bon ange*, or "big good angel," is your life force, and after death it returns to the same well of energy it came from, the one that powers all of God's creation. But your *ti bon ange*, your "little good angel," is your conscience, the special aura that makes you *you*, and it moves on.

Your *ti bon ange* will meet Baron Samedi, the *loa* of death, at the crossroads between this world and the next. The *loa* are the thousand powerful spirits of vodou, each with its own personality, and the baron is quite a personality. He'll make you feel at home by dressing like a corpse himself: a suave black tailcoat, a white top hat, dark glasses, cotton plugs in his mouth and nostrils. His face may be painted like a grinning skull, and he enjoys rum and absolutely filthy jokes.

MEET THE LOCALS

If the baron is smoking a cigar and tempting you with an apple in his left hand, that means he's taken on the aspect of Papa Guede. Papa Guede is the first mortal man who ever died, now nameless, and he's the powerful judge and magician who will conduct you into his realm, variously said to be under the earth, beneath the waves, or above the sky.

Now you join Les Invisibles, the *loa* spirits, as well as the souls of all your ancestors. You're not cut off from the living—in fact, they're counting on you to look out for them and intercede on their behalf. But this isn't your final destination. A year later, you'll be reincarnated on earth in a new body.

Hang in there for sixteen mortal incarnations, and then you get to take the real cruise. You'll cross the ocean to Lan Guinée, or Ginen, a lush tropical land of sunshine, peace, and ease. All the trees and springs here are *reposoirs* (resting places) for powerful *loa*, and the creator god Damballah reigns here with his consort Aida Wedo, the rainbow. Damballah is a great white serpent of seven thousand coils, but don't let that scare you off. He's a wise and patient *loa* who radiates good vibes, so ancient that he'll just hiss or whistle to you gently instead of speaking.

Lan Guinée is named after Guinea in West Africa, and its capital Ife seems to be a reflection of Ife-Ife, an important city in Yoruba myth. Ife-Ife is where the legendary king Oduduwa emptied a snail shell full of sand, creating the first dry land, and planted the first palm nut, creating the first plant life. The dream of vodou is an ancestral memory of Africa, a desire to return home across the sea and reclaim a paradise lost to slavery and the Middle Passage.

During the days of Caribbean slavery, escaping the misery via suicide was a common fact of life among the enslaved. Sugar plantation owners encouraged the belief that enslaved people who killed themselves would *not* return to Lan Guinée, but would remain behind in the Haitian fields, soulless and undead. This is probably the origin of the zombie trope that became well-known in vodou culture and, eventually, took over all of Western pop culture. Halloween and *The Walking Dead* seem a lot less fun when you know that all the shambling, brain-hungry zombies started out as sugar plantation slaves who just wanted to go home.

How Low Can You Go?

LIMBO

Roman Catholicism

"Pope Closes Limbo" read the *New York Times* headline on April 21, 2007. In *Newsweek*, His Holiness "let go of" limbo; in *Time*, he "banished" it. Updates to the afterlife rarely make the front page, but Benedict XVI's endorsement of a long-awaited study by a Vatican theological committee went viral, and suddenly everyone was talking about limbo. But those who read down into the fine print of these articles discovered that the "closure" wasn't so definitive after all, because there wasn't really any limbo to close. All afterlives may be hypothetical, but limbo is *especially* so.

Limbo as a concept was born when the early church fathers ran into a tricky theological problem. If you believe, as Roman Catholics do, that all children are born into original sin, and that only the sacrament of baptism can cleanse us, then at some point you have to reckon with the fact that millions of little children die without baptism, and therefore cannot be saved.

Scripture is entirely silent on what happens to them, but believers tend to be pretty determined *not* to visualize babies screaming in the fiery lake of hell. Parents, especially parents who have lost children, are especially vocal on this point. But if the little tykes can't enter heaven either, then what? Out of this negative space arose limbo, a netherworld between the two final destinations ("*limbus*" is Latin for "boundary") where the innocent-but-unbaptized go. *Limbus patrum* is the "limbo of the patriarchs," the proverbial "Abraham's bosom" where the Old Testament prophets slept before Christ's resurrection allowed them into heaven. But *limbus infantium*, the "limbo of the infants," persisted into modern Catholic thought, as a place where those who died before baptism, through no fault of their own, could escape the sufferings of the damned.

What's eternity like in this netherworld? The problem is that the concept of limbo was never officially defined in Catholic dogma, so any description of life there would be purely speculative. No medieval visionaries seem to have reported a visit to limbo—apart from Dante, who, as we shall see, described it as a pleasant resort perched on the edge of hell's First Circle. The big names in Christian scholarship even disagreed on the basics of limbo life. Augustine wrote that, if sent to limbo after death, you would still experience a mild case of *poena sensus*, the burning torments of hell; Abelard thought that was a little harsh and decided that in limbo, you only feel *poena damni*, the sense of interior loss that comes with being separated from the beatific vision of God. Aquinas, that big softie, wrote that limbo was free from *both* kinds of pain, and that the souls there lived in perfect natural gladness, since they had no knowledge of what they were missing out on in heaven.

But all that is moot; since 2007, limbo has seemed to be an unlikely destination for you, even if you're an unbaptized infant. In their report to the church, the International Theological Commission didn't rule out limbo, but they opined that God's allowing unbaptized infants into heaven is, in fact, consistent with Catholic dogma. If true, that would make limbo unnecessary. This is a disappointment for those who like the broadest possible array of postmortal travel options, but a comfort to a great many Catholic parents.

NARAKA
Hinduism

In Hinduism, hell is Naraka, a temporary state where all your earthly misdeeds are expiated before the reincarnation of the soul. The great Sanskrit epic poems and Puranas describe Naraka in close detail: twenty-eight hells, for a variety of sins large and small. They also outline how you'll spend your next life—again, in forms both large and small. You might leave Naraka as a camel, or you might leave as a worm.

At the moment of death, a virtuous Hindu soul leaves the body through the eyes, ears, nose, or mouth. Unfortunately, you're headed to Naraka, so you'll leave your body through a lower orifice: the genitals or anus. Follow a dark, stinking path covered with hair instead of grass, and flesh and blood instead of mud, where worms writhe and flies buzz in piles of dismembered corpses. Past the boiling river and the forest of thorns, you'll cross a plain of white sand and iron stones, both blazing hot under hell's twelve suns. Finally, after a journey of eighty-six thousand *krosa*s (a *krosa* is about two miles), messengers from Naraka will lead you through the fortress's southern gate, where you'll hear the shrieking of one hundred vixens. You will babble with fear as the governors of hell approach: serpents with the heads of cats, owls, frogs, and vultures. They'll bind you with chains and nooses, smear you with blood, and drag you inside.

Your first walk through Naraka will be a lot to take in. Besides the expected beatings and burnings, you'll spot novel punishments like quicksand, cobras, furious rogue elephants, and the hell of "six bad smells." You'll be pelted by a constant barrage of projectiles: arrows, dust clouds, meteor showers, squirts of acid. It's a real Nickelodeon game show down here.

LOCAL FARE

You might feel some momentary hope as you pass great banquet tables weighed down with mountains of rice and yogurt as well as many cool and fragrant beverages. But when you beg for a taste, the demons will just taunt you. This delicious Indian buffet isn't for you! You didn't give generous sacrifices and charitable gifts in life, so you don't get any here.

Your destination is the court of Lord Yama, the Hindu underworld god who drinks the ocean, swallows the world, and vomits fire. He sits on a great buffalo, surrounded by his attendants Death, Annihilation, Nightmare, Smallpox, and so forth, all armed with fearsome spears and tridents and discuses. Yama is dark as kohl, with blazing red eyes, fearsome eyebrows and mustache, curved fangs, and eighteen arms. He's bedecked in a yellow robe and red flowers. His court will rebuke you for your sins, and then his servants will pick you up by the feet and slam you into slabs of rock. Then you'll be assigned to one of his twenty-eight hells.

There's an astonishing variety and invention to the suffering in Naraka. You might fall down a bottomless well, plagued on all sides by thorns and fire, for 110,300 years. You might spin on a potter's wheel while demons slice away at you with wires. You might be banished to a hell so cold and dark that when you cling to the other damned souls, your teeth freeze to theirs. Generally, these punishments are tied to specific sins. For example, wine bibbers drown in nasal mucus. Thieves get spears and leeches. Men who hit on their daughters-in-law are burned with hot coals. Sellers of milk get beaten with an adamantine chain.

Yes, "sellers of milk." The list of offenses punished in Naraka is long and puzzling. People who cut the canopies off trees get barraged by thunderbolts. Those who mixed with other castes are thrown into boiling molasses. If you ever ate a delicious treat without sharing it, you are force-fed insect poop. Often terrible crimes are expiated alongside the most venial offenses: "he who commits multiple murders of villagers" winds up in the same hell as "he who destroys honey." An arsonist might share a spot with "he who subsists on the trade of fish."

Your bizarre torment won't last forever. Eventually you'll return to earth—but, again, a list of oddly specific sins will determine your fate. If you stole perfume in this life, you'll be reincarnated as a female muskrat. If you stole gold, you'll come back as a human with terrible nails. If you cheated with your teacher's spouse, you might come back as a clump of grass! That sounds dull, but on the bright side, it'll be hard to commit too many terrible sins in your new grass life. Grass can't destroy honey or subsist on the trade of fish!

NIRVANA

Buddhism

THE PARADISE EARTH

Jehovah's Witnesses

In the heaven envisioned by Jehovah's Witnesses, God's chosen are resurrected as immortal spirits and reign alongside Jesus Christ. (Since Witnesses don't believe in the Trinity, the Jesus who governs heaven is not the same as God/Jehovah, but rather His first creation.) The main difference between Jehovah's Witness heaven and the one in mainstream Christianity is population. According to Witnesses, only 144,000 "anointed" Christians will make it to heaven. No more, no less.

This strict afterlife quota isn't a zoning issue. It's based on a literal reading of Revelation chapter 7, in which John learns that "the number of those who were sealed" is "a hundred and forty-four thousand, sealed out of every tribe of the sons of Israel." When the Witnesses were a small millenarian sect in the late 1800s, this cap made sense. But over the following century, the denomination's growth created a problem—not a theological one so much as a math one. There are now almost nine million Jehovah's Witnesses worldwide vying for just 144,000 spots. In other words, heaven now has a more daunting admissions rate than Harvard.

In 1935, Joseph Rutherford, the second president of the Watch Tower Bible and Tract Society, solved this problem by broadening the group's view of the afterlife. He announced that while Jehovah has still reserved a place in heaven for 144,000 elect followers, everyone else gets a very nice consolation prize: the chance to live forever on earth. And not our current, lame earth either. A *paradise* earth.

According to the Witnesses' reading of Isaiah, the Paradise Earth is a perfect place, free of death, disease, and unhappiness of all kinds. Everyone lives in beautiful homes and works together as friends. It's what the Garden of Eden could have been if Adam and Eve had cut out the inappropriate snacking. Its millions or even billions of residents belong to what the Jehovah's Witnesses call the "great multitude of other sheep," and they're not the least bit bummed to miss out on being among the elect running the show in heaven.

If the lush acrylic paintings in every issue of the *Watchtower* magazine are to be believed, your eternity on the Paradise Earth will be something like a laid-back corporate retreat. In these illustrations, groups of multiracial people in polo shirts lounge on the grass amid eye-popping natural splendor. You'll be picnicking, guitar-playing, and having a lot of fun with animals. Often majestic predators like tigers and wolves are pictured chilling nearby, in fulfillment of the biblical prophecy about lions and livestock lying down together.

Paradise will be populated by those who, sooner or later, accepted Jehovah and did His will. What about the wicked? There is no hell in the Jehovah's Witnesses' theology. Remarkably, the dead stay dead. "The dead know not anything," as per Ecclesiastes 9:5. Hell is nonexistence.

As a result, if you're an atheist and two nice Jehovah's Witnesses in severe skirts ever knock on your door, you can tell them you already agree on many things. You believe that atheists like you won't live on in the afterlife—and so do they!

Trolling in the Deep

THE SPIRITUAL WORLD
Swedenborgianism

In 1758, the Swedish mystic Emanuel Swedenborg published *Heaven and Its Wonders and Hell, from Things Heard and Seen*, based on his visions of the afterlife. Though Swedenborg never formed a church, his theology was influential—particularly in America, where famous fans from Johnny Appleseed to Helen Keller spread the good word about his teachings.

In Swedenborg's visions, he saw that the "spiritual world" consists of heaven, hell, and a third realm: the World of Spirits, which will be the first step of your journey. When your heart stops at the end of this life, angels from the Lord's spiritual kingdom will arrive to usher you onward. You'll suddenly have the weirdest sensation, like your left eye is being rolled back toward your nose. That's your vision changing. Now you can see the clear light of a new heavenly color and your thoughts are suddenly spiritual, not natural ones. Welcome to the World of Spirits.

In rare cases, the dead are already "regenerated"—ready to move on to heaven—or they're such malicious liars and hypocrites that they immediately plunge into hell, some headfirst. But most people will spend some time in the World of Spirits sorting out their final destiny. Some will stay a few weeks. Others will be here for thirty years.

This is a world of introspection and instruction, as you gradually get a clearer-eyed view of eternity. At first, you'll find yourself in surroundings so much like this world that you'll tend to forget you're dead. After all, you're the same as ever, still able to think, talk, sense, touch. It'll be as if your burial were just a run to Goodwill, discarding old stuff. Friends who passed on before you will lead you through a series of cities, gardens, and parks. For as long as a year, you'll enjoy this tour, assuming that your outwardly civic-minded life on Earth will guarantee you a ticket to heaven.

But gradually you'll move into a state of deeper awareness as you remember your mortal weaknesses more clearly and become aware of the real intentions behind your acts. Were you *really* a kind and truthful person or just a well-behaved one? At this point the truly good begin to attain real wisdom, while the wicked act out and rebel. Your appearance will even change to match your inner self. If you start to look a little haggard in the mirror at this point, it's not good news.

See, your assignment to heaven or hell *is* a judgment, but it comes from you, not the Lord. Truly regenerated souls yearn for instruction on this matter, and they get a brief, personalized course of study from the angels of heaven, who model the "divine pattern" for them. You will be issued angelic clothing of white linen, and the Lord will lead you to heaven, which will accept you with joy. But evil souls can't help but rebel against this new awareness. They just love carnal things more than divine ones and will follow that love down to hell.

Heaven isn't one gleaming city of God. Swedenborg saw a multitude of communities, each devoted to a different activity of love and faith. There's something here for everyone. Some take charge of souls who died in infancy and rear them to adulthood. Others are tasked with teaching new arrivals or overseeing hell. Many have ecclesiastical or even civic duties. That's because the Divine Being didn't create any angels or devils—heaven and hell are completely staffed by dead mortals.

As you near your community, it will look like a white cloud in the east surrounded by little stars, gradually reddening as you approach and coalescing into human form. Each star is an angel, but the community as a whole looks like an angel too, each member reflecting the whole. In fact, the hundreds or thousands of angels in each of these heavenly offices or departments have a similar facial "look," like family resemblances back on earth.

LEARN THE LANGUAGE

Everyone here speaks and writes in the same new tongue, unearthly but most similar to Hebrew. It lends itself so well to expressions of love and beauty that the simplest conversation or series of pen strokes will bring you to tears.

In your heavenly time off, admire the perfect architecture and landscaping of your community. You'll stay in a series of spacious suites and courtyards, surrounded by lawns and gardens, with lanes and squares connecting your home to your neighbors'. But this layout is largely an illusion. Time and space don't exist in the spiritual world—there's no past or future or east or west, just changes of state. So any journey here can take as little time as you want—or as much, if you're enjoying the walk. Everyone's here: rich and poor, Christian and non-Christian, billions of people from Earth *and* all the other planets in the Lord's creation. Eventually, you may find a member of your community so simpatico with you and your interests that the other angels will throw you a wedding feast, and you'll live together in marriage.

Like heaven, hell is a series of communities, but without the nice plazas and flower beds. Each hell is entered via gloomy gates under cliffs or in rocky crevices in the World of Spirits. All are dark, with a glow like sulfur or hot coals. Some are downward-slanting caverns; others are vaulted crypts, mines, dark forests, animal dens, or burned-out ruins of cities. Milder hells might be shantytowns full of domestic violence and abuse, with thieves lurking in every alleyway, or vast red-light districts of infinite sleaziness. The worst ones are just empty deserts. Each is for a particular flavor of evil, with similar sins bunched geographically together.

Hell emanates a great malevolence and rage. Just as angels have more capacity for good once freed from mortal life, evil spirits have a greater knack for malice and craft! Everyone here is the slave of fear and self-absorption. They look human to each other, as an act of divine mercy, but in reality the savagery and cruelty of their particular sins show through from within, to monstrous effect.

The angels charged with administering hell don't torture the inhabitants; in fact, they spend most of their time trying to moderate and balance hell's torments, so as not to exceed the divine will. According to Swedenborg, it's the damned who torment *each other* with endless baiting and dehumanizing mockery. Hell is a vast internet forum, trolling itself forever.

THE SUMMERLAND

Spiritualism and Witchcraft

Followers of Wicca and other modern pagan religions don't always agree on specifics of theology, but many envision a peaceful afterlife called the Summerland. This is generally a place of rest and reflection, as spirits recover from life's troubles and make plans for their next reincarnation. There you're in the company of the God and Goddess, and you can stay as long as you want—maybe even forever, becoming a spirit guide for new arrivals. In many accounts, the Summerland is a place of abundance: grassy fields and peaceful rivers, never a day of bad weather. To others, it's not a real "land" at all, just a placeless state of communion with the energies of the universe. Wiccans are way too chill to insist on specifics here.

The Summerland, like much about the neo-pagan movements, began with the spiritualists and Theosophists of the nineteenth century. These occultists dreamed up an afterlife that would primarily serve to explain the phenomena they witnessed in their séances and other rituals: ghosts knocking on tables, speaking through mediums, haunting houses, and so forth.

Andrew Jackson Davis, the "Poughkeepsie Seer" who helped create the spiritualist movement, wrote several books of minutely detailed descriptions of the Summerland, which he described as "an inhabitable Sphere or Zone among the Suns and Planets in Space." Davis had his mind blown by new scientific calculations about the immensity of space, like a stoned teen reeling at the night sky above, and was convinced that the Summerland was a blazing belt of ether hundreds of millions of miles above the Earth.

As you rise beyond the clouds toward the Summerland, you'll be traveling at the speed of light or thought through the "celestial current"—but you'll hardly feel any motion at all. Millions of tons of atomic emanations rise from the living every year and float into space on this current, eventually being refined into the higher matter of the afterlife.

When you arrive on the Summerland's shores, you'll see that all these particles have been perfected to form a place of infinite beauty and diversity: velvet soil, lush groves, crystalline streams. The radiant sky above is filled with unfamiliar nebulae and constellations. You'll never forget the fragrance of the Seven Lakes of Cylosimar or the brilliance of the star Guptarion rising above the silver waters of Lake Mornia. In the distant hills, the dead from Venus and Mercury wander in the sunbeams. (Yes, the quadrillions of souls here include plenty of aliens.) Following the great river Nezar to the east, you'll find a less cheery valley: Ara-Elin-Haroun, where angels work to heal the mentally ill, those who took their own lives, and other souls damaged by life.

Different societies and brotherhoods have formed to do good works here, like philanthropists on Earth. At the highest levels, these groups are run by those souls most enlightened in the principles of the Divine Mind—mostly from Jupiter or Saturn. At their yearslong festivals, you will join in the singing and discover that your celestial voice can reproduce all the sounds of any musical instrument. Your wisdom and willpower will have increased as well, so you can still drop in on faraway Earth and communicate with the living, especially to help and comfort them.

Theosophist writers like Charles Webster Leadbeater also described an afterlife where the dead could contact the living, but they assumed that the sunny Summerland of so many visions was just the lower levels of the astral plane, where self-absorbed spirits who are still stuck on mortal life conjure up idealized versions of Earth. If you are a pure person, well schooled in the Wisdom Religion, you will feel no attraction to the grosser matter of the Summerland and will soon be able to rise to a higher plane, the devachan. But those with less occult development may be here for centuries.

> **OFF THE BEATEN PATH**
>
> If you're a truly degraded person, your lower manas will become so enmeshed in earthly passions that you'll separate from the higher ego and haunt the Earth as a vampire or werewolf!

The astral plane is a chaotic place, full of the many different kinds of spirits responsible for various manifestations and hauntings. With your enhanced astral vision, you'll be able to see every aspect of all of them. The oval masses of luminous mist surrounding everyone are their auras, and that includes the living and the dead. (Yes, the living are here—they have astral selves as well.) You'll also see the drifting etheric shells that astral souls leave behind on their way out of life, the shades left over when souls move on to the devachanic plane, nonhuman elementals, nature spirits like gnomes and naiads, the auras of animals, and even nonhuman angelic beings called devas, the regents of the Earth. The most esoteric residents of this plane are the "human artificials" that sometimes get created to replace dead souls that have moved on, but that's a complicated story all bound up in the history of ancient Atlantis. Weird, in other words, even for Theosophy.

THREE KINGDOMS OF GLORY

Latter-Day Saints

Many visions of the world to come, dreamed up in times of brutal subsistence living, promise endless leisure and luxury. But not so the afterlife envisioned by the Church of Jesus Christ of Latter-day Saints. As befits their peach-canning, carpool-driving, casserole-delivering image as the industrious honeybees of the American West, Mormons head to the grave prepared to *keep on working*.

Latter-day Saint cosmology is so elaborate that the church's young missionaries sometimes resort to flowcharts to explain the whole thing. When this earthly sojourn ends, the deceased first enter a temporary arrangement called the Spirit World—conveniently located right here on earth, and separated from the living only by "the Veil," a metaphorical divider of some kind that prevents the living from glimpsing the eternities. Your spirit, which will look just like an adult version of your mortal body, will be "laboring and toiling diligently," said Brigham Young. "Those spirits . . . sleep not."

And what will you spend your twenty-four-hour shifts doing? The dead "walk, converse, and have their meetings" with the souls of the righteous (they occupy the nice part of town, "Spirit Paradise"), busily teaching the gospel to the souls of those who have not yet accepted Christ (they live in "Spirit Prison," borrowing Peter's gloomy turn of phrase in 1 Peter 3:19). This missionary crusade will be more fruitful than the Mormons' door-to-door efforts in this life, because human minds will no longer be dulled by mortality. "Instead of thinking in one channel," wrote early Mormon apostle Orson Pratt, "knowledge will rush in from all quarters; it will come in light like the light which flows from the sun."

TIME-SAVER!

Not having a body is also a big efficiency in the humming prairie-dog warren of the Mormon afterlife, since it allows for teleportation "with lightning speed to any planet, or fixed star, or to the uttermost part of the earth, or to the depths of the sea," as Brigham Young promised.

Despite their new superhuman abilities, wrote one Mormon prophet who had a vision of the Spirit World, "the dead . . . looked upon the long absence of their spirits from their bodies as a bondage." When the Resurrection arrives for all men and women—first the just (including those who were converted after death) and then the unjust—your spirit will be permanently reunited with your glorified, perfected body. The Mormon afterlife is a specifically physical and tangible one.

At the Final Judgment, the resurrected dead are then assigned to one of three "kingdoms of glory," described by the church's founder, Joseph Smith, using a metaphor from 1 Corinthians about the respective brightness of the sun, moon, and stars. The righteous wind up with God the Father and Jesus Christ in the Celestial Kingdom (the glory of the sun); those less worthy will be unable to abide God's presence and will actually prefer the Terrestrial Kingdom (the glory of the moon) or Telestial Kingdom (the glory of the stars).

TRAVEL TRIVIA

Don't bother looking up "telestial" in your dictionary; it's a coinage invented by Joseph Smith that you won't find anywhere else.

You can't really go wrong here; all three kingdoms of glory are world-class destinations. According to Mormon scripture, even the economy-cabin option, the Telestial Kingdom, "surpasses all understanding" to our mortal minds. Contra the claims of the stage musical *The Book of Mormon*, which depicts a "spooky Mormon hell dream" complete with dancing coffees, there is no real hell in Latter-day Saint theology. A small number of "sons of perdition" will be banished to a glory-free sphere known as Outer Darkness, but that's not an all-purpose punishment for everyone who owns a Starbucks card. It's reserved for a select, perverse few who had a sure personal witness of Christ and denied Him anyway.

To enter the Celestial Kingdom and gain "eternal exaltation," said Brigham Young, you must pass angels who stand as sentinels and, as in the Egyptian underworld, give them certain key words, signs, and tokens to get by. (Luckily these are provided in Mormon temple liturgy.) Upon passing through a gate of encircling fire and stepping onto the gold-paved streets of Mount Zion—a.k.a. the city of the living God, a.k.a. the heavenly Jerusalem—you will receive a white stone with a secret new name written upon it, as promised in Revelation chapter 2. This stone will be your "Urim and Thummim," a reference to some kind of priestly gear used for divination in the Old Testament.

The blazing throne of God, which Mormon scripture locates near a star called Kolob, sits on a "globe like a sea of glass and fire." Since Joseph Smith also taught that the Earth itself will be celestialized into crystalline glory, many believers assume that the Celestial Kingdom is a rebooted planet Earth.

Once you're in the heavenly city, is it finally time to kick back, believers? It is not! The Mormon gospel is one of "eternal progression," so working and learning and growth continue even in heaven. So do families: earthly marriage and family bonds persist in the Celestial Kingdom. Joseph Smith said to expect "that same sociality which exists among us here," which presumably would also include neighbors, friends, work friends, Facebook friends, and Facebook friends trying to sell you essential oils.

The biggest news is that there's no limit to progression in the afterlife. Celestial souls can advance so far in glory that they essentially become gods—with the divine ability to create and people their own worlds, many leading Latter-day Saints have taught.

So let's recap the itinerary: spirit prison, spirit paradise, resurrection and judgment, Outer Darkness, Telestial Kingdom, Terrestrial Kingdom, Celestial Kingdom. When Jesus said that His Father's house had "many mansions," He wasn't kidding.

TZROR HA-HAYYIM

Kabbalah

Beyond Gehenna and Gan Eden, even more elaborate Judaistic journeys through the afterlife are possible through the tradition of Kabbalah. This school of Jewish mysticism was *not* founded in the early 2000s by Madonna and Ashton Kutcher, as is popularly believed, but dates back to the publication of an esoteric text called the *Zohar* ("Radiance") in thirteenth-century Spain.

According to the *Zohar*, judgment is a seven-stage process that begins thirty days *before* you die. On your sickbed, you will receive a series of supernatural visitors as you near death. You will glimpse the Shechinah, a female manifestation of God, which will be accompanied by three heavenly messengers, each with a different job description. The first is your guardian angel, while the next two are a pair of angelic Fitbits: the angel in charge of counting down your days and the one who tracks all your good and bad deeds. Deceased friends and relatives will look in on you, and so will your most distant relative: Adam himself, of Adam-and-Eve fame. He'll drop by to remind you that he only sinned once, that whole apple thing, whereas you have a whole lifetime of sins to answer for. Gee, thanks, Adam.

In Kabbalistic thought, the human soul has three parts. Your *nefesh* ("breath") constitutes your lowest animal self. It stays in the grave suffering *hibbut ha-kever*, the trembling, sweaty anguish of your body separating away and then decomposing. Your *ruach*, the spirit of your moral virtues, gets hurled into the afterlife by *kaf ha-kela*, a divine catapult. First, you must be purified for one year in Gehenna, just as in the Talmud. (To this day, Jews say kaddish, the prayer of mourning, for a maximum of eleven months, in accordance with this purgatorial period.)

SAVVY TRAVELER TIP

At least the blazing fires in hell are cooled for you on the Sabbath, and you can avoid some torments by having lived a good life—especially if the angels notice you're a circumcised man!

After your year is up, you'll dip into the purifying, spice-perfumed waters of Nahar Dinur, the River of Light, and move on to Lower Gan Eden.

The third part of your spirit, the *neshamah*, is your "super-soul," your intellect. It can ascend to bliss in the *nicer* neighborhood of heaven: Upper Gan Eden. Your body has now been replaced by a translucent garment of spirit called *guf ha-dak*. Enjoy the dancing and Torah study. You've earned it!

But, unlike in mainstream Judaism, the journey doesn't end here. Kabbalists believe in *gilgul* ("wheel"), the reincarnation and transmigration of souls. When you tire of Gan Eden, you can advance to the Holy King's glory and be bound up in *tzror ha-hayyim*, the "bundle of the living." This is God's storehouse of souls, all waiting to head back to earth. There are two kinds of return ticket possible. You can beam back to earth temporarily to inhabit the souls of the living—either as a helpful *ibbur* or a malevolent *dybbuk*. Or you can return as a newborn for another human lifespan, hopefully fixing some of the mistakes you made last time.

Your spiritual body has 248 limbs and 365 sinews, representing the 248 positive commandments and the 365 "thou shalt not"s of the Torah. Will you look kind of strange? Maybe. But the good news is, once you advance through *gilgul* enough to observe all 613 laws, you can leave the cycle. You'll be physically resurrected in a perfect body and merge with God Himself, in "the very Body of the King." Hopefully God doesn't mind all those new limbs and sinews!

VAIKUNTHA

Hinduism

A much more pleasant Hindu afterlife than Naraka is Svargaloka, a paradise ruled by the god Indra from atop Mount Meru, the golden peak at the center of the universe. There you can relax in the "pleasure valleys" and await your next incarnation. But that isn't your ultimate goal. What you want is *moksha*, release from the law of karma and its cycle of rebirths.

The saints who attain *moksha* ascend to the Vaikuntha planets, the abode of the Lord Vishnu. This realm isn't just in the sky—it's beyond the sky. You're now in the highest heaven, beyond the billions of universes the Lord has created. Your complexion is now a glowing sky blue or diamond or coral, your eyes are like lotus flowers, and you're young again and more attractive than you ever were in life. Also, you have four hands.

LOCAL DRESS

Before you explore, take a moment to change into the customary garb of Vaikuntha: yellowish robes, garlands of flowers, earrings, and medallions strung on pearl necklaces. You can obtain your new wardrobe from the trees around you, which are full of flowers and fruits all year long and will grant your every wish.

The Bhagavata Purana describes Vaikuntha as a transcendental land of forests and palaces beyond time, ignorance, and passions. The ground is made of touchstone and the walls of marble. Madhavi flowers fill the air with a fragrant scent of honey, but you won't even notice because you'll be so busy singing about Vishnu's many great qualities. Exotic birds (cuckoos, cranes, peacocks, parrots) fill the air with music, but even they pause when the king of bumblebees hums a hymn of praise to Vishnu. You have a five-star palace of your own, an opulent home of lapis lazuli, emeralds, and gold. There you'll live with your spouse and many consorts, all of whom have bewitching smiles and "rotund buttocks"—but, once again, even those charms won't distract you from the glories of Vishnu.

Lord Vishnu himself lives in Vaikuntha-puri, a palace you can enter via seven great gates of gold and diamonds. At the last gate, don't be intimidated by two blue, four-armed doormen wielding maces and fresh flowers. Jaya and Vijaya are imposing bodyguards, but they know better than to hold you up. They were once exiled from Vaikuntha for three lifetimes for preventing sages from approaching the Lord.

As you enter, you'll see Lakshmi and other goddesses of fortune laying garlands on the coral-lined edges of pools around the throne, while other attendants shade their Lord with parasols and cool him with fans. Vishnu is blackish in color, with a smile like a blossoming flower and toenails that glow like rubies. He may be wearing a helmet and riding Garuda, the king of birds, or he may walk toward you, his white hair rippling behind him in slow motion. He will wear only a yellow cloth around his waist with a gleaming girdle, but he's also adorned with pendants shaped like alligators as well as many bejeweled crowns and necklaces. Despite all the alluring flowers that grow here, Vishnu garlands himself only with simple leaves of *tulsi*, holy basil. The smell of it will bring a moment of deep enlightenment even for a great sage like yourself!

Outside of Vishnu's palace, the most impressive attraction here is the fleet of *vimana* that fills the sky. In Indian mythology, *vimana* are great palaces and chariots that fly through the air. The poets say that, despite the perfect weather here, the skies resemble a thunderstorm, because the *vimana* tower overhead like great clouds, and the women who fly them are as beautiful and brilliant as lightning. That's right: in Vaikuntha, you will have your own celestial airplane. You will whiz through the heavens forever, long after the material world fades away.

THE VILLAGE OF ANCESTORS

Traditional African Religions

Everyone tends to underestimate the vastness of Africa. It's the second-largest continent on Earth, bigger than the United States, Europe, and China combined. Africa is huge, and its people are far from monolithic, including in their religious conception of the afterlife.

For example, the Nuer and Dinka people of southern Sudan say that immortality is achieved only on earth through one's children and cattle, not for the soul in the hereafter. The Nuer say that a rope once connected heaven and earth, so that the elderly could climb up and become reinvigorated—but the rope was cut long ago by the hyena, and since that day death has been inevitable and permanent. The Yoruba of Nigeria, by contrast, expect a final judgment between bliss in Orun-Rere (the "Good Realm") and torment in Orun-Apadi (the "Realm of Potsherds").

But those beliefs are the exception, not the rule. Despite the continent's diversity, most indigenous African religions do agree on at least the general contours of the afterlife that awaits us. And believers might even quibble about the word "afterlife," because the dead are still a vital part of their family and community life.

Everyone has a specific lifespan allotted to them, but sometimes that accounting goes wrong. If your life was cut short by some misadventure (accident, infant mortality, unclean disease, machinations of a witch), you'll begin the afterlife as a restless ghost, scaring and annoying your former neighbors. You'll pass your days idly throwing stones, unthatching roofs, and harassing your widow or widower's new boo. This can also happen if your body isn't buried properly, so African cultures have generally been careful to gather whatever tiny human remains they can from even the most ferocious fire or animal attack. (If no remains at all are available, there are work-arounds. The Luo people, for example, will bury the biggest sausage-tree fruit they can find in lieu of a corpse.) The Yoruba say that if you end your own life, you'll linger as well, hovering in the treetops nearby like a butterfly or bat.

MAPPING THE JOURNEY

To keep these spectral nuisances from coming back, some tribes remove the deceased from the house by cutting a hole in the wall rather than using a door, or carrying the body to the graveyard in a zigzag path or through thorny thickets. Beware, they're trying to confuse and ditch you!

But even if you have to spend some time in poltergeist purgatory, you eventually continue your journey to the world of the ancestors. This hidden place is variously located underground, across a river, or in the forest, but it always lies down a dark and difficult path. The Chagga of Tanzania say the journey takes nine days, so they anoint dead bodies with fat, fill them with milk, and cover them with animal skins for protection. Then they sacrifice a bull to let the deceased's grandfather in the next world know to keep an eye out for the newcomer.

You now join your ancestors in a realm that's similar to this one, but with fresher air and no hunger or tears or sickness. The Mende still expect to be rice farming; the Luo say there's still joking and teasing. There are rivers, mountains, trees, villages. As you wander through your new town, you'll see that boys are still herding goats and sheep, women are harvesting crops, men are caring for the cattle. When the sun goes down (and rises in the living world), you all gather around the fire for evening discussions. It's just like home.

In fact, it's not really correct to think of it as "life after death," because that implies some break or gap. This world is just a continuation. You're not dead; you're the living dead, still present in the lives of your family. Your job is to watch over them, helping the deserving and rejoicing in their suc-cesses. By the same token, your new moral perfection means you're even more wounded by the bad conduct of the living. When you see someone in your old community who's delinquent in their moral duty, you can punish them with sickness or other bad fortune.

The living will know you're nearby: in the shadows when they lengthen, in a fire when it dies, in the house when it creaks. (Dreamers and diviners may even be able to see and speak to you.) The Kikuyu call you *mwendwo ni iri*, "the people's beloved." Your descendants will leave you offerings of food—and local alcoholic favorites like palm wine or imported schnapps!

But you owe your immortality to their memories of you. After four or five generations have passed, even the most exemplary life is unlikely to be remembered. Your ancestor status will fade. Then it's time to be reincarnated—back into a newborn baby of your own lineage. As the song goes, you might be your own grandpa.

The Yoruba say that you will kneel before Olorun, the lord of heaven, and request a new *ori*, or destiny. The god Orishala, King of the White Cloth, will make you a new body, and Olorun will breathe into it the future you desire: wealth, wives, a good character, a long life, whatever. No rea-sonable request will be refused!

THE WESTERN PARADISE

Pure Land Buddhism

The ultimate goal of Buddhism is nirvana, release from the cycle of rebirth. Nirvana is liberation, but what the word literally means is "extinction." It's an abandonment of self. (If it's any consolation, Buddhism also holds that the self never really existed to begin with. Easy come, easy go.)

But in the tradition of Mahayana Buddhism predominant in East Asia, there's an alternative. "Pure Land" Buddhism provides a shortcut to enlightenment, a sublime realm more accessible *and* more important than achieving nirvana. This is the Western Paradise of the celestial Buddha Amitabha.

Amitabha was an ancient monk who vowed to become so enlightened that the Buddha-field of his perfection would become a peaceful destination for all those who call upon his name in the moment of death. If you sincerely speak Amitabha's name ten times as you leave this life, you won't be reborn into one of the six familiar realms of samsara (gods, demigods, humans, animals, hungry ghosts, and hell). Instead, you'll be reborn far away in the west, in a world of utmost beauty and bliss.

When you awake in the Pure Land, the view might seem underwhelming at first, but that's only because you're inside a golden lotus blossom. The amount of time you have to spend in there, incubating like a celestial Cabbage Patch Kid, depends on your karma from this life. People of great virtue who achieved deep meditation might see their lotus open immediately and find that they're already in one of the highest grades of paradise, with the Buddha nearby. Those who lived impure lives before calling out to Amitabha at the last minute might have to wait five hundred years to get out of their flower—and then find themselves in one of the lowest grades of this realm, with a long spiritual journey ahead of them before they reach the Buddha.

If you're looking for a jaw-droppingly beautiful landscape, this is the heaven for you. The Pure Land is a jeweled forest stretching endlessly in all directions. The ground is beryl, supported by rows of pillars. Everywhere you look you'll be dazzled by your brilliant surroundings: golden paths criss-crossing the ground; bodhi and sandalwood trees of seven glittering colors (purple-gold, white-silver, beryl, coral, crystal, agate, and ruby) hung with golden-threaded nets of pearls and jeweled bells; golden fruit spinning on the branches like firework wheels; ponds covered entirely in blue, pink, yellow, and white lotus flowers. Everything is made of gems, and each gem reflects every other gem, and each facet projects one thousand rays, and each ray comes in eight thousand colors. You might wish you had sunglasses.

The Western Paradise is an ambler's dream, so go for a stroll! Every time you take a step, beautiful fabric will unroll to mark your path. When you step on the flowers, they sink down a full four inches but spring back up as soon as you lift your foot. You'll be blown away by the sheer scale of everything: the bodhi trees are a million miles high and their trunks are forty thousand miles around. The light that beams upward into the sky forms giant floating platforms, each of which supports ten million jeweled pavilions. But once you get used to the size, what's most impressive about the landscape is its perfection. The trees are in perfectly parallel rows, with every leaf in a harmonious position. The eight pure breezes that pass through them produce beautiful pentatonic melodies. Just contemplating these serene sights and sounds will clear your senses and allow new insights into the dharma.

In fact, the whole vibe here is designed to improve your serenity and mindfulness. Sniffing the hundred thousand kinds of aromatic wood will rid you of impurities and passions. If you step in the ponds, the water will adjust to any temperature and depth you wish; in the ripples, you can hear the repeated chanting of any Buddhist teaching you desire. Rare birds like swans and parrots sing songs about enlightenment, monasteries appear anywhere you wish, and the musical instruments on the floating sky-pavilions produce melodic truths about emptiness and impermanence.

I hope you enjoy this life of the mind, because that's about all there is to do here. An amazing banquet of hundreds of delicacies appears every mealtime, but the food is so good that just considering the sight and smell of it will satisfy your hunger. The goal of all your contemplation is to attain Buddhahood yourself, so you'll spend most of your time near the seat of enlightenment, a majestic lotus throne of eighty-four thousand giant petals where Amitabha Buddha sits, flanked by banners each billions of times larger than Mount Meru. When you reach the highest, perfect enlightenment, you too can become the colossal golden centerpiece of your own Buddha-field!

MEET THE LOCALS

Amitabha is a gleaming giant of such radiance that the sun and moon are blocks of black ink in comparison. His face is tender, his speech is kind, his eyes vast and clear as the oceans, the tuft of hair between his eyebrows white like a snowcapped mountain, and his halo the size of the universe.

BOOKS

ASLAN'S COUNTRY

The Chronicles of Narnia

C. S. Lewis's masterpiece was his Narnia series, and whatever you think of the books' religious symbolism, you have to admit one thing: it takes a brave author to end his children's fantasy series by killing all his young protagonists, as well as their parents, *off-screen*.

In *The Chronicles of Narnia*, the fantasy world of Narnia was created by Aslan, a name Lewis borrowed from the Turkish word for "lion." Aslan is an enormous lion, gentle but terrible. He stands as tall as an elephant, and his mane and eyes gleam like gold.

Aslan is the son of the Emperor-Over-the-Sea and comes from a legendary land beyond the Great Eastern Ocean. The living may glimpse Aslan's Country, as the crew of the vessel *Dawn Treader* once did, by passing through the carpet of white lilies in the Silver Sea and looking up above the standing thirty-foot wave of water that circles the world. The lush green mountains of Aslan's kingdom can be seen rising so high that no sky is visible above them. The mountains contain groves of huge, cedarlike trees; flocks of musical birds with rainbow plumage; and streams of endlessly refreshing water.

In *The Last Battle*, when Narnia finally ends in the Armageddon-like Battle of Stable Hill, the seven earth folk who have traveled to Narnia learn that Aslan's Country actually encircles the entire world. So if you're in Narnia, you can travel to Aslan's land by striking out through the mountains of the Western Wild past Caldron Pool and swimming straight up the Great Waterfall. You'll arrive at a garden with a green wall and golden gates atop a towering hill of smooth grass. Enter when the horn sounds, and prepare for an eye-popping surprise! What seems like a small enclosure is vast on the inside, containing within it a perfected and ideal version of Narnia—and England as well, and anywhere else you might come from. Each world in the afterlife is a spur jutting out from the great mountains of Aslan. "There is a way into my country from all the worlds," the Great Lion says.

Once you leave the living world, or "Shadowlands," your journey "further up and further in" can continue forever, in concentric circles that are each larger and more beautiful than the last. Keep an eye out as you get to know the locals! Aslan may appear to you there as a lion, or a lamb, or in his earthly guise, strongly implied to be Jesus Himself. (The Christian allegory in the Narnia books is far from subtle.)

BEST TO AVOID

The enemies of Narnia do *not* get to enjoy eternal peace in Aslan's Country; they get carried off by Tash, the vulture-headed, four-armed Narnian devil. But at least a few misguided followers of Tash are redeemed personally by Aslan, a hint that token "good people" of all religious traditions may merit entrance into heaven.

When the Pevensie children from *The Lion, the Witch, and the Wardrobe* arrive in Aslan's Country after the last battle, Aslan tells them offhandedly that this time they don't have to go back to England—because they and their friends and family all died in a terrible railway accident a few chapters earlier! So that all worked out then.

THE BRIDGE

"Revelation"

There's an old joke that you can tell about Baptists, Catholics, Mormons—any religious group held to be a little dogmatic and smug. St. Peter is ushering a new arrival into heaven and pointing out the gathering places of the various religious denominations: here are the Buddhists, there the Methodists, and so forth. When they arrive at a great wall, he shushes the new arrival and urges him to tiptoe past.

"Who lives on the other side of that wall?" the man asks.

"The [Baptists/Catholics/Mormons]!" says St. Peter. "And they think they're the only ones here!"

The exclusivity of heaven is challenged by many visions of the afterlife, but perhaps none so vividly as the one in "Revelation," a Flannery O'Connor short story published a few months after her 1964 death. O'Connor was a devout Catholic whose grimly funny portraits of the American South often emphasize its eccentrics and its grotesques.

"Revelation" describes a trying afternoon in the life of Ruth Turpin, a large, respectable Southern woman who has thought long and hard about her proper place in society. She often falls asleep at night mentally ordering the human race into a hierarchy of class and merit—"colored people" and white trash on the bottom, of course, and the vanishingly small number of people who are both wealthy *and* well-mannered on top.

On this particular day, Mrs. Turpin is forced to confront a series of indignities both large and small: a poor woman in a doctor's waiting room who insists on making conversation, an unruly child who won't move aside so she can sit down, an angry college girl who lunges at her and calls her an "old wart hog," and Black field hands who now expect friendly greetings and ice water when they pick cotton. As the sun sets that evening, Mrs. Turpin is out back watering the hogs when, without warning, she is struck by a surprising vision of heaven.

In her revelation, the streaks of cloud in the sky at dusk become a long swinging bridge rising from the earth toward heaven "through a field of living fire." An endless parade of souls climbs upward into the stars, singing hallelujahs. But what upends Mrs. Turpin's orderly and self-satisfied universe is the makeup of the horde on the bridge. If you happen to be a respectable white churchgoer like Ruth Turpin, you'll be on the bridge, but you'll be near the *end* of the procession, behind all manner of poor people and Black folks and freaks and lunatics, "shouting and clapping and leaping like frogs."

Sneak a peek behind you while crossing the bridge. The only ones not visibly happy to enter heaven will be the pious, dignified folks bringing up the rear. Like Mrs. Turpin, they will have finally realized how small and expendable their sense of order and decorum is in the eyes of God. "She could see by their shocked and altered faces," wrote O'Connor, "that even their virtues were being burned away."

A Grave Disappointment

THE CEMETERY

Lincoln in the Bardo

The ancient Greek word for a cemetery was "necropolis," literally a city of the dead. And there's a long literary tradition of setting afterlife adventures in the vibrant postmortem communities of cemeteries, stretching from Edgar Lee Masters's *Spoon River Anthology* to Neil Gaiman's *The Graveyard Book*. Why *wouldn't* the next world just be the cemetery where our loved ones wound up? After all, that's where we decided to put them.

In 2017, George Saunders won the Booker Prize for his novel *Lincoln in the Bardo*. It's set in Georgetown's Oak Hill Cemetery in Washington, D.C., on the night of February 25, 1862, following the funeral and burial of Willie Lincoln, the eleven-year-old son of the president of the United States. The shades at Oak Hill welcome Willie, but they expect he will not be with them long. Children don't tend to linger in what they call their "hospital-yard."

See, the most remarkable thing about Saunders's cemetery residents is that *they refuse to believe that they are dead*. Since most have been moldering in the earth for decades, this requires an astounding level of self-deception. They tell themselves that they will soon recover from the mysterious, previously unknown malady that has separated them from family and friends.

LEARN THE LANGUAGE

Speaking the language of the dead fluently requires a lot of euphemism. The shades here call their crypts "homes," their coffins "sick-boxes," and their corpses "sick-forms."

If you choose to linger with the denizens of your resting place, it will be because you have refused to let go of some little piece of mortal life—or "that previous place," as your new friends call it. You might have guilt over past misdeeds or regrets over some unaccomplished dream. Perhaps you are just too attached to the small beauties of earth or fear the unknown to come.

That's not an unreasonable fear! One churchman buried in Oak Hill Cemetery found himself being judged in a vast hall made of diamond. An emissary of Christ sat at a banquet table, lit by a jagged chunk of topaz on a gold stand. Luminous beings of light touched their forehead to his and asked, "How did you live? Tell it truthfully." They produced a bejeweled mirror and a scale to test the verdict, by weighing each soul's heart. The pure were admitted to feast with the Lord in a white silken tent, while the guilty entered a pavilion made of human flesh, in which the damned were flayed by a terrible beast and his fiery escorts. The churchman fled the judgment-bar in fear and decided he was content to stay in his cozy cemetery.

Your ghostly form here will mutate to reflect your earthly attachments. If you miss your beloved children, their likenesses may float about your head as gelatinous orbs. If you were a person of property, your prone body may spin like a compass arrow, pointing to your various real estate possessions as they occupy your thoughts in turn. If you died with a traumatic wound or even an erection—well, your ghost will transform accordingly.

It's tiresome to spend all day in a casket with your decaying body, only emerging by night. It's lonely never to be touched and deathly dull never to visit anywhere new. Your ability to interact with the world is so limited—occasionally raising a small dust storm or scaring an animal is all the shades can manage. Nevertheless, you'll consider yourself one of the brave elite, the wise few who have not given up the struggle for life. And you will become more of a rarity the longer you linger, because the vast majority of the dead eventually move on.

Occasionally, a warm breeze will enter your cemet—er, "hospital-yard," followed by a rush of good smells and visions of flowers, fruit, food, and drink flowing through the grass like rivers. Beings of light disguised as loved ones will try to tempt you to give up your grip on mortality, so stand firm. Those who succumb will disappear in an explosive flash that the dead call "matterlightblooming," accompanied by the crash of a "fire-sound." Remnants of their clothing will rain down from above. You will ridicule those men and women of weak resolve. Enjoy the local custom of miming urination or defecation on their grave!

But perhaps in some future moment of crisis you too will be convinced by the beckonings of the world to come. Your ghostly physical form will flicker through every stage of your life, from infancy to extreme old age—even if you never lived to see some of those years. As you disappear in a burst of fire, you will realize how silly this all was. You were never really you, or your life. *That* was the illusion; now all is real and possible and beautiful. Time will slow and then stop, as you live forever in one eternal instant.

THE EMPYREAN

Paradise Lost

John Milton set just as much of his 1667 epic poem *Paradise Lost* in heaven as he did in hell—which isn't a theological problem, but it's definitely a literary one. Satan is a terrible role model, but he's a much more interesting character than God. By the same token, Milton's "Empyreal Heaven" is a lot duller than his volcano-choked hell.

At the end of *Paradise Lost*, the archangel Michael promises that God will eventually blast Satan's hell out of existence and raise up the new heaven and earth promised in the Book of Revelation. Presumably that's where you'll end up if you choose a Miltonian paradise. But let's assume it will look more or less like the pregame heaven described in *Paradise Lost*.

If that's true, you'll arrive at a realm ringed by a crystal wall and enter through the blazing portal of its golden-hinged gate—which will open and close for you automatically, like at a grocery store. Pause to check out the superb views of the "clear hyaline" of the firmament and the earthly plane visible below. Then turn and follow the broad road into heaven, paved with stars and golden dust. From beneath, you once knew it in the night sky as the Milky Way.

Below its crystalline sky, heaven has hills, dales, rocks, waters, and woods. The grassy carpet under your feet is a green "sea of jasper" dotted with celestial purple roses. The road leads to the Holy Hill, on which sit two thrones. You can probably make out the Son sitting on His Father's right hand, but the big man Himself will be hidden in a golden cloud—God's glory is so bright that even the Seraphim shade their eyes with their wings. When He speaks with His voice of thunder, an ambrosial fragrance fills the Empyrean; when He's angry, smoke and flames wreathe His throne.

> **OFF THE BEATEN PATH**
>
> Some of heaven's best and most unusual attractions lie off the main highway. When you have time, wander over to the cave where Day and Night live, alternating their visits to earth. Or follow your nose to the golden altar where burning incense is used to perfume the prayers of the righteous before Christ presents them to His Father.

As an angel, you'll spend most of your days sitting in "fellowships of joy" around the Fount of Life and the River of Bliss, an amber stream that flows over Elysian flowers. A flower called amarant was transplanted here from Eden when Adam fell, and you'll weave its blossoms into your golden crown. When trumpets sound, you'll congregate at God's throne with the Heavenly Quire. You'll probably have a golden harp hanging at your side like a quiver of arrows; if the harp's not your thing, you can join in with "soft tunings" of organ, pipe, or dulcimer instead. Countless other angels accompany the hymns by dancing around the sacred hill in an intricate, mystical ballet that mirrors the harmonious motion of the heavenly spheres. At designated break times, banquets miraculously appear, the tables laden with heavenly fruit and rubied nectar in cups of gold and diamond and pearl. In the Empyreal twilight, pavilions appear on the plain where all can sleep—except God, of course, and those assigned to praise Him all night in shifts.

But that chill vibe can change in an instant if heaven needs to go to war. Then the heavenly host forms into ranks and companies: Thrones, Potentates, Dominations, Princedoms, Virtues, Powers, and so forth. Literally millions of banners circle the throne, each one inscribed with the great deeds of "zeal and love" performed by the angels who hold them. Two brass mountains nearby are where God keeps the armory of heaven—His chariots, His fiery steeds. The memory of Satan's rebellion means this is an unusually militarized paradise. You're in the army now.

THE FIVE LESSONS

The Five People You Meet in Heaven

In 2003, flush with the confidence that must come from selling fourteen million copies of *Tuesdays with Morrie*, Detroit sportswriter Mitch Albom decided he was ready for a *real* challenge: writing his first novel and revealing what really goes on in the afterlife. The resulting book, *The Five People You Meet in Heaven*, spent almost two years on the bestseller lists and was even adapted into a TV movie starring Jon Voight.

Albom posits a heaven where nobody wastes time lolling around on clouds, because "scenery without solace is meaningless." Instead, people go to heaven to find peace by finally understanding their lives. What was really going on down there on earth all that time anyway? This new perspective comes from learning one lesson each from a quintet of people, each occupying a different "pocket" of heaven.

After your death, you'll find yourself floating in a sky of shifting colors, from brilliant turquoise to cotton-candy pink. Soon you'll see rainbow waters swirling below you and the far-off sands of a golden shore. Splash! The sea will envelop you, and that's how you arrive in heaven.

The five pockets of heaven you visit, and maybe even the specific lessons you learn, will belong to the five people you meet. Some may be recreations of places familiar to you from your life; others will not. At first you won't be able to speak, but that will wear off soon. Your body will recover its youth, though that too will wear off. As the five lessons advance, you'll re-advance through life and age as well.

That's because time, as we understand it, doesn't exist in heaven. When you arrive, you've been dead a minute, a day, ten thousand years. Some of your five lessons will feel like brief conversations; others might be joyful reunions with loved ones that seem to go on for weeks.

Albom based his dead protagonist, an amusement park maintenance guy, on his own uncle Eddie. In heaven, Eddie meets a sideshow freak from his childhood, his old army CO, a diner waitress who reintroduces him to his abusive father, his own late wife, and a Filipino girl killed by his unit during World War II. They offer small epiphanies like "Forgiveness is important" and "You did more good than you know," so temper your expectations of solving life's mysteries. No one offers to tell Eddie which religion was the correct one, for example, or whatever happened to Amelia Earhart.

All the little aphorisms you hear are meant to convey heaven's "secret": that we are all connected and every person's story is part of one big story. Once you understand that, you float upward into the sky and hear the voice of God saying just one word: "Home." But the Almighty has plans to put you to work. You're headed to your own pocket of heaven now, but you'll spend your time waiting in line for some other soul to die, so you can join four other folks in telling your stories to them.

HALF-LIFE

Ubik

Philip K. Dick's acid-trip science fiction explored both the future of technology and the inner mysteries of human consciousness. But one of his best works, the 1969 novel *Ubik*, charts a path into the afterlife as well.

Ubik is set in the far-flung future of 1992, but in this 1992, everyone is really into psychic phenomena instead of grunge music and Malcolm X caps. It's a world of precogs and teeps (telepaths) and people with every other paranormal gift you can think of, most of which are being used against one another in corporate warfare. The wealthy live extended lives thanks to "artiforgs" (implanted artificial organs). And even when they die, they're not really dead.

As an affluent resident of the North American Confederation in 1992, you can choose, upon death, to send your body to a "half-life" moratorium, where the deceased are stored in misty glass caskets, a process called "cold-pac." A protophason amplifier tuned to your cephalic activity will allow you to communicate with your loved ones for a certain number of postmortal hours. They'll visit you in consultation lounges, where you'll be revived and speak to them via microphones and earpieces. You can use your visitation hours all at once or dole them out over centuries, your choice.

What is half-life like when you're not being revived for a chat? You dream, with no sense of time passing between consultations. At first you'll still feel the pull of gravity and your earthly identity, but that will fade over the years. Through a kind of psychic osmosis, the dreams of your casket neighbors will blend into yours, and you can interact in a shared virtual world.

Most of *Ubik* takes place in a shared half-life simulation, after the characters are abruptly killed in a bomb blast on the moon. Before you assume that you've survived a deadly accident or illness, look for the telltale signs that you're actually dead and frozen in half-life. Do you feel chilly all the time? Are you hearing mysterious voices on telephones? Is your environment gradually breaking down in small ways, sliding inexorably into the past?

That last phenomenon will be the most shocking to you. Suddenly, the coins in your pockets might start to change to antique liberty dimes and buffalo nickels. The groceries in your fridge will all be spoiled, your books years out of date. Objects will be replaced by their predecessors from Plato's realm of pure forms; for example, a television will turn into a radio, not a lump of raw plastic and glass.

Through mental focus, you may be able to push back the aging: un-sour the cream in your coffee, turn your gramophone back into a stereo. But that's just temporary. Soon entropy will come for you as well. You'll feel an oceanic pull downward, an urge to get away from people and stretch out. Don't give in! Your half-life compatriots will discover your mummified body the next morning, dead for good this time.

This accelerated virtual aging is actually being caused by one or more of your moratorium neighbors, who have discovered how to cannibalize your own life-energy to preserve *their* cephalic activity a little longer. What you need is new, improved Ubik! Puts zing in your thing! Safe when taken as directed!

Ubik is a consumer product that may enter your visions in the form of an aerosol can labeled in big golden letters. Give Ubik a spray, and a shimmering vapor full of dancing metallic flecks will provide an immediate reality support, pushing back the crumbling of your constructed world. You see, you have allies sleeping near you in cold-pac, and they've figured out how to ionize the anti-protophason particles that are sapping your dream vitality. Ubik is the opposite of entropy. It is creation. It is God. "I am Ubik. Before the universe was, I am."

But a can of Ubik won't last forever. The longer you dream, the more you will dream of other times, other identities. That's a sign that your time in half-life is coming to an end. You'll see lights around you in the darkness, other wombs in which your soul can reincarnate. Just like in the Tibetan bardo, you should look for a bright pink one, not a smoky red one. That's how you know your next full life will be better than your current chilly half-life.

THE INBETWEEN

The Lovely Bones

Alice Sebold's 2002 bestseller *The Lovely Bones* borrows a trick from movies like *Sunset Boulevard* and *American Beauty*: the dead narrator. From heaven, fourteen-year-old Susie Salmon watches life move on after she is murdered by a creepy neighbor. And it's not just Susie. This is a perfect heaven for voyeurs; everyone likes to watch.

"This wide, wide heaven," as Susie describes it, encompasses all your desires, no matter how simple. It's a house that has all the little architectural details you yearned for in life, an ice cream shop where your favorite flavor isn't seasonal. It can be anything you've ever dreamed—"Nova Scotia or Tangiers or Tibet." It you want something *and understand why*, you will get it. Because Susie died so young, her particular afterlife is the low turquoise-and-orange buildings of a typical 1960s-era American high school campus—but there are no teachers in the classrooms. It is heaven, after all.

An intake counselor will be assigned to show you around heaven when you arrive. Roads will appear to new destinations as you choose to follow them. Perhaps you'll want a joyful reunion with dead relatives or just a roommate to hang out with. Heaven can be as social as you want; you see other people any time your idea of heaven overlaps with theirs. But be warned that they may be (understandably) obsessed with death. "How to Get Away with Murder" is a popular parlor game there.

That's probably because so many of the dead spend their days in "the blue, blue Inbetween," the horizon where heaven and earth meet. You can look down at all the people inching along like ants, as if from a skyscraper, or envision yourself hovering among them.

SAVVY TRAVELER TIP

For the most interesting aerial views, try the roofs of places like hospitals and old folks' homes. There you can watch the souls of the newly dead float upward and spin like fireflies or snowflakes.

More often, you'll probably watch those you knew in life. There's a little pleasurable thrill that comes when one of the living says your name, a pinprick of sorrow when someone remembers how you died. The voices you hear around you are other dead souls chatting with the loved ones they watch, in long one-sided conversations. Susie calls it "the noise of our longing." Some of the watched living get so popular in heaven that they actually have giddy fans, like teenagers cooing over a copy of *Tiger Beat*.

Most of the time, earth life will come to you as an image; you'll have to imagine yourself standing in the old familiar places. It can be frustrating. But occasionally, contact is possible. The living might shiver when you pass by, or feel an unexplained breeze or hear a faint whisper. You might be able to affect the weather or make plants bloom. Push hard enough in the Inbetween and you can even be seen, though the living may glimpse you with ethereal strings waving outward or a cheeseclothlike veil stretched over your features. Kids will just think you're an imaginary friend; sensitive adults might know better.

On very rare occasions, a dead soul can switch places with a living one and briefly inhabit a body. When Susie does this posthumous *Freaky Friday* trick, she finally hooks up with her high school crush by inhabiting the body of her friend Ruth. In the meantime, Ruth streaks up to heaven and performs a spoken-word piece for her adoring deceased fans. It's probably best not to examine this part of the book too closely.

The living are so important to the dead that the title of the book, *The Lovely Bones*, doesn't actually refer to Susie Salmon's remains—which are never found, by the way. It's a reference to personal connections, the framework of a body of people that gets formed by her absence. In this heaven, the real lovely bones are the friends we made along the way.

Abandon all hope, ye who enter here.

—*The Gates of Hell*

INFERNO

The Divine Comedy

Dante Alighieri's masterpiece, the *Commedia*, recounts his journey through all three kingdoms of the afterlife, but most readers skip the sequels and focus on his garish and gruesome tour of hell. In theory, the Inferno should hold hundreds of millions of unbaptized humans from all over the planet, but somehow Dante mostly runs into his favorite literary characters from antiquity and his political opponents from thirteenth-century Florence, now receiving their various comeuppances. That's the great thing about hell: nine huge circles, but it still feels like a small town.

Dante's Inferno is a literal pit, a narrowing funnel-shaped abyss that steepens dramatically at its bottom, where it approaches the center of the Earth. A spiral path will take you through each of the terraces along its edge, the fabled nine circles of hell. Each realm holds a different kind of sinner, neatly arranged according to Aristotelian ethics. The first five circles are punishments for the sins of incontinence—that is, lack of self-restraint. The lower concourses are reserved for the more serious sins: violence and fraud.

When you arrive in hell through its iconic gate—don't miss the famous gloomy inscription!—you'll be presented to King Minos and confess your sins to him. Watch carefully as he wraps his serpent's tail around his body, because the number of coils will convey which of hell's circles you'll get to experience.

TOP ATTRACTIONS

THE CITY OF DIS—On the Fifth Circle of hell, you can light a flame in a tower battlement, and Phlegyas will appear to ferry you across the river Styx to Dis. (Phlegyas, like many Dante characters, is a king from Greek mythology that nobody remembers or cares about.) What's Dis? Why, it's a spectacular city of minarets, glowing from the hellish furnaces below. Avoid Medusa and the Furies guarding its walls, or you'll be turned to stone. Once inside, you're in for a surprise: the whole city is one vast, bleak cemetery, with flames emerging from a sea of open tombs. (This is the Sixth Circle, where heretics burn forever.)

THE CENTRAL WELL—Don't stop your downward spiral before you see the Ninth Circle, the very bottom of hell! The core of the universe is a frozen lake where the worst sinners of all, the treacherous, are trapped in ice. The three outer regions hold those who betrayed family, country, and guests. The fourth is reserved for those who betrayed their lords, and Lucifer himself is here, a gigantic torso emerging from the ice. This is where he landed when God cast him down from heaven. His six flapping bat wings produce the cold that air-conditions the pit, and his three monstrous faces are red, yellow, and black. In each of his mouths, he chews up one of history's great traitors: Brutus, Cassius, and Judas Iscariot.

OTHER MUST-DOS

THE CIRCLE OF VIOLENCE—Take your time scrambling down into the Seventh Circle of hell, because it takes a while to get used to the smell. You might catch a glimpse of the Minotaur, who guards this level just as he once guarded the Labyrinth of Crete. In its first ring, murderers of various kinds boil in the Phlegethon, a river of blood. The second ring is the Wood of Suicides (see page 117). The third is for those who committed violence against God and nature: blasphemers, usurers, and (according to Dante) sodomites. They lie, crouch, or wander in a sandy waste where flakes of fire fall like snow, futilely trying to shield themselves from the heat.

THE MALEBOLGE—The Eighth Circle of hell, or Malebolge ("Evil Pockets"), is actually ten circles in one: concentric circular chasms separated by high rock ridges and each holding a very different sinner ecosystem. Here's a brief rundown. In the first chasm, demons with whips march pimps and seducers around in circles. In the second, flatterers flail in human excrement. The third chasm is for greedy, corrupt religionists—but you'll only see their feet! The rest of their bodies have been crammed headfirst into round holes in the rock. The fourth is a slow parade of fortune-tellers with their heads jerked around backward, crying big, fat tears that run down their backs into their butt cracks. In the fifth chasm, graft-loving politicians are boiled in pitch and jabbed with hooks and claws by torturers above, and the sixth chasm is for hypocrites, whose monastic-looking robes are heavier than lead. The seventh chasm is the destination of thieves (see page 117) and the eighth is for evil counselors, each imprisoned in his own flame. In the ninth chasm, sowers of discord are chopped up continually by a demon with a bloody sword. The tenth is a pile of festering, sick bodies: various kinds of deceivers. Quack alchemists are now lepers, imposters are madmen, counterfeiters have dropsy, and perjurers burn with fever.

WHERE TO STAY

Compared to hell's six nether circles, described above, the upper realms of the incontinent seem downright welcoming.

THE FIRST CIRCLE—An easy "first" choice in accommodations, but it's crowded and books up fast. This is hell with an asterisk; it's actually limbo for all the folks who somehow lived virtuous lives *despite* being godless pagans. They all hang out in a majestic castle that rings a lush, green meadow. So many great leaders and thinkers are here: Homer! Aristotle!

Caesar! Too bad they all had the terrible luck to be born before Jesus, when it was a lot harder to be Christian.

THE SECOND CIRCLE—Lust must be the least serious sin, because this is the Inferno's mezzanine level, right below the lobby. It's a dark cavern where the famously horny (Cleopatra, Paris, and Helen of Troy) are beaten and blown around by a great tempest, just as their hormones must have battered them in life.

THE THIRD CIRCLE—A stinking bog of muddy rain, hail, and snow. Travel tip: if the hideous Cerberus tries to flay your flesh here, stuff its three mouths with handfuls of dirt to briefly stay its hunger.

THE FOURTH CIRCLE—Plutus, the god of wealth, rules this realm where the greedy are punished. (Yes, it's confusing that this Christian hell is full of figures from pagan mythology!) Misers and wasters push great weights back and forth here, shouting at each other all the while. Many are clergy.

THE FIFTH CIRCLE—This is where the wrathful snarl and bubble in a stinking mire of the river Styx. Finally, something to be legitimately mad about!

GETTING AROUND

You'll cross into hell over the river Acheron in the boat of Charon, a grizzled old man with flaming eyes. The circles of the Inferno are normally well connected by paths and causeways, but the great earthquake that shook the pit when Christ was crucified has left landslides and rubble. If you hit a dead end, you may need to think creatively. To get from the Seventh Circle down to the Eighth, for example, you can hop on the shoulders of Geryon, a flying monster with a scorpion's tail who now makes a pretty good elevator. Once you're down on the Eighth Circle, you can practice your parkour like Virgil once did, surfing down the steep walls of the pit in a controlled slide. Just don't ask locals for guidance! Malacoda, who leads the demons of the Eighth Circle, loves to give bad directions that leave wanderers trapped at the bottom of a chasm.

MEET THE LOCALS

Malacoda does have one amazing talent: he can summon his demonic troops by farting a military fanfare. You have to admire his sphincter control.

EATING AND DRINKING

At mealtimes in hell, you're not typically the diner, unfortunately. You'll be on the menu.

THE VESTIBULE—Just inside the Gate of Hell, this misty waiting room holds the spirits of people (and even angels) who chose neither good nor evil. As they run in circles, pursuing a whirling banner, this noisy rabble gets swarmed by wasps and hornets. The blood and tears produced by their stings feed the worms you'll see writhing at your feet. Yuck.

THE WOOD OF SUICIDES—This dreary, tangled forest in hell's Seventh Circle seems lonely at first—but the trees are actually the damned, trapped forever in wooden trunks for the sin of self-violence. Flocks of Harpies nest in their branches, feeding on their sensitive leaves.

THE CHASM OF THIEVES—This ring of the Eighth Circle is teeming with snakes, who bind and coil around the sinners. If a serpent takes a bite out of you, you'll transform into a reptile while it takes on your form in turn—and the cycle of torment will continue.

This Twain Is Bound for Glory

THE KINGDOM

"Captain Stormfield's Visit to Heaven"

The last story published by Mark Twain before his death was "Extract from Captain Stormfield's Visit to Heaven." This was an excerpt from a longer satire he'd been revising for almost forty years, about a crusty old sea captain who expects to go to hell when he dies and is surprised to find himself in paradise. The story went unpublished for decades because Twain's wife, Livy, found his depiction of heaven to be irreverent.

After leaving his lifeless body, Captain Elias Stormfield finds himself zooming through space at the speed of light. Take care not to make the same mistake he does! It's tempting to chat too long with your fellow voyagers and race the comets that will whiz by you, delivering brimstone to hell. Stormfield gets so distracted by his thrilling cosmic adventure that thirty years pass, and by the time he finally arrives in the hereafter, he's at one of heaven's most remote gates, light-years from Earth. All the clerks are confused and all the arriving souls are sky-blue aliens with seven heads and just one leg.

Pay attention and you should spot a heavenly entrance nearer to *our* solar system. It's hard to miss the spectacular jeweled gates to the Kingdom: miles high and set into an infinite wall of gold. Line up and tell a clerk the name of your home planet. He'll use a balloon to sail up his giant star chart and find Earth among the billions of worlds in the cosmos. If you're at the wrong gate, like Captain Stormfield, you can use a red wishing carpet to transport yourself to the right part of heaven. Otherwise, the clerk will issue you a harp, hymnal, wings, halo, and palm branch on the spot, and you can head for your cloud bank. You're in!

But if you're a believer in a traditional heaven, Twain says you'll still have some surprises ahead of you. The clouds of the Kingdom are littered with discarded halos and hymn books, because new arrivals soon tire of them. The big, feathery wings are unwieldy for actual flying, and singing in the heavenly choir gets old after the first day. Eventually, everyone chooses an occupation and earns a living. There must be work and pain and suffering even in heaven, or no one could appreciate happiness by contrast.

You can choose to be whatever age you like in heaven, and you'll be tempted at first by eternal youth. Surprisingly, almost everyone in the Kingdom eventually chooses a very advanced age—even those who died young! The shallowness and conceit of youth start to pall pretty quickly once you've tried the quiet life and early bedtimes of old age.

MAPPING YOUR JOURNEY

Our part of the Kingdom has the same geographic contours as Earth—but at a scale billions of times larger. If you're white, don't be surprised if white folks are rare, even within heaven's equivalent of North America. After all, as Captain Stormfield is reminded, people of color filled most corners of the globe for millennia before white people showed up there.

As you should be able to tell from its name, the Kingdom is not a democracy. There are a hundred orders of nobility, from viceroys and princes and grand-ducal archangels on down to the masses. This means there's a surprisingly TMZ-like celebrity culture in heaven, and commoners will spend thousands of years hoping to catch a glimpse of Moses or Buddha or Muhammad—or even bigger names, interstellar poets like Saa and Bo and Soof—at one of their rare public appearances.

Luckily, heaven is full of prophets you've never heard of who are just as exalted as the great religious teachers. Anonymous normal folks who quietly helped others or made great art just for themselves finally get their reward alongside Confucius and Shakespeare and Homer and all the big names. Take Richard Duffer, a humble and saintly sausage maker from Hoboken. He was shocked at the grand reception he received in the Kingdom, having suspected he hadn't been good enough for heaven and was headed to the other place. Maybe you too will be in for a pleasant surprise!

KING'S CROSS

The *Harry Potter* Books

In the waning years of the twentieth century, London's King's Cross station became a popular destination for Harry Potter fans in search of "Platform 9¾," the magical railway platform where Harry and his friends board the "Hogwarts Express" for their wizard school. (Even though wizards can teleport, they also like slow, old-timey locomotives. Maybe it's a steampunk thing?) So in 1999 the real-life train station obliged, adding a magical luggage-cart photo op (and eventually a gift shop) for fans. But how much of a Potter fan are you? Would you follow Harry to the big King's Cross in the sky?

J. K. Rowling was always a bit cagey about life beyond the grave in the magical Harry Potter universe. You can't walk ten feet in Hogwarts Castle without running into a ghost like Moaning Myrtle or Peeves, but these silvery apparitions are the exception, not the rule. Ghosts are those rare wizards who chose to leave a pale imprint of themselves upon the earth rather than "move on." The Gryffindor house ghost, Nearly Headless Nick, admits to Harry that he was afraid of death and now second-guesses his decision to remain behind. Similarly, the walls of Dumbledore's office are decorated with walking, talking portraits of past Hogwarts headmasters, but these are just memorials and not actually the souls of the late professors themselves.

The afterlife has long been studied by the Department of Mysteries, a kind of magical Area 51 on the ninth floor of the Ministry of Magic, where top-secret employees called Unspeakables explore the great forces of nature. The Death Chamber, where they study the greatest mystery of all, is a large amphitheater with a crumbling stone archway at its center. The arch is hung with a tattered black curtain that flutters in invisible breezes, a manifestation of the veil between life and death. Listen closely, and you may hear the seductive whispers of voices from beyond. (Or you might not. Hermione didn't hear them, perhaps because of her inner rationality or her lack of firsthand experience with death.) But don't succumb to your urge to pass through the archway! It's a death portal, duh. Those who enter never return.

A magical artifact called the Resurrection Stone is one of the legendary Deathly Hallows of wizarding lore. Turn this ordinary-looking rock over three times and you can bring back shades of the dead. Are these really your loved ones? Maybe, sort of. But they are sad and cold, and suffer upon being returned to the mortal world. When Harry Potter briefly brings back his parents, Sirius Black, and Remus Lupin, they appear as their much younger selves and act as his protectors, insubstantial as they are.

Later that day, when Voldemort hits Harry with a Killing Curse, they both find themselves in an empty world of light and vapor. If you arrive in this same afterlife, you will probably be able to form your surroundings any way you want. Harry arrives naked but finds robes as soon as he thinks about them. As he looks around, the vapor gradually coalesces into a deserted version of King's Cross railway station. The late Albus Dumbledore appears to him and explains that, because he sees this limbo realm as a station, he could probably catch a train there that will take him "on." Voldemort, however, is trapped here as a shuddering, deformed child curled on the ground. His soul can't move on from National Rail limbo, because he spent his noseless life being pretty awful.

It's "warm and light and peaceful" in Heavenly King's Cross, and time is hard to judge. Are hours passing or moments? Happiness radiates from those you meet there, and it appears you can stay as long as you like. When Harry asks if all this is happening just in his head, Dumbledore replies, "Of course it is happening inside your head, Harry, but why on earth should that mean that it is not real?"

MANSOUL

Jerusalem

We live in a universe of three known dimensions: length, width, and height. But what if there was a fourth spatial dimension, extending outward in some impossible-to-visualize *new* direction, at right angles to each of the other three? And what if that new dimension was the afterlife?

Alan Moore's massive 2016 novel *Jerusalem* covers millennia of history in his lifelong home of Northampton, England. But it also spends hundreds of thousands of words describing the dimension of Mansoul, the Second Borough, the eternal afterlife above the city of Northampton. Well, not "above" exactly.

When you head "Upstairs" at the moment of your death, you'll feel like you're rising toward the ceiling, and that its corners are suddenly protruding, not receding, like one of those weird optical-illusion drawings of cubes. As you move through the fourth-dimensional hinge (or "crook door") into Mansoul, deceased relatives will be there to greet you. It might be hard to talk to them at first, until you gain your "Lucy-lips." Fourth-dimensional speech unfolds its meanings in densely packed verbal geometries we don't have on earth, and even the grammatical tenses are different. You'll need a verb like "wizzle," for example, to mean "was" and "is" and "will be," all at once.

That's because every moment happens at once in Mansoul. Alan Moore is a believer in eternalism, the notion that all time—past, present, and future—is part of a complex solid that already exists and can be viewed as a single whole from outside itself. So when you emerge from your mortal life, you'll be able to see the whole thing from the Attics of the Breath, a roofed arcade a mile across and receding to a seemingly infinite distance on either end. The floorboards frame a vast grid of openings, through which you can look "down" into a series of spaces in the same earthly neighborhood. Each frame is a single moment in time, like a comic strip panel or movie still. Colorful trails will mark a few seconds of movement from each of the human souls present. To see a different space from the same region, move across the arcade. To see the same place a moment earlier or later in time, move up or down along its length. If you get lost, remember the mnemonic, "West is future, east is past / All things linger, all things last." Mansoul isn't really an afterlife; it's a before-during-*and*-afterlife.

The architecture of this arcade, like the rest of Mansoul, will be a radiantly jumbled version of the point on earth it's directly "above," because it's all formed from the dreams of the living, who can briefly wander Mansoul in their sleep during their "25,000 nights." (That's how the dead refer to mortal life.) Pigeons and sometimes cats can get to Mansoul as well, via steep passages called Jacob's ladders.

As you walk along the Attics of the Breath, you'll be a time traveler, moving through bands of day and night. Vast trees may rise up out of time in your path, because trees are the only objects whose three-dimensional appearance matches their four-dimensional growth in time. Walk far enough east into the past and the floorboards will eventually become rock. Head west into the future, and the arcade will eventually change as the architecture begins to reflect the visions of mankind's posthuman successors: purple hairless bipeds, then giant photosynthesizing land whales with horns, four-foot crabs, octopi the size of trees, and anthill hive minds. The corridor will eventually end in an awful precipice: the end of everything, the heat death of the universe.

This is a working-class heaven. Mansoul is administered by seventy-two Builders, apron-clad "angles" who maintain the universe on a cathedral-like factory floor called the Works. Chief among them are Gabriel (who represents authority), Uriel (severity), Michael (mercy), and Raphael (novelty). These four play a never-ending table game called "trilliards" with alabaster cues, enacting not just the celestial collisions that shape the universe but also the interpersonal ones that shape mortal lives. Just as our three-dimensional essences fold up into the higher geometry of these builders, they in turn fold up into the five-dimensional wholeness of the Third Borough—that is, God.

BEST TO AVOID

Another seventy-two builders were cast down into two-dimensional flatness. You've probably heard of them: Satan, Belial, Beelzebub, Asmodeus, and the rest. Their writhing forms can be seen tessellating the floors of Mansoul.

Some of the dead are afflicted with a certain "constipation of the spirit" and can't bear to leave earth for someplace with no rank or status. These restless "rough sleepers" inhabit the "ghost seam." You'll know you're in the ghost seam if the world is bleached of color and you leave a series of flickering afterimages behind you as you move.

LOCAL FARE

The best time to tunnel into the ghost seam is when you feel hungry. While you're there, keep an eye out for growths of the odd fairy fruits called Puck's hats (or mad apples, bedlam-Jennies, or Minerva's truffles), an intoxicating afterlife treat.

Eternalism means that everything happens at once, in one glorious super-instant. Your life is a book already written. That's why nobody stays in Mansoul long: it's too tempting to grab the book for a reread. It's not uncommon for the dead to jump back into their newborn selves and relive their life a thousand times—with no memory except for the occasional flashes of recognition we know as déjà vu. As with any good book, you'll find something new in it every time.

THE NULL

Revival

In Christianity, "universalism" is the belief that God will save all souls—in other words, that everyone ultimately goes to heaven. I'm not sure there's a name for Stephen King's variant of universalism, as proposed in his 2014 novel *Revival*. What do you call an eschatology in which every single human soul ultimately goes to Lovecraftian Ant Hell?

Revival is the story of a Maine musician whose life crosses paths many times with that of his childhood pastor, Charlie Jacobs. Jacobs gradually becomes obsessed with a powerful "secret electricity" that he believes can heal any sickness, and perhaps even death. At the end of the book, the secret electricity gives us a vision of what awaits us beyond death. As you might expect in a King novel, it isn't particularly cheery.

Per *Revival*, death is a small door that we shrink to approach, leaving everything behind but our mind and spirit. At the moment of your death, you may perceive the transition as a literal door, hidden behind dead ivy in a gray stone wall. The ominous voices drifting through the rusty keyhole are your first clue of what awaits you in the Null.

The Null is the plane where you'll spend the rest of eternity, the *real* existence behind the flimsy, comforting illusion of our world. It's a barren landscape dotted with ruined cities, now just piles of massive, uneven basalt blocks. Look around: everyone you know is here! Unfortunately, they're all being endlessly marched through the waste by an army of horrifying ant men. When you join the stumbling column, your expression will soon match the blank horror you see on all the faces around you. Your new insect masters sometimes crawl, sometimes walk like men. They are black and dark red, with gnashing mandibles and horrible but clearly intelligent eyes. When you fall, they'll punish you with bite wounds that hurt but don't bleed.

Above this charnel kingdom, what at first appear to be stars in the night sky are actually holes. The light emerging from them is a glimpse at the power behind the sky: malevolent ancient gods called Great Ones. Because you're serving them forever—no death, no light, no rest—you're guaranteed to eventually see the Great Ones. The sky will rip like black paper, revealing insane lights and swimming colors not meant for mortal eyes. If the god who emerges is the one called Mother, she'll have giant black limbs with spiny fur. Her body is an enormous groping claw made of screaming human faces. Not quite the God you imagined in Sunday school.

You're now a permanent slave to this tyrant, tormented by her giant ant soldiers for eternity. Settle in and get ready to march! After all, Mother knows best.

PANDEMONIUM

Paradise Lost

Milton's *Paradise Lost* is the granddaddy of fan fiction—and the blueprint for all subsequent bestsellers that retell a beloved classic from the perspective of a supporting character, from *Rosencrantz and Guildenstern Are Dead* to *Wicked*. What if the Bible, wondered Milton . . . but from Satan's point of view?

Paradise Lost opens with one of the most vivid depictions of hell in all of literature. Satan and his followers, having been cast out of heaven, find themselves chained to a fiery, sulfurous lake. It burns forever but is never consumed, and its flames somehow give off darkness rather than light. They stumble up to the dry land of this horrible dungeon, a blasted heath that glows like lava. The air is foul and polluted, and floods and whirlwinds of fire wash across the landscape.

Milton's hell is missing one important element: damned sinners. At the time in which *Paradise Lost* is set, mankind has not yet fallen from Eden, and therefore nobody has died and gone to hell yet. But should you choose this Stygian abyss as your final destination, you'll likely see many of the same sights in hell that Milton described from its heyday. Hell probably hasn't gentrified much.

The main change in today's hell is more convenient access. When God created hell, it was surrounded by a dark void, but now a smooth, broad causeway connects Satan's realm to earth. (It's paved with stones of adamantine, not good intentions.) Originally, hell was guarded by Satan's offspring, Sin and Death, and their own progeny, a pack of hellhounds. Sin is a beautiful snake woman, and Death is a fierce crowned shadow armed with fiery darts. But when Adam and Eve fell, Sin and Death left their posts, raised up this high arching bridge to Eden, and headed upstairs to wreak havoc on our world.

So you'll likely arrive at hell only to find its entrance unguarded. The open gates have nine layers: three of brass, three of iron, and three of adamantine. Their intricate portcullis of bolts and bars will be unlocked, with the key to hell still in the lock where Sin left it when she departed to tempt humankind.

Dodge the belching flames and head into the infernal world. You'll cross a battered landscape of rocks, fens, bogs, dens—a whole "universe of death." Don't miss the four rivers of hate, sorrow, weeping, and anger. Farther off, the watery labyrinth of Lethe is guarded by horrible Gorgons, so the dead can't use its gift of forgetfulness to escape their torment. Beyond these rivers is a frozen continent of snow and ice, the better to shock the damned with the contrast of heat and cold.

Great volcanoes pour out molten gold into a series of canals and foundries. When they first arrived, Satan's minions used this ore to build up a great temple of Doric pillars and golden ornaments, so gaudy that even Babylon would pale in comparison. This is the capital of hell: Pandemonium, meaning "all demons."

HISTORY BUFFS!

Pandemonium was designed by the fallen architect angel Mulciber, who also planned the great palaces of Milton's heaven (see page 104.) And its construction was suggested by Mammon, the greediest of Satan's followers. Mammon has the worst posture in hell—if you see a demon walking with his back hunched over and eyes on the ground, that's Mammon, obsessed as always with spotting any valuables that might be underfoot.

Inside Pandemonium you'll see a vast vaulted space hung with the bejeweled banners of Satan's (failed) military campaign and lit by rows of magic floating lamps fueled by hell's own naphtha and asphaltus.

There's room here for Beelzebub, Moloch, Belial, and all the millions of other princes of hell to meet in dark conclaves—but only if they magically shrink down to mini-demon size as they enter. When Pandemonium is full, it hums like a beehive as the tiny infernal peers take their golden seats.

At the far end of the Plutonian hall is Satan's high throne, set under a regal canopy. When hell's dread emperor first arrived here, his head still blazed with false glitter, but after Eden fell, God transformed all the hosts of hell into complicated, serpentine monsters: horned snakes, two-headed snakes, half-scorpion snakes. Satan himself is now a giant, sinewy dragon. You may see some of them outside, twisting on the branches of hell's only grove, placed outside Pandemonium by God to punish the sinners there. It's a parody of the tree Satan used to tempt Adam and Eve in the Garden of Eden, but I'd steer clear of the fruit. Just like sin itself, it looks delicious on the outside but tastes of bitter ashes.

PARADISO

The Divine Comedy

Like the first two books in his *Commedia*, Dante's *Paradiso* envisions heaven as a nine-level journey. Unfortunately for the tourist, everyone in heaven is so pure and good that the nine levels are all basically the same. Paradiso may not be a land of contrasts, but there sure is a lot of light and singing!

Instead of laboriously trudging upstairs like in purgatory (see page 137), visitors to Paradise shoot upward through the heavens like a crossbow bolt. (Presumably that's the fastest object anyone could imagine in Dante's time.) Every sphere is represented by a different heavenly body, each brighter and more beautiful than the last. In a bit of dubious cosmology, these stars and planets all orbit the Earth below. The first level is the moon, a dense pearly cloud wherein dwell the righteous who were not quite perfect in their vows. (Their inconsistency is symbolized by the light and dark spots on the surface of the moon.) Above them, on Mercury, the souls of the ambitious glow and dance like sparks. (They had big dreams, so they get the littlest planet.) But nobody minds being in heaven's budget accommodations: they're still blissfully content with God's will!

Venus is the heaven of lovers, and their souls wheel through space like flaming torches. Above them is the sun, where you can talk turkey with all of history's great theologians, dazzling flames who will hover around you in the shape of a crown. But *every* level of Dante's journey is filled with long theological monologues, so if you like pedantic arguments about angels and predestination and stuff like that, you can't really go wrong here. Paradiso is the heaven for you!

CELEBRITY SPOTTING

Even though a lot of the big names (the Virgin Mary and the Apostles) lie ahead in the higher levels of Paradise, there are a surprising number of A-listers in the Fourth Sphere as well. Keep an eye out for Thomas Aquinas, the Venerable Bede, and King Solomon himself!

The red glow above you is fiery Mars, the fifth heaven, where the souls of righteous warriors are glowing jewels in the shape of a cross. Above Mars, on Jupiter, you'll meet the souls of just rulers like Constantine and King David and even the Roman emperor Trajan! (Dante learns that some righteous pagans were still predestined for heaven even if they never converted to Christianity.) These souls are like a big college marching band, flitting around to spell out words in gold letters against the silvery surface of Jupiter. They might even shift into the shape of a giant eagle and speak to you collectively from its beak.

Saturn is a vast golden crystal and a realm of contemplation, where songs of praise are sometimes interrupted by a thunderous cry as the blessed briefly think about sin or something upsetting like that. An endless ladder leads upward, with souls streaming up to the two highest heavens. The eighth heaven is the sphere of the stars, a dazzling cocktail party where you can hobnob with Peter, James, John, and other nobles in Christ's court. The ninth heaven is the Primum Mobile, the outermost sphere moved only by God. Here the nine orders of angels can be seen as rings of fire circling the divine essence itself, which will appear as one brilliant point of light.

Outside the geocentric universe is nothing but the Empyrean: the mind of God, full of pure light, love, and transcendent joy. At first, it may look to you like a river of light flowing between flowered banks. The ruby and topaz flowers you'll see are the souls of the blessed, while the sparkles shooting out of the river are angels. Look closer and the floor plan will change to a vast arena where the faces of the righteous form the petals of a radiant white rose. On one axis, the rose is divided into men and women; on the other, Jews and Christians. The lower levels are filled with unbaptized children, saved by predestination. The highest thrones are reserved for John the Baptist, on one side, and the Virgin Mary, on the other.

When Dante gazed into the light of the Empyrean and finally saw the face of God, words failed him. The best he could muster was to compare Him to three circles, each of a different color but somehow occupying the same space. Granted, God is mysterious and hard to describe under the best of conditions, but if Dante is correct, you still might be surprised to see Him looking so much like an M. C. Escher engraving or 1980s computer graphics demo.

THE PARISH

The Third Policeman

If you were an avid cyclist in life, your postmortem options for continuing your hobby are limited. Only the Irish writer Brian O'Nolan has dared to envision a bicycle-based afterlife—but to get there, you will have to put up with a setting that owes something to Lewis Carroll and something more to Franz Kafka, all filtered through a lot of Joycean blarney.

At his 1966 death, O'Nolan left behind his unpublished masterpiece, a short novel called *The Third Policeman*, which he wrote in 1939 under his pen name Flann O'Brien. *The Third Policeman* is about a man who murders his neighbor for money and then later, trying to retrieve his ill-gotten gains, finds himself in a strange county patrolled by three bicycle-obsessed policemen. "When you get to the end," O'Nolan explained in a letter to William Saroyan, "you realize that the hero . . . has been dead throughout the book and that all the queer ghastly things which have been happening to him are happening in a sort of hell."

At first, O'Nolan's afterlife looks much like an idyllic Irish countryside: fine boglands under serene skies, farmers driving carts and tilling fields, sheep, heather, "considerate cows." You'll enjoy the smell of hay and the buzzing of bees. But this parish might seem a little *too* perfect: the fields greener than any you remember, the air more intoxicating, the arrangement of trees a little too picturesque.

Don't be alarmed if you don't remember anything when you arrive in the parish; your memories—with the exception of your memory of your own name—will return in time. You will also find that you can now converse internally with the voice of your own soul, who will helpfully orient you to your new life.

This district is apparently run by a County Council, but the only authorities you are likely to meet are the policemen who live down the road. Their barracks will look false and flat to you, with both its front and back somehow visible at once; it is evidently missing some dimension that buildings in this life possess. The constabulary there—a large sergeant called Pluck and his subordinate MacCruiskeen—are prone to saying absurd things in a very grave and careful way. "It is a difficult pancake," they often remark about a case that's confusing them.

Most of Pluck and MacCruiskeen's elliptical chatter concerns bicycles, bicycle accessories, and bicycle-related crime. They regularly hide citizens' bikes and related "clues" so they will have new bicycle crimes to investigate. To be fair, the bicycles in their jurisdiction are practically people. Through a freak effect of physics here, the atoms—and therefore the souls—of bicycles and their riders are always commingling. A resident of the parish who is more than half bicycle will walk stiffly, lean on walls, and tip over if moving too slowly.

The policemen are also enthusiasts of strange devices and scientific theories based on a substance called omnium, the fundamental energy that makes up the universe. You will probably never meet the unseen third policeman, a mysterious figure called Fox who lives in the walls of other people's houses. He has hoarded for himself four ounces of omnium, which he secretly uses to exert a God-like power over the entire parish.

Duck into the small back bedroom of the police station and peek upward. The cracks you see in the ceiling there are actually a map revealing the secret lane that leads to "eternity," a strange place of which the policemen are caretakers. Using the map to follow the hidden lane through the thicket, you'll arrive at an old, mossy stone church containing a steel lift, which descends into an underground realm. There ironclad corridors wind for miles, lined with tiny cabinets and obscure machinery. While you are down there, time stands still. Clocks stop, beards don't grow, and you won't get hungry. The machines there can produce any object you desire: gold, bananas, underwear, or even impossible things, like a magnifying glass that will enlarge objects so much that they become invisible, or a weapon that turns men into purple powder.

SOUVENIR SHOPPING
Warning: Don't try to bring any of this stuff up out of eternity with you! The lift will open like a trapdoor if you weigh more upon exit than you did when you entered.

Presumably you did something to deserve this strange eternal destiny, so you won't be able to complain when you find yourself nonsensically condemned to death (again), returned to earth as an angry spirit, or even placed in an endless time loop. Round and round you will go, like the wheel on a bicycle. It is all a very nearly insoluble pancake.

PURGATORIO

The Divine Comedy

Many believers in the afterlife have long been puzzled by deathbed confessions. Can you really live a depraved life and then repent just as the game clock runs out? In his *Purgatorio*, Dante's answer is a definite yes—but before you go to heaven, you're still going to have to pay for all your pre-deathbed sinning. And what better place for your cleanse than a giant mountain in Polynesia?

Instead of accompanying Charon across the Acheron into hell, "saved" sinners catch a high-speed cruise to Purgatory that departs regularly from the mouth of the Tiber River, near Rome. (What happens if you don't die near central Italy? Dante doesn't seem to have considered that wild possibility.) You'll sing hymns as your boat, propelled by the wings of an angelic ferryman, speeds you to the Southern Hemisphere, where Purgatory is found.

The island of Purgatorio is located antipodally to the holy city of Jerusalem—that is, straight through the center of the earth from Palestine and out the other side. That would place it about a thousand miles south of Tahiti in the South Pacific. It's a towering mountain pushed upward from the sea when Satan fell from heaven—the same impact that created the pit of Dante's *Inferno* way up on the other side of the planet. As you purge your sins there, you'll move up the slopes of the mountain toward God, metaphorically as well as literally.

The lower slopes of the mountain are "Ante-Purgatory," where your journey begins. Those who repented too late must wait there for the same length of time they put off their penitence, while excommunicated souls wander there for *thirty times* the length of their separation from the church.

SAVVY TRAVELER TIP
If you're eager to ascend to the rest of Purgatory faster, both sentences can be shortened by the intercessory prayers of your loved ones.

While you're waiting, don't miss the Valley of the Princes, a beautiful mountain dell where not-great rulers rest on flower-covered lawns. It's the low-security prison of Purgatory, for well-connected white-collar criminals.

Once you're ready to move on, ascend the three steps of white marble, black stone, and red porphyry that lead to Purgatory's gate. The angel there will let you in with his silver and gold keys, but he may also use his sword to scar the letter *P* in your forehead (for "*peccata*," meaning "sin") up to seven times. After you enjoy this delightful local custom, climb up a zigzag shaft in the rock into Purgatory proper.

Purgatory consists of seven terraces, each about fifteen or twenty feet wide, ringing the side of the mountain and connected by narrow stairs. Each level represents one of the seven deadly sins which is purged there. On the first terrace, the proud walk in circles, crushed into twisted deformity by the huge stones they carry. If you can bear to look up, enjoy the remarkably lifelike carvings on the cliff face, depicting biblical and classical scenes of great humility. (If you can't look up, similar scenes of pride brought low are etched into the pavement at your feet.)

Each time you ascend one level in Purgatory, the climb will seem easier—and angel wings will erase one of your forehead scars. On the second terrace, the envious huddle against the cliff, nearly invisible because of the dirt-colored hairshirts they wear. Their eyelids will be sewn shut with iron thread, to keep temptation down. Above them on the third terrace, the wrathful are surrounded by a canopy of thick, acrid smoke. The fourth terrace is a never-ending fun run, as the slothful sprint around the ring at top speed. They can't stop—it would get in the way of their fitness journey!

The fifth terrace cleanses avarice, as the greedy lie prone, weeping and praying all day. They're staring at the ground, just as they were overly fixated on earthly things in life. One level up, the pallid, emaciated gluttons run in a pack just like the slothful—but their hunger and thirst are heightened on every lap, as they pass sweet-smelling fruit trees and clear mountain springs that they just can't reach. On the seventh terrace, the path is lined by a great wall of flame, from which the lustful cower. As they pass each other, each announces their sexual sins with a little slogan. Gays have to yell "Sodom and Gomorrah!" while straights name-check Pasiphaë, a queen from Greek mythology. (That's weird, because Pasiphaë's sin was actually bestiality!)

The fire is so hot that you'd jump into molten glass to escape it, but it's got to be crossed if you want to reach the final stair, which leads to the Earthly Paradise at the summit of the mountain. This was Eden, before the fall of man. It's a divine forest, where the floor is dotted with yellow and red wildflowers. If you're lucky, you might catch a glimpse of the mystical procession that wanders these woods. Seven candlesticks lead the way, leaving a rainbow trail of color behind them. Then you'll see twenty-four elders garlanded with lilies (representing the books of the Old Testament), then four heavenly beasts (the Gospels), then more old men garlanded with roses (the books of the New Testament). In the center, a griffin pulls a chariot (representing Christ), surrounded by dancing nymphs (the Virtues).

> **TIME-SAVER!**
> Once the folks in this weird parade stop at the Tree of Law, they'll put on a long pageant representing the history of the medieval church. You may want to leave early; it's a bit of a snooze if you don't care about heresies and antipopes.

Look for two crystal-clear streams rippling the grass as they flow by you. Both rise from the same spring: one is Lethe, erasing memories of sin, and the other is Eunoë, restoring memories of good deeds. Baptize yourself in these waters and drink deep. When your soul is ready to move on to Paradise, you'll know—and so will everyone else, because Purgatorio gets rattled by a great earthquake *every time* someone ascends. That must get old.

A Cast of Billions

RIVERWORLD

To Your Scattered Bodies Go

Imagine there's no heaven, no hell below us. Instead, everyone who has ever lived is resurrected at once along the banks of a fourteen-million-mile river. How was this done, and why? This is the irresistible premise of Philip José Farmer's Hugo Award–winning 1971 novel *To Your Scattered Bodies Go* and its four sequels.

On resurrection day, you will find yourself lying on the grass of Riverworld, back in your body as it was when you were twenty-five or so. You will be naked and as hairless as a baby, but your hair (aside from facial hair) will grow back in time. Women have their virginity "restored"; men, curiously, are all circumcised.

> **TRAVELING WITH KIDS?**
> Those who died younger than their midtwenties are resurrected on Riverworld at that younger age. These so-called Rivertads stop aging around twenty-five, and from then on everyone on Riverworld stays the same age forever.

Your fellow humans—all 36,006,000,637 of them—are waking up all around you, shocked that every single one of their beliefs about the afterlife has turned out to be incorrect. On such a vast planet, the likelihood of ever meeting someone you knew in life is extremely low, but they're all there somewhere, if they died between 97,000 BC and 1983 AD. (A second phase of the project is planned for baby boomers and up.) The only people absent are those who died before the age of five or had serious mental disabilities; it turns out that a separate afterlife, Gardenworld, has been prepared for them.

The River winds back and forth across this new planet through a long grassy valley. Above the lawnlike meadow where you awoke are hills covered in familiar plants, like bamboo, as well as strange ones, like the indestructible, vine-draped ironwood tree. By the time you get two miles away from The River, the hills become impassable ten-thousand-foot mountains rising nearly vertically above the valley floor. The stars at night are strange and lit with brightly colored nebulae. The weather is generally sunny and warm, with a brief rainstorm once a day (midafternoon in temperate zones, late at night in the tropics). There are no seasons, no insects—in fact, no animal life of any kind beyond the worms and River fish necessary to keep the ecosystem humming (read: keep the planet from piling with human poop).

Strapped to your wrist, you will find a light metallic container that the resurrectees (or "lazari") come to call a Grail. This is an afterlife lunch pail that can be placed into a cylindrical hole in the Grailstones, large mushroom-shaped stone platforms that line both Riverbanks every mile or so. Three times a day, the Grailstones flare to life with an electric discharge, and Grails that have been set atop it miraculously fill with a meal's worth of food. The Grails also provide pieces of fabric with magnetic tabs that can be snapped together to form clothing, personal items like combs and cosmetics, and a variety of minor vices that betray the book's 1970s origins: cigarettes, liquor, instant coffee, marijuana.

LOCAL FARE

Most days, the meals in your Grail will be drawn from your earthly milieu, so take care to die someplace with good food, like Vietnam or Portland. But watch out for the stick of gum that comes with your dinner: it's "dreamgum," a powerful hallucinogenic that can produce intense spiritual, sexual, or even violent experiences.

About two-thirds of the people resurrected in your area will come from the same earthly time and place, with a smaller minority from some second era, and a tinier fraction scattered from all over. Neanderthals will lunch next to Spanish conquistadors and Chinese peasants and ancient Egyptian merchants and 1950s American suburbanites. In that atmosphere of diversity, new pidgin languages will thrive, and eventually Esperanto, a failed artificial language of the nineteenth century, will catch on across the planet. So too will new religions, in the absence of all the old, seemingly invalidated ones. The Church of the Second Chance is made up of gentle pacifists who believe that Riverworld is a temporary state provided for humankind's ethical advancement.

Eventually, settlements and cities will spring up, in a primitive style that comes to be called Riverine Polynesian. States and governments will form, and many will make war on each other. (Remember, every warlord and dictator who ever lived is here too, consolidating power.) At first, those who are killed get re-resurrected the following morning at some other random spot on The River, but these "translations" end about thirty years AR (After Resurrection). Riparian life becomes much more peaceful after all the would-be conquerors kill each other off.

The river flows from the north of Riverworld, winds for millions of miles (aided in many places by artificial gravity), and eventually returns to the same misty polar sea. That sea hides an enormous tower, home to the "Ethicals," the mysterious beings who resurrected mankind.

How was the mass resurrection accomplished? Through pulp sci-fi tropes, of course! As it happens, no living being in the universe was actually self-aware until ancient aliens created synthetic energy fields called *wathan*s, which attach to intelligent life and give them their "souls." Those aliens and their descendants then seeded infant planets with vast underground machines that could generate and collect *wathan*s. Earth was seeded in Paleolithic times, and that's why you were born with a *wathan* (and therefore sentience). When you died, your *wathan* held on to your memories and consciousness, which could then be implanted into a newly cloned body in the twenty-third century, on a terraformed exoplanet called Riverworld.

So that's it: there is no God and souls are artificial. But the Ethicals who designed Riverworld are watching your *wathan* to track your moral and spiritual progress. After a century of observation, those who excelled in their second life will be granted *permanent* immortality. About 40 percent of the human race will be allowed to return to Earth—that is, a future Earth that's been freshly scrubbed after the neutron-bomb wars of the twenty-first century. So be nice to your fellow lazari on Riverworld, and share your Grail cigs with your neighbor in need—whether he's Attila the Hun or Mahatma Gandhi.

THE THIRD SPHERE

What Dreams May Come

Sci-fi fabulist Richard Matheson dreamed up some of the most vivid fantasy landscapes of the twentieth century, from the urban zombie wasteland of *I Am Legend* to the claustrophobic airplane cabin of *The Twilight Zone*'s "Nightmare at 20,000 Feet." But only his 1978 afterlife adventure *What Dreams May Come* comes packaged with an earnest vow that the story is completely factual—in Matheson's italicized words, *"derived exclusively from research."*

In *What Dreams May Come*, Matheson describes the death and afterlife of TV writer Chris Nielsen, an account that supposedly comes to light when a psychic delivers a convenient postmortem manuscript to Nielsen's cousin. This never actually happened, of course. When Matheson brags about his research, that doesn't mean he actually *died*. He just got really into Theosophy and read a lot of 1970s paperbacks about the paranormal and near-death experiences.

What Dreams May Come warns that becoming "disincarnate" (the book's preferred euphemism for "dead") is a difficult transition. Some people spend years or even centuries in the murky borderland between life and death before their astral self finally breaks the binding to its physical and etheric bodies. The best way to "move upward" is to visualize an ideal place in your memory. In Nielsen's case, a peaceful glade in the California redwoods does the trick.

At that point, you'll find yourself in a *real* ideal locale: the Third Sphere, one of perhaps seven concentric realms radiating outward from our earthly reality. Residents call it Heaven, Homeland, Summerland, or (because you reap the results of earthly life) Harvest. Harvest will be your own conception of perfect happiness; to Nielsen, it looks a lot like New England in early summer. A guide—your guardian angel from back down on earth—will show you the amenities. Everything here is a little better than life: sunlight has no shadows, meadows have no weeds, the oceans are tideless fresh water, nights are dim and restful but not dark. In the 1998 Robin Williams movie adaptation of *What Dreams May Come*, the deceased's wife is a painter, and so the jewel tones of the afterlife are made to look like one of her impressionist landscapes come to life. Everything around you will glow with a refreshing energy.

You'll be glowing yourself, with a colorful aura visible to all the other "disincarnates" but not to yourself. Materialists have a red aura; those who mourn have a pale yellow one. (Shoot for lavender, the color of spiritual enlightenment.) The state of your aura also informs your new wardrobe—typically a robe-and-sash combo with a style reflecting your own growing spiritual advancement. Your astral body can appear any age you choose, but most prefer to look about twenty-five, for obvious reasons.

TRAVELER BEWARE!

Don't get too cocky about your hot new summer(land) bod. There's no sex in heaven, so your genitalia will eventually fade and disappear from your astral body. Hope you weren't too attached to them! Your astral body doesn't need food either, so your heavenly dream house, which you will mentally create from a raw "matrix" of astral matter, won't have a kitchen or a bathroom.

You can check in on your fellow disincarnates with your new powers of telepathy and telescopic sight, but to commune with them face to face, head to Harvest's towering alabaster city. In the movie adaptation, the city looks like Maxfield Parrish discovered Cirque du Soleil, but Matheson's version is much more boring: it's a smog-free version of a big-city performing arts center, with broad avenues, marble buildings, lawns, and fountains. Visit the efficient Office of Records to check in on the arrival dates of your earthly loved ones, or browse the Hall of Literature to find history books that are actually accurate for a change, as well as books that have yet to be written on earth. The Hall of Music offers performances of posthumous works like Beethoven's Eleventh Symphony, accompanied by vivid light shows that translate the music into visual architecture.

Below the Third Sphere are other, darker realms peopled by those whose earthly delusions still blind them into thinking no heaven is possible for them. All of them will rise eventually, but some will suffer for millennia. Chris Nielsen descends into this etheric world, Orpheus-style, to save the soul of his wife, who killed herself in mourning for him. If you retrace his steps past the borders of Harvest you'll find that hell is a vast, dark crater miles wide, surrounded by mindless gluttons and violent mobs. You'll descend the pit itself via a stinky, decaying fissure crawling with many-legged creatures and enter a mass of writhing, skeletal bodies covered in flies. Until they realize they're bringing this punishment on themselves, the damned have to stay in their own custom limbo, but hopefully you can escape back to a higher realm. Why not recover from your misadventure with a short stay in the city's Hall of Rest, with its vaulted blue ceilings, lounging couches, and thick shag carpeting? (Remember, this is a novel from 1978.)

There's a lot to see in the Third Sphere, but try to think of it as merely a stopover. There are higher spheres, after all, which end with the soul's reuniting with the essence it came from: God, in effect. But earth is the best testing ground to get that kind of advancement, so everyone in the Third Sphere eventually decides to get reborn into the physical world. What amounts to a celestial computer dating service matches souls with their new infant bodies (either before, during, or after childbirth) and a spirit "physician" oversees the rebirth from the astral plane. You can even sketch out your new life in advance, planning your whole education and career arc like an overly serious high school student. If you and your life partner have auras that resonate on the same frequency, you might just be "soul mates," destined to be linked throughout eternity. Most earthly relationships don't last into the astral plane, but if you have a soul mate, you'll definitely be seeing each other again—both in and out of the Third Sphere.

THE TIME BUBBLE

Before I Fall

Lauren Oliver's bestselling 2010 YA novel *Before I Fall* is the story of Sam Kingston, a Connecticut high school junior who dies in a car accident on her way home from a party . . . and then she wakes up. She's back in her bed at home and it's February 12 again, the morning of the day she died. She spends the book living out the last day of her life over and over and over again. "Maybe when you die time folds in on you, and you bounce around inside this little bubble forever. Like the after-death equivalent of the movie *Groundhog Day*," Sam decides, generously crediting the Bill Murray film from which the novel has lifted its premise.

If you enter a time bubble like Sam Kingston's after your death, you'll find yourself in a dreamlike state of falling endlessly in cold and darkness. Suddenly you'll wake up, and everything will be just as it was on the morning of the day you died. (This must be a bummer for people who died at, say, ten in the morning. They land in a very short and repetitive cycle.)

You will retain all your memories of having lived this day before, but no one else will. The constant repetition—of events, dialogue, even weather—can seem claustrophobic, but it's also an opportunity! Feel free to try out any number of new life philosophies in succession: nihilism, hedonism, escapism, altruism. The small choices you make can, like the flapping of a butterfly's wings, unloose whole new chains of events on that single day. Note that, should you manage to prevent your own death, it won't really matter. If you survive through the end of your last day on earth, you'll still just wake up again on that very same morning.

The repetition may help you start to appreciate the small pleasures in everyday life and become the whole person you were meant to be. In Sam Kingston's case, she realizes that she and her group of popular friends have been quintessential "mean girls" for years, the terrors of Thomas Jefferson High—but that it's not too late to make amends.

As you get closer to finally getting your last day "right," things will change. The falling dream that precedes each reset will be replaced by one of floating, and eventually you'll dream of flying above pink clouds and sunny green fields, surrounded by a rainbow of butterflies. The last time you die, the greatest hits of your life will flash before your eyes, but they'll mostly be quiet, comforting moments, not big life-changing ones. Your final realization will be that time doesn't matter at all, because these moments go on forever. You'll be surrounded by sound and warmth and light, arcing up into a tunnel, and your last sensation will be of music and laughter and moving upward into what comes next. At least it'll be something different!

A Million Ways to Die in the West

THE UNDYING LANDS
Middle-earth

When Frodo and Bilbo boarded the White Ship at the end of the *Lord of the Rings* trilogy, and Annie Lennox crooned and they all sailed from the Grey Havens into the Uttermost West, you probably assumed they were heading for eternal life in Tolkien Heaven. (Ditto for Samwise and Gimli, the other mortals who, according to J. R. R. Tolkien's voluminous appendices, were later allowed to make the journey across the Sundering Seas as well.) After all, the Blessed Realm across the ocean, the continent of Aman and the Lonely Isle of Tol Eressëa, are often referred to as "the Undying Lands." So no one there dies, one might imagine.

But that's the same lie that Sauron fed Ar-Pharazôn the Golden, king of Númenor, when he sought immortality at the end of the Second Age! (You remember your *Silmarillion*, right?) The Undying Lands are so called because the bulk of those who live there are immortal creatures who do not age. But a voyage to the Undying Lands does not automatically confer immortality on mortals. "There you would but wither and grow weary the sooner," wrote Tolkien. He called Frodo's voyage there "only a temporary reward: a healing and redress of suffering."

The continent of Aman is indeed a heavenly place for the Elves and Ainur (the Valar and Maiar, Tolkien's pantheon of gods) who have left Middle-earth. In Valinor, the country of the gods, you'll find must-visit spots like Valmar, the city of many bells and golden roofs, and the Gardens of Lórien, where silver willows and drowsy pines droop over fields of poppies and pools lined with glowworms. Go for a ramble there at dusk to enjoy the soothing song of the nightingales in the trees.

> **HISTORY BUFFS!**
> Outside the western gate of Valmar, look for a green mound of grass. This is Ezellohar, where the Two Trees of the Valinor, one gold and one silver, once stood before Melkor destroyed them. The silver tree Telperion, which glowed for seven hours every day, is the ancestor of the iconic White Tree of Gondor.

One particular place in Aman is less idyllic, though all travelers must pass through it on their itinerary. The halls of Mandos are located on the western shores of Valinor, on the edge of the Outer Sea. Mandos is the Doomsman of the Valar, and his vast, echoing caverns descend below the Shadowy Seas. They are the domain of recently departed spirits.

Mandos himself reigns with his consort Vairë the Weaver in a sable throne room with columns of jet, lit only by a few drops of dew from Telperion. The gloomy halls of his kingdom are draped in Vairë's storied webs, which record all the events of history like tapestries.

This may sound problematic today, but the state of your *fëa*, or spirit, in the Houses of the Dead will depend on your racial origin. Elves do not age as Men do, but they can be slain in battle or die of grief. If that happens, their *fëar* experience a time of waiting in Mandos's realm, where they socialize little but undergo whatever correction or comforting is required before they can be reborn as a little pointy-eared Elvish baby. Some stubborn Elvish spirits may choose to forgo reincarnation and stay with Mandos forever.

If you're a Dwarf, you receive a separate hall in Mandos where you patiently await the end of the world. Then, you believe, you will be called upon by Aulë the Creator to help rebuild the earth.

If you belong to the race of Men, your itinerary is a little more vague. Those who die under some great curse may live on for a time as a ghost, haunting the site of their final shame or regret, as we learn when Aragorn travels the Paths of the Dead in *The Return of the King*. Once the souls of Men pass on to Mandos, Tolkien originally envisioned the queen of the dead judging them in a hall of basalt and bat's wings, keeping some with her, dooming others to the Hells of Iron in Angamandi, and placing still others on the black ship *Mornië*, which sails to the dusky plains of Arvalin. A select few are borne up in chariots to feast with the gods in Valmar.

But Tolkien later decided to play it coy about what happened to the souls of Men once they left Mandos. He always wanted to have it both ways with his cosmology: there's a polytheistic pantheon of Ainur, like the ones in the Norse sagas he loved, but all are ruled by Eru Ilúvatar, a single omniscient supreme being consistent with Tolkien's Catholic beliefs. According to *The Silmarillion*, Eru willed that Elves should stay in an endless cycle of reincarnation but that Men should "seek beyond the world and should find no rest therein." Whatever fate awaits them when they leave their purgatory in the halls of Mandos is beyond the Music of the Ainur, and unknown.

If you are a Hobbit, Tolkien's mythology is utterly silent about your fate. Maybe you can only hope for a cozy heaven full of vests, fireplaces, pipe tobacco, sautéed mushrooms, and annoyingly twee flute music.

Let It Go

THE VALLEY OF THE SHADOW OF LIFE

The Great Divorce

C. S. Lewis titled his 1945 dream vision of the afterlife *The Great Divorce*, as a nod to William Blake's *The Marriage of Heaven and Hell*. In Lewis's mind, heaven and hell represent two very different outlooks on life—and they are never, ever, ever getting back together.

Your journey to this heaven will likely begin with your arrival at the civic center of the Grey Town, a dismal, rainy city of dingy shops and lodging houses. Billions live here in the endless twilight, but you'll rarely see them. In this place, you can create your own neighborhood, your own street, your own house, with just a thought, so the city lights have sprawled out for millions and millions of miles. Everyone here is tense and quarrelsome, but luckily no one has close neighbors.

The only way out of town is by bus, but many find excuses not to take the journey. If you're one of the few to make it aboard, you'll have a surprise: the bus will rise into the air and soar over the rooftops of the Grey Town. Soon you'll be floating in a pearly abyss, and a cruel, unflattering light will begin to glow ahead. The bus will rise over a sheer cliff face, so tall that you can't make out its base below you.

You'll emerge onto a broad grassy plain dotted with forests and a wide river, like a summer morning on earth. The landscape and sky will seem to stretch wider somehow than they ever did in life. But the big difference is that everything here is eternal, while you are still impermanent and ghostlike by comparison. Try to walk on the grass, and its unmoving, diamond-hard blades will poke painfully at your feet. Try to examine a leaf or petal, and it'll be so heavy that you'll barely be able to lift it an inch.

Then how do you cross the meadow and get to the mountains rising off in the distance? Look for the helpers! The Bright People are glowing spirits who have delayed their journey deeper into heaven in order to help you begin your own journey. Time in heaven has made them as solid and substantial as the grass and trees, and you can lean on them as you gradually toughen up and become eternal as well. With their help, you can enjoy the highlights of heaven's outskirts, which they call the Valley of the Shadow of Life. If you're lucky, you might spot lions playing on the grass, herds of unicorns with flashing red eyes and indigo horns, and a tree of golden apples, drenched by the spray of a mighty waterfall—which is no normal waterfall, but also a laughing, angelic giant.

Look back behind you *very* closely and you might see a little crack in the soil. That's the "cliff" you saw when you arrived here! Heaven isn't just "above" the Grey Town. It's also infinitely larger.

Yes, the Grey Town is hell—or at least purgatory, since many of its residents are eventually able to move on. The only thing holding them back, you'll learn, is themselves. They need to change, to let go of earthly concerns and weaknesses, and most of us resist abandoning our crutches. Maybe you miss mortal life too much or want reassurances that your old talents and priorities will still matter now. Maybe you feel unworthy of heaven, or distrust it, or want to "improve" it in your own image. Maybe you liked fooling around with questions better than hearing answers. Whatever the flaws that hold you back may be, they're probably not the ones that religionists predicted. False idols like art or patriotism or even love of family can be more dangerous than lust or anger, because they don't always *seem* like sins.

Some of these weaknesses may even take physical form, as a little lizard clinging to your shoulder. But you need to agree to burn off your lizard and move on. As you journey into Deep Heaven with the celestials, you'll find a Lethe-like fountain whose water will help you lose all sense of pride and ownership in your own works. Then you can *really* start growing into a person, by letting go and saying to God, "Thy will be done." As the celestials will tell you, *everyone* is surprised by heaven and realizes they were wrong about it all along. The secret is to stop pretending you were right.

MOVIES

You Have Sunk My Battleship

THE BOGUS JOURNEY

Bill & Ted

Bill & Ted's Excellent Adventure is a cult comedy classic, but its 1991 sequel is even more ambitious. In *Bill & Ted's Bogus Journey*, the titular slackers take a grand tour of the afterlife, including visits to a most non-heinous heaven and a most non-*non*-heinous hell.

When it's your time to go, hopefully you don't get pushed off Los Angeles County's Vasquez Rocks by an evil robot duplicate version of yourself from the future, like Bill and Ted do in the movie. But however you die, it'll be a big adjustment. Your surroundings will be tinted blue, your skin pasty, your voice filtered through a weird reverse-reverb effect, your clothes suddenly a dull monochrome. (You'll be invisible and intangible, by the way, so when someone walks through you, you'll stretch and bounce around like jelly. The only way to communicate will be to possess the living, by flying into their bodies through their ears.)

But the dead giveaway, as it were, will be the man looming over you in a black robe and carrying a scythe. "You will come with me," Death will command in deep, echoing tones.

There are two ways to, as Bill and Ted put it, "ditch" the Grim Reaper. You can temporarily stymie him by yanking on his robes and giving him a "melvin," which is a most egregious type of wedgie. But for a permanent escape, you'll need to challenge Death to a contest, like the game of chess from Bergman's *The Seventh Seal*—and win. Be warned that Death has only ever been defeated once—and he was a super-poor sport about it. In the movie, Bill and Ted beat him at four different challenges (Battleship, Clue, Electric Football, and Twister) before he finally lets them return to the world of the living.

If your challenge fails, Death will sentence you to one of two final destinations, depending on how bogus or bodacious a person you were during your earthly sojourn. Bill and Ted briefly tour both before their final Twister game with Death. The hell they visit is an abyss so deep that you'll fall for minutes on end before landing in a dark, smoky cavern. A constellation of great rocks floats in the void, tethered by chains to massive infernal machinery. Watch out for the huge metal dragon head breathing fire!

A giant, horned Beelzebub will open the trapdoor that drops you into a maze of low subterranean tunnels. Every door opens onto a new torment, all filtered through a nightmarish lens of German expressionism and each tailor-made for you. Is there a particular childhood memory that traumatized you or secret fear that haunts your dreams? They're all here! Choose your eternity!

Heaven, on the other hand, is a glittering Art Deco city in a white void, surrounded by floating discs radiating Day-Glo green and purple. The *Bill & Ted* films were convinced that the future would be a perfect 1980s utopia—why shouldn't heaven be as well?

Walk past the rows of superb white pillars along with your fellow saints. You'll all be dressed in white and lavender versions of your earthly attire. A row of greeters in flight attendant uniforms will hand you a leaflet warning you that only the most serene and enlightened souls can enter. In front of a giant gate, you'll see a sentry who looks a lot like blues legend Taj Mahal, with his white quill poised over a gilt book. This is the angel in charge of deciding who merits heaven.

> **LOCAL CUSTOMS**
> If the gatekeeper asks you a tricky question like "What is the meaning of life?," don't worry. Bill and Ted get away with quoting Poison lyrics.

In the big atrium beyond, you might see a lively game of charades between Albert Einstein and Ben Franklin. The wide white staircase ahead of you leads upward into a blinding light. Scope it out: it's totally resplendent. That's the throne of God, and you'll find Him to be a most excellent deity.

CANINE HEAVEN

All Dogs Go to Heaven

The universe, as we've seen, is full of complicated and bewildering afterlives, but this one is a straight shot. If you're a dog, you go to heaven. Full stop. It's right there in the titles of the 1989 Don Bluth cartoon and its low-budget sequel!

If you're fortunate enough to be a dog, then you are naturally good and loyal and kind, unlike human beings. When you die (or "when you're sent to a farm upstate," if your owners prefer), you'll find yourself rushing through a tunnel of stars and bubbles before arriving in a bank of pastel-pink clouds, bedecked with jewels and beads in the night sky. A blast of Gabriel's Horn will materialize a set of golden gates through which you enter.

SAVVY TRAVELER TIP

If you're bringing with you the object that led to your demise (the chicken bone you choked on or appliance cord you chewed through), be warned that it will be gently confiscated at this time. You can't take it with you!

This is the Great Hall of Judgment—but the "judgment" is just a formality. You'll place a pawprint onto your page of the Book of Records, displayed on a marble table, and then a high-ranking angel will usher you into heaven, issuing you your robe, wings, and halo. Maybe you'll be assigned to Annabelle, the cute dancing whippet!

After that, you can do whatever you want, forever. Though we briefly see lions chilling with lambs in the clouds, this seems to be mostly a pups-only paradise. Take a tour by following the endless network of golden sidewalks and ramps. You'll see dogs sunbathing and getting massages—but never scratching. (Fleas go to the other place.) There are whole fields of food dishes, and when you dig a hole in the clouds, a geyser of delicious bones will erupt. By day, there are lots of little ceremonies where the deceased get jeweled pins for being such good boys. By night, weirdly, there are fireworks shows. Don't dogs hate fireworks?

For most dogs, this is the good life. But some find that it gets old fast—too perfect, too quiet. If you're fed up, there are two options. First, you can return to earth. Near the entrance to Canine Heaven is a sea of floating timepieces, all of them stopped. Each one represents the life of a late doggo. Find the clock or watch labeled with your name (you're a dog who can read, right?) and wind it up. You'll be whisked back to earth when it starts ticking, but you can almost certainly never return.

And your second option? Despite the title of the franchise, there also seems to be a Canine Hell—a lava pit beneath a blasted volcanic plain—though its theology is murky. In a couple nightmare scenes in the first movie, a dragon-dog with bat wings navigates his bone ferry on a lake of fire there. But in the second movie, hell seems to be run by cats (which would make a lot more sense to dog lovers). Specifically, the head demon is a panther type named Red who commands a legion of little skeleton imps with rodent ears. Whatever goes on down there, hell is connected to heaven by a handy pay phone. You may be able to scheme your way out of heaven by literally making a deal with the devil.

But beware! The first movie ends with the villainous Carface Carruthers—a cigar-smoking pit bull mix who is neither good *nor* loyal *nor* kind—entering heaven, like the rest of his species. But when his schemes don't pan out in the sequel, Carface gets dragged down to hell! So much for the title and premise of the movie. Hashtag not all dogs.

Twist of Fate

DENIAL

The Sixth Sense

As we'll see on page 169, in some movies the dead go to Iowa. But the Hawkeye State isn't the only state with its own afterlife—there's also the state of denial. If you're afraid the hardest part of the world to come will be the depressing realization that you're dead, why not skip that step altogether? Clueless oblivion is the destination for you!

Tales about ghosts who think they're still alive go back to at least the seventeenth-century Chinese folktales of Pu Songling. Later authors like H. P. Lovecraft (in "The Outsider") and Ambrose Bierce (in "An Inhabitant of Carcosa") seized on this idea for the same reason Pu used it: it makes for a killer twist ending when your protagonist realizes he's the haunter, not the hauntee. And in 1999, an unknown young director named M. Night Shyamalan scared up almost $700 million at the box office with (SPOILER!) the exact same twist, in his movie *The Sixth Sense*.

If you choose a *Sixth Sense*–style haunting for your afterlife, you'll probably find yourself orbiting the same people and places you knew while alive. They won't pay much attention to you, of course, as you're now invisible, but you'll find ways to explain that to yourself. That'll be easy because the dead only see what they want to see. You won't see any other ghosts, for example. That would break the suspension of disbelief. Your spirit form might still bear the marks of the illness or incident that killed you (burns, a hangman's noose, uncontrolled vomiting), but you won't even notice.

Ignorance is so blissful that rationalization will become second nature to you. Family and friends not talking to you anymore? You're just going through a rough patch in your relationships. (This gives "ghosting" a whole new meaning.) Is all your stuff now boxed up in the basement? You must have moved it down there for some reason. Don't have your house keys? You forgot them somewhere. Just rematerialize on the other side of the locked or blocked door and pretend there's nothing weird about that.

LOCAL DRESS

As you go about your daily routine, you'll see yourself in a typical out-fit from your earthly life, probably a variation on the one you died in. You'll imagine access to your personal effects, so you can putter around with a briefcase or whatever. The only exception might be an emotionally weighted accessory like a wedding band—there's no conjuring that up. It's gone for good.

With effort, you can hold and move objects, but not while anyone's directly looking. Your voice can be recorded on tape, but at such a low volume that no one is likely to hear. People might chat with you if they're lightly asleep, but they won't remember. A small number of people *can* see the dead, and you'll find yourself drawn to them. (Try to resist the temptation to physically abuse these sensitives, as many ghosts do. If you're nice to them, they can be a huge help.) But as for reaching the rest of the living, the most you can do is make them put on a sweater. Temperatures will drop abruptly when you're around, as much as fifteen or twenty degrees, especially if you get agitated.

And you'll probably be agitated a lot. People who wind up in this after-life limbo have unfinished business—they just aren't admitting it to them-selves. Once you accomplish your mission, probably by helping someone, you'll feel a palpable sense of liberation and be ready to depart into the light. Where are you headed? Who knows. But at least you won't be mop-ing around the basement anymore.

THE FACILITY

After Life

You can only take one memory with you to the next life. What will it be?

In Hirokazu Kore-eda's 1998 film *After Life*, the dead emerge from a white mist and enter a complex of low, rather run-down concrete office buildings as a bell chimes in the distance. Give your name to the employee at the window and proceed to the waiting room. You'll be ushered in turn to a conference room with one of the facility's three caseworkers, who will confirm your name and birth date. "You died yesterday," the counselor will say. "I'm sorry for your loss."

Enjoy your one-week stay at this way station with about twenty other guests, relaxing in your private dormitory room and wandering the forested grounds. The facility we see in the movie has an all-Japanese staff and clientele, but there must be many, many more of these places dotting the borders between our world and the next. It's unclear who runs this organization, but their corporate logo, which we see on flags and paperwork, is a white swirl of two interlocking discs on a blue background. At a glance, it looks a little like a bubble or cloud.

You will have three days this week, Monday through Wednesday, to think back on your life and select just one memory, the most meaningful and precious, to bring along as your sole souvenir from the living world. This is a daunting task! Many new arrivals feel they have too many good memories to choose from; others say they have none. If you're having trouble narrowing your choice down, your caseworker can have a box of VHS cassettes brought in—one tape for each year of your life—to help you review all your mortal highlights.

It's important to select your memory by midweek, because the staff will spend all day Thursday and Friday physically re-creating your experience for you, via the magic of movies! That's right: one building in the complex is a crowded little studio, where a film crew will rehearse and shoot a short film clip of your favorite memory. (Why don't the videotaped archives of your life suffice for this process? It's not clear. They just don't.) The staff takes their job seriously, spending a full day location-scouting for reference photos in the living world, building sets, assembling props and costumes, and even casting actors.

Don't expect a big Hollywood budget, however. These hardworking folks don't have unlimited resources. The model of car or plane at your shoot might not be exactly period-accurate. Potted plants and a painted background may stand in for a beautiful landscape, and the clouds might be big wads of cotton wool. You're going to be carrying into eternity a very Wes Anderson version of your life.

On Saturday, you and your fellow guests will file into a screening room with seven rows of comfy orange-upholstered seats, and everyone's scenes will be unspooled in turn. In the darkness, you'll literally enter your memory, the way moviegoers can only do metaphorically on earth. When the lights come back on, all the deceased are gone. Where do you go? To a place "where you can be sure of spending eternity with that memory."

Unless you didn't choose one at all! If you don't make a movie, you will stay on at the facility as a staff member or assistant caseworker. Now you'll be one of the quiet functionaries filing papers, mopping the squeaky wooden floors, practicing at lunch with the office brass band. Congratulations on landing a steady government job.

FORT MORGAN

The Ballad of Buster Scruggs

The notion of death as a horse-drawn coach is a familiar one in our culture, from the Cóiste Bodhar of Irish legend to the leisurely carriage ride past the sunset in Emily Dickinson's "Because I could not stop for Death." But the death carriage from "The Mortal Remains," the last segment in the Coen brothers' 2018 Western anthology *The Ballad of Buster Scruggs*, is a lot more efficient: it's a roomy Old West stagecoach that comfortably seats five or six. But they don't seem to know that they're dead.

If you find yourself aboard the Coens' stagecoach to Fort Morgan at some point, you will probably be surrounded by a motley assortment of humanity—because that's just how death is. In *The Ballad of Buster Scruggs*, two bounty hunters sit across from three oldish passengers: a grizzled trapper, a chortling French gambler, and a formidable church lady traveling to be reunited with her Chautauqua-lecturer husband. The three squabble about the nature of love, life, and sin. Wistful Irish death ballads are sung, ghost stories are told, and the bounty hunters describe their violent trade. The "cargo" they are ferrying to Fort Morgan on the stagecoach roof, it turns out, is the body of a wanted man they have killed, one Mr. Thorpe. It may be that some of your companions on your last carriage ride are not your fellow deceased at all, but "reapers" and "harvesters of souls" like these two.

As you journey, night will fall and the moon will rise, but the cloaked coachman, faceless beneath his wide-brimmed hat, will not stop the horses. He never stops. ("Policy," one of the bounty hunters explains.) Later that night, you will finally arrive at Fort Morgan, a small cluster of dark clapboard buildings. The coach will drop you in front of the Fort Morgan Hotel, a gloomy gaslit establishment with a dark green Victorian façade. As you climb the front steps, pause to admire the two symbols atop the double door: a heavenly cherub on the left side, and a demonic goat's head on the right.

The parlor will be dark, with heavy velvet furniture and a few Tiffany-style lamps. There is no front desk visible, just a staircase at the rear of the lobby leading upward into ethereal light. If you are rethinking your stay at this point, it's too late. You'll hear the stagecoach driving off into the distance as you enter your final destination.

HOTEL HADES

Cabin in the Sky

Modern cinema afterlives generally boast a studied diversity, but an integrated heaven wasn't always a palatable option for American moviegoers. In our defense, that was only because we were very, *very* racist.

In the early days of Hollywood, studios were eager to hop on the bandwagon of newly popular genres like jazz and blues, and so they green-lit half a dozen musicals with all-Black casts. The scores were always by white composers, of course. On the one hand, all wrote with obvious respect for the "Negro music" they loved and finally gave good parts to dozens of talented performers who deserved better than their usual lot in Hollywood. On the other hand, it's impossible to watch these movies today (and for Black audiences, even at the time) without cringing at a bunch of the dialect and stereotypes.

Perhaps the best of the bunch is 1943's *Cabin in the Sky*, in which Eddie Anderson, most famous for his role as Jack Benny's valet Rochester, plays Little Joe, a loving husband who has a hard time keeping on the straight and narrow. His wife, Petunia (Ethel Waters), tries to get him to church on Sunday, but she never knows when he might escape out the back door for a quick game of dice. When Little Joe is shot by a big-time gambler to whom he owes money, his soul is caught between heaven and hell. (Or at least the heaven and hell that white writers imagined a Black audience would imagine in 1943.)

Hell is the "Hotel Hades," staffed by cigar-smoking imps with bell staff uniforms and their hair sculpted into devilish horns. The pitchfork-wielding Lucifer Jr. runs the hotel's Idea Department, an air-conditioned office where the staff wears white terry-cloth robes. A much cushier posting than shoveling coal in the boiler rooms below! But the idea men (including Louis Armstrong!) have long been coasting on the torments they dreamed up ages ago, like houseflies or the cruelties of the biblical Pharaoh. Lucifer Jr. worries that his unseen "Pappy" won't be happy if his asbestos chariot loses another soul.

We never see "the Lord" either, but His army of dignified angels dresses in white military uniforms with lots of braid and epaulets. They can read thoughts, summon miraculous aid, and zip to heaven and back in a matter of minutes—if there's a tailwind.

If you merit the gospel-choir heaven of *Cabin in the Sky*, endless flights of stairs will lead you upward from the place of your death. You'll pass plenty of naked cherubs leaning on pillars. They look just like the ones in Renaissance paintings, except that they're all Black. *Did we just blow your mind, white people of 1943?*

Little Joe wakes up on his deathbed before he can enter the pearly gates—it was all a dream! (He probably should have figured this out when the General of the Lord looked just like his preacher and Lucifer Jr. was the spitting image of his gambler pal Lucius—*Wizard of Oz* style!) So our only hints about what goes on inside heaven come from "Cabin in the Sky," the title song that Petunia sings to Joe early in the film. She envisions a tiny celestial homestead with "an acre or two of heavenly blue to plow." It's not great that white moviemakers imagined Black folks as menial laborers *even in heaven*, but at least the lyrics were changed to establish that Petunia plans to "sing and pray" in her cabin. On Broadway, she vowed to "eat fried chicken every day." Which would be delicious, obviously, but not exactly a victory for civil rights.

People Will Come

IOWA

Field of Dreams

As surely as *All Dogs Go to Heaven*, the afterlife decision chart is equally easy if you happen to be a deceased professional baseball player from the early twentieth century. In that case, there's a very exclusive heaven waiting for you right here on earth: the titular baseball diamond from the 1989 movie *Field of Dreams*.

Wander out of the cornfield at this real-life tourist attraction in Dubuque County, Iowa, and step onto the manicured outfield grass. Miraculously, you'll be supplied with your original uniform and glove. Everything will still fit, as your body has been restored to the prime of your career with, you know, the St. Louis Brown Stockings or whoever. Don't be alarmed by the big towers of lights! A lot has happened while you were in corn limbo. The major leagues have night games now.

Take batting practice, shag a few fly balls, or even join in a pickup game with other past all-stars who have been waiting decades for the chance to play again. You may see old rivals or your *real* enemies—the umpires, who can also emerge from the afterlife and call the game for you. There will always be more dead ballplayers than spots in the lineup, so you may have to wait your turn. And if you were an asshole in real life (like, say, Ty Cobb), the boys may never give you a shot.

Not all the living will be able to see your athletic feats on the field, because they don't all believe in the magic of baseball, the "thrill of the grass." But many will! The bleachers will probably be full of tourists who answered a silent call to Iowa and got to see their heroes play one more time. It will be a blissful afternoon for them—as James Earl Jones says in the movie, "as if they'd dipped themselves in magic waters."

> **TRAVELER BEWARE!**
> Don't fraternize too much with the living. They can cross the gravel border at the edge of the field, but you can't. Step off the grass and you'll lose your youth and roster spot all at once. You'll vanish, just like the ballplayers walking back into the cornstalks at the end of every practice, but you won't be able to return.

On rare occasions, even baseball lovers who never made the bigs are allowed to join the teams for a game. Ray Kinsella, the Iowa farmer who plowed under his corn to build the field, learns at the end of the movie that the universe really just wanted him to play catch one more time with his estranged father, at which point every emotionally repressed male watching cries manfully into his popcorn.

"For me it's like a dream come true," says his dad, surveying his son's field. "Is this heaven?"

"It's Iowa!" replies Ray.

"Coulda sworn it was heaven."

JUDGMENT CITY

Defending Your Life

What if Final Judgment wasn't final after all? What if you could just keep retaking the test until you passed? In Albert Brooks's 1991 rom-com *Defending Your Life*, the afterlife begins with an efficient five-day stopover at Judgment City, where a hearing determines whether each dead soul should return to earth for reincarnation or is advanced enough to move "onward."

After your demise, you'll find yourself sitting in a wheelchair wearing a hospital gown. The chairs will be pushed three abreast by orderlies down a long series of ramps to a fleet of white trams. You'll still be a little dazed from your journey, so don't be alarmed by your dead-eyed affect or inability to even raise your arms. Helpful staff will usher you onto the correct tram and then to your hotel room.

Judgment City will probably seem familiar to you. It's a generic place, designed to remind you of your earthly life and provide a stress-free transition. Albert Brooks's character is a Los Angeles ad exec, so his city is the one that processes arrivals from the whole western United States—2,500 people per day. It looks just like a medium-sized American city, albeit one with a strong retirement-community vibe. Your fellow arrivals are mostly old folks, of course. (Children who die don't require a hearing at all, and teens are so rowdy they get their own destination.) You'll see billboards for golf courses, horseback riding, and hot spots like Sid's Steakhouse, the Bomb Shelter comedy club, and Judgment Lanes bowling alley. Don't miss the Past Lives Pavilion, where your host, a holographic Shirley MacLaine, will give you a peek at your previous incarnations on earth.

Back in your hotel room, enjoy the five TV channels airing postmortal soap operas, talk shows, game shows, and weather. (It's 74 degrees and perfectly clear in Judgment City . . . every single day.) Why not order up some room service? For the first time, you can eat whatever you want and not gain a pound.

> **LOCAL DRESS**
> The closet in your room will be full of identical white caftans called tupas. They fit everybody! You'll never have to worry about what to wear here.

You're not in Judgment City to relax, though. On your first full day there, hop an Inner City tram to Defenders Circle for a meeting with your advocate. This is the legal counselor who will argue at your hearing that you deserve "full onward movement" to become a citizen of the universe. This examining period happens after every lifetime, and the people who have grown enough on earth—learned stuff, overcome their fears—get to move on to more exciting destinations. The afterlife administrators, Judgment City's "residents," are former humans like us, but they call us Little Brains because they use a much larger percentage of their minds than we do. They're so advanced that they eat incredibly unappetizing brown clumps for food and communicate in binary digits.

Your hearing will take place at a large office building called Judgment Center, where your advocate and a prosecutor take turns replaying scenes from your life. The flashbacks appear on a screen so lifelike that you'll be sucked right into your past. After four days of arguments, a two-person judicial panel will hand down its judgment in thirty minutes or less, and you'll know where you're headed.

Return to the transit station, where a row of trams will be headed toward eight tunnels in rocky cliffs. The two tunnels on the right lead "onward," while the six on the left take you back to be reborn on earth. If you're still a Little Brain, don't sweat it. Some people return to Judgment City almost one hundred times before they get it right.

Remember me, though I have to say goodbye,
Remember me, don't let it make you cry.
—*Héctor Rivera*

THE LAND OF THE DEAD

Coco

Pixar has long made animated movies designed not to inspire the wonder of children but to indulge their sentimental parents. Kids don't want movies about outgrown toys, lonely robots, overprotective clown fish dads, grieving widowers, ex-superheroes in midlife crisis, or Route 66. Kids will watch anything! That stuff is all parent-bait, sincere but thinly veiled boomer nostalgia. And in 2017, Pixar took the next logical step, moving on from children's cartoons about old people to children's cartoons about dead people.

Coco begins in a small Mexican town on Día de los Muertos, the Day of the Dead. While the living honor their ancestors, a series of unlikely shenanigans lands young Miguel in the Land of the Dead, where he discovers that his ancestors live on and wait eagerly all year to visit the living world on their special day.

This Land of the Dead is a candy-colored metropolis of stacked houses spiraling upward to dizzying heights, linked by a web of colonnades, trolley tracks, and gondolas. In the shadows of these towers is a maze of cobblestone streets, where you can wander through quaint stucco archways or relax in cool cantinas.

You and your fellow souls here are skeletons—but fun Pixar ones, not scary ones! Your eye sockets have eyes, you can put on wigs, and your skull will even mimic the fleshy pooching of your cheeks and chin from life. You control each of your bones separately, so you can reassemble yourself if you fall apart or even send your head or an arm off on a mission separate from your body.

HISTORY BUFFS!
The Land of the Dead was built piecemeal over the centuries to accommodate the burgeoning population of the afterlife. As a result, just getting around town can be a fascinating archaeological expedition. The lower levels of the city are ancient stone pyramids, with strata of successively more modern buildings built above them as more and more generations of newcomers arrived.

TOP ATTRACTIONS

THE SUNRISE SPECTACULAR—On the Day of the Dead, the hottest ticket is this all-star blowout at the city's bullring-like central stadium. Get there early to grab some *elote* and gawk at the skull-shaped fireworks.

THE ARTS DISTRICT—Venture into this bohemian neighborhood of brick warehouses converted into vast studio spaces and you might be rewarded with a glimpse of some favorite artists at work. The late Frida Kahlo has a loft here where she prepares new installations, each wilder than the last. Check out the thirty-foot-tall papaya she's working on!

***ALEBRIJES*—**These neon-colored animal companions resemble the fantastic creatures of Mexican folk art. Your personal *alebrije* may be a tiny beetle or butterfly or fennec fox, or a more exotic hybrid: a winged snake, a frog-bunny, a giant jaguar-eagle with ram's horns. These spirit guides have useful, unexpected powers, like breathing fire or tracking footprints. But watch your step, because they poop *everywhere*.

WHERE TO STAY

It's best to stick to the crowded and relatively safe *centro*, where lights are strung on every parapet and candles glow from recesses in the stone walls. Don't follow the city downhill to the dark shacks by the water. There "the forgotten" dwell.

You see, this entire realm is powered by the memory of the living. As long as your descendants remember you, you can enjoy a lively afterlife. But as memories of you expire above, your old bones will weaken, then finally glow orange and fade. At this "final death," your spirit moves on like a cloud. No one knows where.

GETTING AROUND

You can get anywhere in town from Marigold Grand Central Station, the city's massive transit hub. It's an architectural destination in itself, an Art Nouveau masterpiece of cast iron and stained glass. But to visit your next of kin in the living world, you'll need to clear an elaborate border-crossing process run by the Department of Family Reunions. If the bureau's facial recognition system reveals that your surviving family has put your photo on their Day of the Dead *ofrenda* (home altar), you're allowed to cross over on giant causeways of marigold petals arching into the clouds. Just get back before dawn! But if your posterity didn't remember you this year, you'll be stopped at the crossing or sink into the orange petals on the bridge. This isn't a great afterlife for the "child-free."

EATING AND DRINKING

PLAZA DE LA CRUZ—This bustling square, named for legendary Mexican singer/actor Ernesto de la Cruz, is lined with street food vendors by day and packed with merrymakers by night. If you're lucky enough to be in the plaza on the Day of the Dead, grab a spot down front for the annual talent show, a battle of the bands.

ERNESTO'S PENTHOUSE—If you can swing an invite, hop a funicular up to de la Cruz's floodlit high-rise and gawk at his guitar-shaped swimming pool. Stacks of guitars, baked goods, and liquor bottles—offerings from his fans in the land of the living—tower to the sky. Eat your fill and duck out before Ernesto reveals his true colors. Like most movie stars, he's super evil!

THE REGRET

The Discovery

What if you could fix the one thing you regretted most about your life? Wouldn't that be the greatest gift?

Not necessarily. In the 2017 sci-fi film *The Discovery*, Robert Redford plays Dr. Thomas Harbor, a scientist who has managed to prove that the afterlife exists. That is, he's invented a machine that can detect brain wavelengths "on a subatomic level" leaving the body after death. (I know, but bear with me here.) He can't say where they go, but that doesn't seem to matter. His discovery leads to a global suicide wave, as four million people—from the terminally ill to the merely curious—eagerly kill themselves to "get there," wherever "there" is.

Eventually, Harbor is able to fine-tune his machine so that he can see what people see when they move on. (Maybe he was inspired by watching the movie *Flatliners*?) In flickering, juddering black-and-white video, we watch first-person snippets of this "new plane of existence" where the dead go. They all seem to be set on earth in the relatively recent past—but with a few changes.

When you die, according to Harbor's research, you will find yourself reliving some past moment of your life, the moment that became your biggest regret. There may be small differences about you or your surroundings (a new tattoo, for example) reflecting a now-altered conception of yourself. But for the most part, the afterlife is a precise reenactment, a second chance to right something that once went wrong. In *The Discovery*, all three afterlife regrets we see revolve around death: either preventing a death or letting down a dying loved one. Presumably there are people with less melodramatic regrets—an unfortunate prom dress, a Twitter typo—but this is a mournful indie drama with chilly blue color grading, so we don't see any fun ones. Once you've fixed your biggest mistake, you're ready to move on to an unspecified final destination.

Maybe this kind of redemption sounds ideal, but there's a catch: in the afterlife, you won't remember having done this all before. You might have momentary flashes of déjà vu when a person or a situation seems familiar, but that's it. If you fail in your attempt to change the past, time will loop back again and you'll get a third chance. And a fourth. And so on.

In other words, no matter what you accomplished in your life, or loved about life, you might spend the afterlife fixated on the very worst moment of it, perhaps even living it over and over forever. *The Discovery* isn't the discovery of heaven after all. It's pure hell.

Day-O the Dead

SATURN

Beetlejuice

The idea that the dead might not move on at all, instead just hanging around their last earthly mailing address, can be traced back two thousand years to the ancient Greek philosopher Athenodorus. But these stories usually imagine that the dead don't want to be there; something bad happened and the unhappy spirits need to be "freed." Tim Burton's 1988 movie *Beetlejuice* is more practical. Its cosmology is built around two assumptions: first, that the dead are *happier* just staying put in their old earthly homes, and second, that the goal between the living and the dead should be peaceful coexistence.

Beetlejuice begins with a nice married couple played by Geena Davis and Alec Baldwin dying in a car accident and returning to their lovingly remodeled country home in Winter River, Connecticut. If your afterlife is a *Beetlejuice*-style haunting, you will walk in your own front door with no memory of the trauma of death or how you got home. Things will seem normal at first, but you may gradually understand that you no longer possess a corporeal form. You'll feel cold, and even open flame won't warm (or burn) you. You won't have a reflection in mirrors. You'll find yourself levitating off the ground without even realizing it.

> **LEARN THE LANGUAGE**
> Since you don't have a real body anymore, the correct term for your physical self is now your "manifestation."

Most dramatically, you'll find that your appearance is now entirely malleable. Stretch your face into a horrifying mask, pop your eyes onto your fingertips, sever your own head. You might be tempted to use this ability to create frightening tableaux for the inevitable new occupants of your home—but it may not work. They're unlikely to see you and might be more fascinated than terrified if they do.

They probably won't move out, but neither can you. The "functional perimeter" of your manifestation is likely to confine you to the walls of your home. Take just one step outside and you'll be transported to a waste of yellowish-green dunes and weird, red coral-shaped rock formations. Huge, horrifying striped worms with two sets of jaws glide through the sand. The dead call this place Saturn, but as we know, the real Saturn is a giant gas planet that doesn't even have a surface, let alone sandworms. Perhaps this is actually one of Saturn's moons, or a place not entirely within our dimension. The view of strange planets looming above can be tempting, but don't linger! For every second you spend on Saturn, hours will elapse back on Earth.

If you get frustrated by your new state of affairs, consult the *Handbook for the Recently Deceased* that was issued to your domicile. Sure, it's poorly organized and about as readable as stereo instructions, but there's a lot of good information in there. For example, you'll learn that you have an afterlife caseworker available to you—but you only get three Class One D-90 intercessions to spread out over a century or more, so don't use them too quickly. In any event, your caseworker is likely to be an overworked bureaucrat with a full waiting room of bizarre applicants. (Here in this murky part of the afterlife, the spirits mirror all the indignities suffered by their disfigured bodies, so expect some gruesome scars and amputations.) If the line is long, the number you take when checking in at reception might run into the millions. Still, even if your haunting is going badly, it's best to work within the system. Do *not* fall for the ads you may see for a freelance "bio-exorcist" named Betelgeuse. He's sleazy, he's obnoxious, and he gives the hammiest 1980s movie performance this side of Al Pacino in *Scarface*.

Somehow, you'll need to claim your own space without word of life after death getting out among the living, so subtlety and plausible deniability should be your watchwords. If you get the living too riled up (interrupting an important dinner party with an elaborate calypso routine, for example), they may call in an exorcist. And when the dead face exorcism they become miserable wraiths, eternally trapped in the Lost Souls room. You don't want that. Just stay in the attic, avoid the new family as much as possible, and hope that one of their kids grows up to be a goth.

THE SHEET

A Ghost Story

Beetlejuice follows in the tradition of the Haunted Mansion at Disneyland, depicting a haunted house not as a dark and scary place, but as a rollicking, convivial ghost playground, a Chuck E. Cheese for the dead. But don't count on that vibe for your own haunting! If you feel so connected to the places you love that you plan on sticking around after death, let the 2017 indie movie *A Ghost Story* serve as a cautionary tale.

In *A Ghost Story*, a musician played by Casey Affleck is killed in a sudden car accident, leaving behind a grieving widow played by Rooney Mara. He always loved the little rental home where they started their life together, to the point where he shut down emotionally when his wife tried to discuss moving. After his death, he rises from a slab at the morgue, taking his white sheet with him, and follows her back home.

That's right: according to *A Ghost Story*, you will spend the afterlife draped in a bedsheet from the time of your death, complete with cut-out eyeholes like a lazy Halloween costume. No one can see you, of course. (Maybe children, very occasionally.) You will be able to touch and even move objects during moments of great emotion, but your fine motor control won't be the best—possibly because you're trying to handle things through a layer of bed linens.

You're also confined to the walls of your old house, and there's the rub. In choosing this afterlife, you haven't reckoned with time. There will be hours of standing motionless in rooms watching your loved ones grieve and then move on, and those will be painful enough. But there will also be the longer hours staring out of windows, like a dog waiting for its owner to come home from work. You will have no one to talk to, except for other ghosts in nearby homes, with whom you can trade greetings if you glimpse them at windows. Your only ways of affecting the living (making lightbulbs flicker or books fly off shelves) will quickly pall.

Time will become fluid; weeks and months will pass as you keep your silent watch. At some point, your next of kin will move out, and you'll still be too attached to the space to leave. You might lose yourself in repetitive tasks trying to unearth some relic of your loved ones' time there, or even forget what you're doing there altogether. If the house gets torn down, you'll stand in the wreckage. If a new building replaces it, you'll wander its halls instead.

Even if you regret your decision to stick around your old digs, you can't just leave. You can attempt to escape by, say, jumping from a high part of the house, but the dead don't die. You'll just travel back in time—still stuck in the same geographical spot. You might even have to relive centuries of your home's past, for as long as it's been an inhabited place. The only way to leave is to let go. You must come to the inner realization that waiting was futile, that they're not coming back, that you can never go back. Then your sheet will drop to the ground, empty, and your vigil will finally end.

So if, after your death, you see a white square opening in the air like an old television screen, you might want to step into it. It's time to move on—no matter how much you like your apartment.

STAIRWAY TO HEAVEN

A Matter of Life and Death

At the movies, gritty reality is traditionally in black-and-white, and fantasy—whether it's a soapy Douglas Sirk melodrama or the Emerald City of Oz—is in lush Technicolor. But what this afterlife presupposes is . . . maybe it's not?

Between 1941 and 1951, Michael Powell and Emeric Pressburger co-wrote and co-directed a series of strange and remarkable British films. *A Matter of Life and Death* (from 1946, retitled *Stairway to Heaven* for its American release) is the story of Squadron Leader Peter Carter, a British airman who bails out of his burning plane over the English Channel with no parachute. He somehow survives and falls in love with the American radio operator who received what he thought was his last transmission. But there's a catch: in another world, alarm bells are ringing. Carter was supposed to die in that plane crash, and now his very life hangs in the balance between two powerful forces: true love and the eternal laws of the universe. The other world, shot in black-and-white, is never called heaven, but it's a pearly realm where the skies shimmer with celestial light and the deceased are issued wings. "Any resemblance to any other world known or unknown is purely coincidental," a title card winks.

The movie is careful to give a purely rational explanation for the existence of this not-heaven. Doctors inform our hero that he is suffering from "vascular meningeal adhesions" on his brain, causing hallucinations and complex seizures. The life-and-death struggle he faces is real, but its cosmic particulars may very well be a product of his imagination.

Whether it's all in the mind or not, this eternal realm is reached via a long marble staircase that ascends like an escalator through space. You'll pass sculptures of the great geniuses and lawgivers of history: Caesar, Shakespeare, Plato, Muhammad, Lincoln, Solomon, Chopin. At the top, new arrivals register at a "training center." After picking up your wings off the rack, use the sliding glass door under the weird three-handed clock to head on to "Instructions."

LOCAL FARE

During World War II, the busy air crew section received a constant stream of pilots of many nationalities; the American airmen in the movie are excited to see a Coke machine at check-in. (The movie avoids the tricky question of whether any Axis pilots are there as well.)

Don't worry if the process sounds complicated; this is an orderly afterlife. A vast records office, glimpsed a mile below through circular portals in the waiting room, assigns each new arrival a number and ensures that everyone gets where they're going. Every thousand years or so, the records don't add up—perhaps, as in Peter Carter's case, a guardian angel (or "conductor") missed his pickup. In that case, a tribunal may be called to settle the matter. Gatherings like these are held in a huge amphitheater carved into the notch of a ring of cliffs. From above, the judgment seat looks like the center of a spiral galaxy.

The deceased souls we see in *A Matter of Life and Death* are all dressed in the costume of their earthly time and place, so this eternity looks a lot like some kind of cosplay convention or middle school history fair. Peter Carter's guardian angel is Conductor 71, an eighteenth-century aristocrat who died on the guillotine during the French Revolution. When he visits earth, we can see that he clearly misses the full color palette of mortal life. "One is starved for Technicolor up there," he sighs, gazing at a perfect red rose.

Only (Some) Angels Have Wings

THE STARS

It's a Wonderful Life

In this somewhat depressing version of heaven, located in the skies above Bedford Falls, New York, you can be dead for well over two hundred years and still be a wingless "AS2"—angel second class. You're at the mercy of your stuffy superiors, not to mention the bell-ringing whims of those still alive on earth below.

In Frank Capra's 1946 holiday classic *It's a Wonderful Life*, a man named George Bailey suffers a business setback after a life of seemingly pointless drudgery, disappointment, and sacrifice, and decides to throw himself off a bridge. You see, his absentminded business partner, Uncle Billy, has misplaced $8,000 in company funds. You have to admire a Christmas movie that starts with the festive spectacle of a drunk, bankrupt failure contemplating suicide on Christmas Eve.

But George's guardian angel—a former clockmaker named Clarence Odbody, b. 1653—is dispatched just in time, by two gossipy senior angels named Joseph and Franklin. Their heaven is a sparkling firmament in which Joseph and Franklin appear as majestic spiral galaxies, while Clarence is a tiny white dot whose every movement is accompanied by the strains of "Twinkle, Twinkle, Little Star."

> **CELEBRITY SPOTTING**
>
> "Franklin" is unnamed in the movie, but in an early draft of the script, he's identified as Benjamin Franklin, still puttering away at his inventions in the afterlife.

In Capra Heaven, you'll enjoy wide-ranging powers over time and space. Clarence convinces George Bailey that his life has meaning by shunting him into a parallel universe in which George never existed, his town is a slum, and one of his friends is a prostitute. (More Christmas cheer!) It's unclear why Clarence doesn't just tell George what Uncle Billy did with the missing $8,000. Seems like that would be a lot simpler.

In your downtime as a guardian angel, you'll still be able to enjoy earthly pursuits. Mark Twain, we learn, is up in heaven writing away, and Clarence owns a copy of Twain's *Tom Sawyer*, despite having died over a century before its publication. You even keep the outfit you die in for eternity. (Try not to die in the nude.) Money and alcohol, however, are both verboten.

Angels in this heaven can fly—but just the high-ranking ones. Wings are only conferred for meritorious service, and Clarence has apparently seen a lot of suicides on his watch before successfully averting George's. He finally "earns his wings" at the end of the movie. An angel earning their wings is marked by the chime of a bell on earth below. Given the frequency of earthly bell-ringing, Capra Heaven must still be minting hundreds of thousands of new angels every day—maybe more, if ringtones count.

Goodbye, Cool World

SUICIDELAND

Wristcutters: A Love Story

Dante imagined that people who kill themselves have their own gloomy afterlife, a Harpy-filled forest in which the dead are tortured forever while trapped in the trunks of trees. The 2006 indie fantasy *Wristcutters: A Love Story* imagines a more prosaic afterlife for suicides: a world where everything is largely the same as it is here. It's just a little worse.

Suicide is *never* the answer, of course, but if you do enter the afterlife this way, you'll bear the scars of your self-inflicted death forever—in some cases, literally. Wrist scars and visible head wounds aren't uncommon here. Drowning victims tend to burp a lot, while gas-inhalation suicides often have a bluish tint to their faces. Guessing how your fellow suicides "offed," as the local slang has it, is a popular social pastime.

You'll find a place to live in a run-down city surrounded by desert and dry, scrubby mountains. In real life, suicide rates are actually highest among people in their fifties, but *Wristcutters* depicts a suicidal afterlife populated mostly by twentysomethings, drawn from all over the world. Their daily lives are extensions of the dreary existence of insolvent young people everywhere: couch-surfing, lousy jobs, cheap beer, beater cars.

Some changes from mortal life are evident immediately, and as a result the first few months in your new home can be a tough adjustment. The night sky is starless. No one ever smiles or exchanges good-humored chat. This general dismalness doesn't seem to be a *punishment* for the suicides. It's just how things naturally are in a society organized and populated entirely by people whose lives went so badly. "If anybody here had a clue," someone in the movie observes, "we wouldn't be here in the first place."

Just because your world is a drab limbo doesn't mean there are no highlights to visit. The railroad shantytown called Kneller's Camp is worth a stop, if only to witness the tiny miracles that are possible there when you're not trying for them. (Nothing major: brief levitations, objects changing color.) Nearby is the castlelike mansion of the Messiah King, a cult leader intent on escaping this world with a *second* suicide.

> **BEST TO AVOID**
> Think twice about traveling too far from the city, because the veneer of civilization fades quickly. The wasteland is filled with trash: rusting metal, tires, old shipping containers. Cars have no license plates; businesses hand-letter their signs. Cops seem to be a self-appointed force with uniforms they assembled at thrift stores.

This world does have an elusive authority tier called the PIC, or People in Charge. They wear white outfits with black caps and can be spotted in rare emergencies arriving by van or even parachute. (Their agents also go undercover to mingle with the locals.) The PIC have a file on you in their vast, alphabetized warehouse, and in very rare cases might even stamp you a visa back to earth—but don't get your hopes up. In fact, that's a pretty good rule for this place in general.

TELEVISION

Ya basic. And that's okay.

—*Eleanor Shellstrop*

THE BAD PLACE

The Good Place

No religion has described the afterlife accurately, but they all get about 5 percent right. Only Doug Forcett, a stoner from Calgary, Alberta, experiencing a wild mushroom trip in October 1972, correctly predicted what happens when we die.

When humans move on to their next phase of existence in the universe, they're sorted into one of two places, a "Good Place" or a "Bad Place." In either realm, you'll be grouped by nine-dimensional immortal beings into a "neighborhood" of 322 residents. But will you face torture or eternal bliss? Your destiny depends on the sum total of your actions in life. See, everything you did on earth has a positive or negative ethical value. When you help an aging parent install a printer or give out full-sized candy bars on Halloween, your numerical score goes up. When you root for the Yankees or tell a woman to smile, your score goes down.

So life is a big video game and only the highest scorers (those with, say, a million points or so) get into the Good Place. Unfortunately, modernity has made it so difficult to do real, untrammeled good that nobody's earned a spot in the Good Place since the late fifteenth century. Under the points system, you're pretty much guaranteed to be one of the thirty billion humans who have been dumped into the Bad Place—and it's weird as fork there.

TOP ATTRACTIONS

DEMONS—It's a tiny bit racist to call them "demons," but that's the traditional term for the lava monsters, acid snakes, and six-thousand-foot-tall fire squids who operate the Bad Place. You won't see their full life cycle (larva to slug monster to spooky little girl to teenage boy to giant ball of tongues to social media CEO to demon), and in fact you might not even see them in their final forms. That's because the Bad Place's Bureau of Human Affairs often clothes the demons in human bodies ("skinsuits"), the better to understand and plan tortures. As a result, your tormentors might appear at first to be regular humans named Trent or Lance: sleazy douchebags in graphic tees who love *The Bachelor*, the Red Hot Chili Peppers, selfie sticks, and Hawaiian pizza. They wear a weird scent of Axe body spray that smells the same way *Transformers* movies make you feel, and you can expect to hear Richard Marx, Puddle of Mudd, "Grandma Got Run Over by a Reindeer," and the 877-Kars-for-Kids jingle on endless repeat on their playlists. They drink pig urine and snort the concept of time like cocaine. They're awful.

ENDLESS TORTURE—Here's *The Good Place*'s list of the torments that will rack essentially the entire human race for eternity: electric shocks, disembowelment, acid pits, fingernail removal, getting twisted in half, the ol' penis flattener, flying piranhas, college improv, food that turns to spiders in your mouth, four-headed flying bears, bears with chain saws, lava bees, bees with teeth, spastic dentistry, lightning that tears off your flesh, three to four days of mouth fleas, enormous butthole spiders, volcanoes full of scorpions, scorpion diapers, holiday week at Ikea, eyeball corkscrews, getting your brain batted around a stadium like a beach ball, getting your arms peeled like bananas, getting busted open like a piñata so demons can eat your goo, getting turned inside-out by a demon reaching down your throat and grabbing your butt from the inside, and children's dance recitals.

JANET—The foundational mainframe for your neighborhood will be a Janet, an anthropomorphized vessel of knowledge who will appear with a "ping" whenever she's needed. In the Good Place, Janet is a cheery informational assistant who can provide any answer or item you want at any time. In the Bad Place, she wears leather, offers bored insults while looking at her phone, and farts a lot.

OTHER MUST-DOS

BAD PLACE HEADQUARTERS—If you're ever allowed a tour of the Bad Place's administrative center, linger at the Museum of Human Misery, which commemorates our many follies (and resulting tortures). The highlight is the Bad Place's least disturbing room, the Hall of Low-Grade Crappiness. Here you'll see animatronic tributes to the trailblazing humans who thought up annoying new misdeeds: sending dick pics, flossing in an open-plan office, and calling ultimate Frisbee "ultimate."

WHERE TO STAY

THE MEDIUM PLACE—If the Good Place is out of your range, the best afterlife accommodation option by far is Mindy St. Claire's, a solitary ranch house located in a vast desert between the two realms. Mindy was a coked-up 1980s corporate lawyer who did one massive good deed on the day she died: she started what became the world's largest aid organization. As a result of her unusual ethical position, Mindy was assigned to a compromise Place, neither Good nor Bad. In the Medium Place, you can have your favorite beer—but it's warm. You'll hear your favorite songs, but only in the form of live Eagles covers. The books are all Anne Rice paperbacks with water stains, and at night you can relax by watching *Cannonball Run II* on VHS tape. It's eternal mediocrity, but at least there are no bears with chain saws.

NEIGHBORHOOD 12358W—Not long ago, a Bad Place "architect" named Michael decided to pilot a new kind of Bad Place torture. He stole a Good Place Janet and used her to create a simulacrum of a Good Place neighborhood: a quaint lakeside town of cobblestone streets perched at the foot of picturesque mountains. Here he planted four humans, surrounded them with 318 disguised demons, told them they were in the Good Place, and tried to create perfect conditions for the foursome to torture *each other*. But it all went wrong when the humans, despite their flaws, began to grow personally and improve one another. No matter how many times he "rebooted" the neighborhood, the humans kept figuring out the deception, and eventually they convinced Michael and his overseers that the existing points system was unethical. (See "Day Trips," page 197.)

GETTING AROUND

Within the Bad Place, travel is accomplished via a charming (but swelteringly stuffy) replica steam train called the Trans-Eternal Railway. You can hop trains between neighborhoods or stay aboard through miles of trestle across inky blankness until you arrive at the terminal, Bad Place HQ. But to leave the Bad Place, you'll need to step through a Portal. These are big bank-vault-style doors that lead to a nauseating ride between realms. (You'll need an official Bad Place lapel pin, with that classic thumbs-down logo, to get through the door.)

SAVVY TRAVELER TIP
There's a door back to earth at the central hub of the afterlife, but it's guarded by Jeff the Doorman. The key is made from the first atoms of the Big Bang, and Jeff *might* look the other way and let you use it if you find him a frog-themed gift. Jeff loves frogs.

EATING AND DRINKING

When you set aside all the corkscrews and penis flattening, much of the suffering of the Bad Place takes the form of banality and gradual disappointment. Endless *Pirates of the Caribbean* sequels play on movie screens. Parties are catered with problematic regional cuisine: soul food from Maine, bagels from Arkansas, egg salad from hospital vending machines. To that end, humans in the Bad Place are tortured with rows of punnily named eateries all serving the same disappointing menu item, usually frozen yogurt. *So* much frozen yogurt.

DAY TRIPS

NEUTRAL TERRITORY—A neutral zone is used to house administrative functions for both afterlife realms: accounting, a Janet storage warehouse, and so forth. The big attraction here is a visit to the Judge of the Afterlife. She's a powerful immortal being almost as old as the universe—in fact, her name is Gen, short for "hydrogen," the only thing that existed when she was born. In her tasteful wood-and-granite Deco chambers, she rules on cases involving the destinies of human souls. She also eats burritos and binge-watches a *lot* of TV.

IHOP—The neutral zone boasts an IHOP, but this IHOP is an Interdimensional Hole of Pancakes, a ten-D crossroads of space-time. If you venture inside, you'll perceive it as a disorienting sea of floating blue discs, where size and direction are constantly changing. If possible, stay far away from the Niednagels (green glowing slug things) and the Time Knife (hopefully self-explanatory).

JANET'S VOID—A few lucky travelers may be able to visit the boundless void where each Janet "lives": a subdimension outside of space and time at the nexus of consciousness and matter. Good Janets have empty white voids; Neutral Janets have beige ones. But if you glimpse a void here in the Bad Place, it'll probably belong to a Bad Janet, and will therefore be full of trash and tire fires.

THE GOOD PLACE—Thanks to a ruling by the Judge of the Afterlife in favor of Michael and his human subjects, the points system of the afterlife has recently been overhauled. The Bad Place has abolished torture and is now a series of tests designed by Good *and* Bad Place architects to help you see and address your shortcomings in life. The test will "reboot" as you advance, until finally you hear the soothing chime that allows you into the Good Place. On that day, you'll enter the pleasant landscaped gardens of the Welcome Center, which looks a little like a community college campus or retirement complex. The Good Place will provide an endless series of rewards: it always smells like your favorite smell, any item you want will instantly appear (men over fifty always request a magical guitar that plays itself), pee evaporates as soon as it leaves your body, and you can step through sparkly green doors to visit any time or place, real or imagined. Dishes offer metaphysical treats like "the energy you had when you were twelve," "a hug from Grandma," and "the ability to understand *Twin Peaks*." You'll stay for millennia, but at some point you'll realize that even eternal perfection can pall after a while, and you'll want an ending for your journey. On that day, you can hike out into a beautiful forest, where an archway of twisted branches between two trees leads to final peace. Sit and wait for a sense of quietude, then step through the last door.

WHEN TO GO

When scheduling anything in this afterlife, remember that time isn't linear here relative to earth. For some reason, it loops around in a pattern that looks like the words "Jeremy Bearimy" written in cursive.

Let's Rock.

THE BLACK LODGE

Twin Peaks

For many people, hope in the world to come is the promise of answers: finally, a definitive explanation for all the mysteries and uncertainties of life! But that kind of afterlife holds no appeal for oddball writer-director David Lynch. His afterlife is just like his movies: perfect for people who *enjoy* having no idea what's going on.

Twin Peaks, created by Lynch and his collaborator Mark Frost, took the world by storm in 1990. It was set in a small Washington State logging town, and nothing like its mix of low-art soap opera and high-art surrealism had ever been seen in prime time before. Ratings started to sag long before the show solved its tantalizing central mystery ("Who killed Laura Palmer?"), but its mythology has since sprawled to include a film prequel, multiple bestselling books, and a 2017 TV revival.

In its second season on NBC, *Twin Peaks* delved into legends about two otherworldly domains: the Black Lodge and the White Lodge. According to the Native tribes of northeast Washington (in the *Twin Peaks* world, anyway), these were two opposing places through which the human soul journeyed on its path to perfection. The White Lodge was a place of goodness and love, where nectar rained down from heaven and fawns gamboled happily. But its shadow self, the Black Lodge, was a place of darkness and nightmare. While the inhabitants of the White Lodge were benevolent helpers of humanity, the Black Lodge was peopled by angry, evil spirits prone to terror and violence. In the Black Lodge, travelers encounter the Dweller on the Threshold, a personification of their own darkest impulses. Only by confronting this doppelgänger with courage can the soul move on.

Entry to the Black Lodge seems to be granted through a kind of parlor or "waiting room." The living can glimpse this place in dreams, or by passing through mystical portals like the one behind the sycamores of Glastonbury Grove in the forest outside Twin Peaks. It's a strange, shifting place with red velvet curtains instead of walls and a distinctive zigzag floor. The rooms and passages are decorated with armchairs, lamps, and Greek statuary. Strange shadows pass behind the curtains. Beneath the floor is water; beyond the curtains waits an endless black void.

SOUVENIR SHOPPING

If you see a gold-and-green ring on a table in the waiting room, grab it. It's a powerful talisman that allows passage between the worlds.

Time has little meaning here. You may encounter others who entered the Black Lodge long before or after you, and the voices you hear will sound strange and garbled, like the back-masked "Satanic" messages on heavy metal albums. Some of the spirits who speak to you—a gaunt giant called the Fireman, a little dancing man called the Arm—may provide helpful wisdom about the future in the form of cryptic riddles about owls and chewing gum. But beware their doppelgängers, strobe-lit malevolent twins with opaque white eyes.

Your encounter with the double who guards the threshold will be crucial, because defeat in this purgatory means annihilation of your soul. But it could endanger the world of the living as well! The spirits of the lodge might implant a golden, orb-shaped seed into a cloud of your organic material and create a *tulpa*, a hollow duplicate of you that will wander back out into the world with your memories. Or one of them might possess your body, return you to life, and carry out unspeakable crimes.

That's all pretty nerve-racking. But on the plus side, at least that gum you like is going to come back into style.

Tabula Rasa

THE FLASH-SIDEWAYS WORLD

Lost

Within hours of ABC's *Lost* first hitting the airwaves in 2004, viewers were dreaming up their own theories to explain the show's mysteries. Why did Oceanic Airlines Flight 815 crash on an uncharted Pacific island? Why was there a polar bear in the tropics? What's the deal with that monster made of black smoke? This continued for six years, even after viewers gradually realized that J. J. Abrams and his collaborators enjoyed creating puzzle boxes but hadn't actually figured out any answers to the questions they posed.

From early on, many viewers suggested that the survivors of Oceanic 815 had in fact died, and that the island was their purgatory. The show's producers quickly shot down this theory in interviews and eventually established that the mysterious island was a kind of geomagnetic anomaly with mystical powers over good and evil—but one located very much on our plane of reality.

But then *Lost*'s final season aired in 2010. The show's characteristic flashbacks (who are these people and how did they get to the island?) and flash-forwards (what will happen once they are rescued?), with their familiar whooshing sound cue, were replaced by interludes that fans came to call "flash-sideways." The final season jumped back and forth between our heroes' final days on the island and an alternate timeline where Oceanic 815 never crashed at all. In this timeline, everyone on the doomed flight arrived safely in Los Angeles and got on with their lives.

Lost coyly hinted that the "flash-sideways" might be a parallel reality caused by the detonation of a nuclear device, but the finale revealed the truth: the "flash-sideways" world was, in fact, the afterlife purgatory that viewers had long suspected the island to be! The castaways' time on the island was so important to their lives that, even in death, their spirits had created a way to be together again.

This didn't make a lick of sense, of course, and the finale is not fondly remembered in the annals of early-2000s "prestige TV." But it's an intriguing view of the afterlife: could the souls of you and your loved ones somehow mentally collaborate on a shared reality that strips you of your memories, asks intriguing what-if questions about your time on earth, and allows past guest stars to show up in cheeky fan-pleasing cameos?

In your "flash-sideways" purgatory, don't expect a straight reenactment of your life with a single point of divergence. As in a dream, you will not be the least bit surprised if your background, family, or career has shifted substantially. (WHOOSH! Jack was married to Juliet? Jin and Sun are having a secret affair? That scofflaw Sawyer is a *cop*?) Old enemies may now be friends (WHOOSH! Locke loves his dad? Desmond is working for Widmore?) Time isn't linear here, so you'll be hanging out with people who died before you and some who died long after. (There's also a population of simulated people who fill up this little word but aren't really here in spirit and may never have existed.) But your mind and illusory "body" know on some level that this isn't real. You may be troubled by déjà vu or even physical manifestations of the thing that eventually killed you—like Jack Shephard's pesky bleeding neck.

You will stay in this purgatory until you all "wake up" and realize where you are. This usually happens when you're brought together with one of your loved ones from life. Memories will flood back, and then you'll all come together for a big reunion and move on—unless you're one of the souls who can't "pass over" yet and stays stuck on the island, whispering mysteriously in the jungle.

In the *Lost* finale, grinding plot gears manage to put all the "flash-sideways" characters together at a museum benefit concert, and then they all gather in a church next door. The church is apparently Catholic, but its interior has been scrupulously re-dressed with religious universalism in mind. The Virgin Mary stands between a statue of Buddha and a painting of Vishnu; a stained-glass window displays so many different religious symbols from around the world that it looks like a "Coexist" bumper sticker.

Jack's dead father explains that a collaborative afterlife is important because "nobody does it alone. You needed all of them and they need you . . . to remember and let go." Then a bright light from beyond transfigures the room, and the crash survivors all move on together, though they don't know where they're going. Just like the *Lost* writing staff.

THE GREAT BEYOND

The Twilight Zone

Rod Serling's classic TV anthology *The Twilight Zone* took viewers, in the words of its title narration, to "another dimension—a dimension not only of sight and sound, but of mind." The borders of this vast dimension were always somewhat murky, as the show's little morality plays covered a broad swath of fantasy, science fiction, horror, and social commentary. But it was always clear that Serling's Twilight Zone, whatever it was, encompassed the afterlife in its metaphysical realm. At least a dozen episodes from the show's original run concern the mystery of death—and what lies beyond.

The Twilight Zone posits that your immortal rest will be personalized, that it will likely feature an ironic twist, and that the twist will be explained by Rod Serling himself, lurking somewhere nearby in a neatly tailored suit and aphorizing to the camera through clenched teeth. But beyond that, there's almost no limit to what might await you in this "dimension of imagination."

Many *Twilight Zone* accounts agree that death will arrive as a personal emissary who explains your new postmortal situation and delivers you into the afterlife. In "The Hitch-Hiker," Death is a laconic gray man haunting the shoulders of an American highway. In "Nothing in the Dark," he's a handsome policeman—played by a very young Robert Redford! In "One for the Angels," he's a bureaucrat with a little notepad, annoyed about possible delays on his rounds. In each case, it's clear that no one but the deceased can see Mr. Death, and he must contact each person directly—using trickery if necessary—to usher them onward. In "One for the Angels," Mr. Death explains that reprieves are rare but can be granted in cases of family hardship, unfinished business, or impending achievements in science or politics. But if the deceased is reluctant, Death may claim a substitute soul, just to keep his ledger balanced.

In rare cases, aged travelers may initiate their own voyage. In "Passage on the *Lady Anne*," a group of oldsters charters an about-to-be-scrapped luxury liner, the same one on which they all honeymooned, to ferry them into the afterlife. A young couple is mistakenly allowed to book passage as well, but they are abandoned on a lifeboat in the North Atlantic before the *Lady Anne* disappears into the fog.

In more violent cases, where death arrives unheralded, you may not even realize you're dead—at least not at first. In "A Passage for Trumpet," the dead inhabit a simulacrum of their earthly city life, silently going through the motions of their nine-to-five jobs. If you are particularly stubborn or guilty, this limbo may last forever. In "Death Ship," a trio of astronauts keeps crash-landing onto the same alien planet, unwilling to accept that they are now interstellar ghosts. And in "Judgment Night," a Nazi submarine captain spends eternity reliving the night in 1942 when he sank a British merchant ship—but this time as a helpless passenger aboard the freighter.

Other individual hells are delivered by the devil himself, who appears as a character in many episodes. But stay alert on your travels, or you might find yourself in one of those *Twilight Zone*s where heaven and hell get ironically confused. In "A Nice Place to Visit," a small-time hood is gunned down by cops, only to find himself in a glittering city where he lives in a lavish apartment, scores all the beautiful women he wants, and never loses at the casino. His guide Pip quickly corrects his misunderstanding: this dull existence isn't heaven, of course, but a personalized hell. And in "The Hunt," a backwoodsman refuses to enter heaven when he is told by the gatekeeper that his trusty coonhound can't accompany him. As it turns out, this gate actually leads to hell—where dogs are banned, lest they smell the brimstone and warn their owners.

But angels are also real in *The Twilight Zone*. Gabriel himself gives trumpeter Jack Klugman a second chance at life in "A Passage for Trumpet," and it's generally implied that most travelers go on to a peaceful reward. Death is "no shock, no engulfment, no tearing asunder," Robert Redford's Mr. Death explains to an old woman. "What you thought was the end was the beginning." If you merit heaven, you can expect one individually tailored to you: the hillbilly from "The Hunt" gets an eternity of coon hunting and square dances, while the overworked ad exec in "A Stop at Willoughby" lands in a quiet American town circa 1888, complete with a bandstand, a fishing hole, friendly neighbors, and some of those bicycles with one big wheel and one tiny one.

But the thin barrier between life and death in *The Twilight Zone* means that even in heaven, you may not know permanent peace. The classic episode "A Game of Pool" follows the life and death of a pool shark played by Jack Klugman.

TRAVEL TRIVIA
Yes, Jack Klugman again! He appears in no less than three afterlife-set *Twilight Zone*s, tied for the lead with actress Gladys Cooper.

Klugman defeats his idol, a pool champ played by Jonathan Winters, in a tense billiard-parlor duel . . . but when he replaces Winters as the top dog, he spends an eternity shooting pool in the sky and is forever getting dispatched to earth (via an announcement over heaven's public address system) every time some two-bit hustler challenges his skills. Irony always trumps theology . . . in *The Twilight Zone*. (Cue spooky theme music.)

HEAVEN INC.

Miracle Workers

Heaven Inc. isn't the best workplace in the omniverse. Each galaxy has its own afterlife corporation charged with administering life on the planet(s) below, and some do a great job. But not the outfit managing Earth. Heaven Inc. is a run-down industrial setting with a checked-out divine CEO, an apathetic HR staff, unionized angels on the warehouse floor, and a Department of Bug Control that's never managed to control a single bug. But if you're randomly assigned there, you'd better make the best of it.

In the first season of the TV comedy anthology *Miracle Workers*, starring Daniel Radcliffe and Steve Buscemi, heaven looks like a refinery, with Earth looming impossibly large in the blue sky above. After death, you'll find yourself nude and middle-aged, packed in with other souls five across and four deep in an elevator. Once you arrive at the ground floor, you'll be issued a gray sweat suit and a blue orientation folder and be welcomed to Heaven Inc. You're now an angel, and it's your job to keep Earth running smoothly.

You'll soon be assigned to one of Heaven Inc.'s many departments, each overseeing a tiny slice of creation in accordance with shelves of corporate manuals and handbooks. There's a Department of Clouds, a Department of Body Odor, a Department of Dirt, a Department of Volcano Safety, even a Department of Male Nipples. (Male nipples were originally supposed to dispense orange juice, but it's been millennia and the team still hasn't cracked the problem.)

On your breaks, why not skip the employee cafeteria and explore a little? You have nothing but time. The murky sub-basements are full of surprises. The Department of Mammoths has been closed for centuries, but you could still plug in the tusk-analyzing machine to see if it works. Nearby is the Department of Answered Prayers, where a single employee receives a delivery of two million petitions from Earth every day and generally gets to three or four of them. (He picks easy problems like lost car keys, even though the bulk of the prayers are for impossible things like world peace or reliable Wi-Fi.) Even Death itself lurks around a corner here, in the form of a breaker box flickering with bolts of purple electricity.

Don't miss any chance to visit the executive suites upstairs! These boxy white palaces float above the factory, tethered only by elevator shafts. You'll emerge in what looks like a gleaming hotel lobby, where the executive archangels and their assistants work.

It's surprisingly easy to take a peek into the office of the CEO. (His jaded assistant, Rosie, will probably be distracted by a Sudoku.) The grand piano and the vaulted skylights are impressive, but you'll immediately see why Heaven Inc. is in disrepair: God checked out long ago. He sits on a white couch in His undershirt and pajama bottoms all day, watching Earth on an infinitely tall wall of TVs and popping root beer jellybeans from a crystal bowl. He's just a slob like one of us.

GOD GUIDE

Here's the Supreme Being's problem: He's a black sheep. When His family gathers in their mansion on a floating island in the sky, they can compare successes in their respective galaxies—but our God's creation pales in comparison. He only got one planet in our solar system to work, most of it is too hot or frozen all the time, and He forgot to finish the middle so it's just full of fire. His family *definitely* doesn't understand why He gave His creations free will. Rookie mistake!

HEAVEN VS. HELL

South Park

As you might expect from a TV series that has killed off one of its main characters ninety-eight times, *South Park* visits the afterlife frequently. This is a cartoon that spends a lot more time and thought on its theology than on its animation.

You're probably most familiar with the show's version of hell, since it got so much screen time in the 1999 *South Park* movie. Hell is a smoky, lava-filled cavern of rocky spikes, where you'll need to watch out at all times for the fiery droppings of dragons circling overhead. The demons jabbing you with barbed spears or roasting you over a spit will range from horrific animal hybrids to little dark imps with hollow eyes. But don't miss the occasional special events, like Luau Sunday! Satan himself might provide your fish dinner personally, by throwing nets into a nearby lava pool.

The Dark Lord is a red, barrel-chested daddy type with furry black goat legs and a skull belt buckle that's actually pretty metal. He once lived in the River Styx Condominiums on hell's affluent West Side, where he carried on a tumultuous affair with Saddam Hussein. It didn't work out: Saddam was a cruel sadist, while Satan proved to be a big softie with a Hummel doll collection and a deep need for nurturing and cuddles.

Today Satan lives in a more conventional stone castle, surrounded by lava fountains and bleached skulls. His lieutenants include his assistant Demonius; slain child beauty queen JonBenét Ramsey, who advises him on matters of the heart; and the serial killer trio of Jeffrey Dahmer, John Wayne Gacy, and Ted Bundy, a Three Stooges–like combo of depraved violence and nyuk-nyuk-nyuks. In fact, the *South Park* residents of hell are always a cavalcade of famous names, from obvious choices (Hitler, Kim Il-sung) to celebrities who happened to have died recently when a particular episode aired (Princess Di, Michael Landon, Gene Siskel).

That's because, in *South Park* eschatology, virtually everyone goes to hell. Across the Plains of Limbo, behind a filigreed golden gate guarded by St. Peter, rises heaven, a vaulted city of gold and marble atop a summit of gleaming clouds. Design-wise, it's somewhere between a domed basilica and a Tibetan lamasery. For most of *South Park*'s run, its only residents were chipper Mormons, all wearing white short-sleeved blouses or dress shirts. If you're lucky enough to spend eternity in wholesome activities with them, there's never a dull moment: playing charades, making things out of egg cartons, singing family favorites while someone strums a guitar. And there's always cookies and punch afterward.

God, you might be surprised to find out, is a snaggletoothed hippo-esque creature with cat's ears, squirrel paws, and elephant feet—or at least that's how humans perceive His ineffable nature. In recent decades, God decided to allow non-Mormons into heaven, in order to bulk up its military. Specifically, He invented the Sony PSP console and a video game called *Heaven vs. Hell* to learn which humans would be the most

---

CELEBRITY SPOTTING

The *South Park* afterlife also offers a purgatory option, but, like hell, its clientele is packed with recently deceased celebrities. In one 2009 episode, celebrity ghosts begin haunting South Park because they're trapped on a temporary plane of existence. In fact, this plane looks like a *literal* plane, one that's pushed back from the gate but can't take off. You'll sit in rows of seats in a foggy waste for months as a flight attendant keeps announcing delays. You will get no update from the pilots, no use of the lavatories, no drinks. The only baggage on board is your emotional baggage. (In 2009, the delay was due to Michael Jackson's ghost's refusing to admit that he was dead, so keep an eye out for the culprit grounding your flight.)

skilled tacticians against Satan's armies of Soul-Rippers, Black Knights, and Demon Dragons. When Kenny McCormick was placed in charge of heaven's angels, this *Last Starfighter*–inspired gambit proved successful, and Kenny earned heaven's greatest prize: a life-size gold statue of Keanu Reeves.

Resurrection may be an option as well, but if the strange case of Kenny McCormick is any indication, no one will even remember you were ever gone.

LAKEVIEW, BY HORIZEN

Upload

The year is 2033, and the best days of your life could be after it's over. Welcome to Upload!

In Amazon's 2020 comedy series *Upload*, the corporations of a declining near-future America have staked out a new arena for consumer control: the afterlife. Hospitals have Upload rooms ("URs") near the ER; get yourself into one before breathing your last and your consciousness will be uploaded into whatever virtual heaven you can afford. Your head will be vaporized in the process, but that's the price of immortality.

If you choose to Upload, your first postmortem sensation will be a world forming around you in monochromatic macro-pixels. You'll feel pins and needles in your extremities as the program finds your nerve endings. Focus on the reality of your own consciousness; that should get you through. You'll wake up in the afterlife you or your next of kin purchased. Hopefully you were able to afford a luxurious spot like Lakeview, the afterlife where *Upload* is set.

Lakeview is a mountain resort modeled on the grand Victorian hotels of North America. This digital paradise adds thousands of new floors every year, but you only see guests from your own five-floor increment of rooms, so the hotel never feels crowded. A customer service rep, or "angel," will give you a personalized welcome and can be called on to service you (or any of their forty-seven other clients) at any time. If your avatar seems a little off—say, due to an unexpected cowlick or Australian accent—that's your angel's fault.

This bougie vacation paradise is full of earth's finest amenities and then some: maple bacon doughnuts at the breakfast buffet, a thermostat that lets you adjust the seasonal view out each window, memory parlors where you can watch anything that ever happened to you in life, pet therapy where the pets actually offer spoken advice. Farts smell good here, and your pee never misses the toilet bowl, no matter how hard you try. In fact, life is so monotonously perfect that some residents pay extra for lifelike inconveniences like head colds.

HISTORY BUFFS!
Lakeview has come a long way from its primitive first version, in which uploads couldn't eat, defecate, or blink. Nowadays, regular updates introduce elaborately programmed additions like whales, unicorns, and umami taste buds.

Yes, that's the not-so-hidden secret of Lakeview: extras cost extra. There are lots of free activities, but Horizen will bill you (or your estate) if you swipe on any of the ever-present upgrades or "in-app purchases" that hover above minibars and concierges. Want to add avocado to your breakfast selection? That'll cost you. Want to fight the hotel staff, an army of irritating identical redheads, using "Game Mode"? Want to limit adbots, or keep Horizen out of your hair with "Privacy Mode"? That'll cost you.

Never forget: you have sold your consciousness to a major corporation. They now have eternity to data-mine your memories or market to you. Every leaf on every tree of the resort is marked with a Horizen bar code. If your monthly payment ever bounces, you'll quickly lose all your hotel privileges and be demoted to life with the "2-Gigs," the pay-as-you-go uploads who live in the white, fluorescent-lit utility corridors in the bowels of the hotel. There the rooms are bare, the dining hall is sponsored by Lean Cuisine, and even books are blank except for a few sample pages. The 2-Gigs always display above their heads the amount of data they've used in the last billing cycle, and once they run out, their avatars freeze in monochrome until next month. Try to avoid activities that use too much data—like thinking too hard or experiencing emotions.

SAVVY TRAVELER TIP
There are ways to get around your new corporate overlords. Look for a flickering gap in the hedge surrounding the Lakeview grounds. That's the entrance to the Grey Market, a neon-lit silo where any postmortal dark-web commodity you can imagine is for sale. You have one hour to buy any hack you want (like avatar upgrades or contraband celebrity memories) before Horizen notices you're missing and wipes your file.

Uploads can still contact "bios" (the living) virtually, via video calls or even conjugal visits, if your romantic partner wants to insert themselves into Lakeview via a full-body "hug suit." But stay away from the Torrent, a glowing stream of light that connects Upload to the real world. It's suicide. Your brain was vaporized when you died, and now you're just ones and zeroes. There's no going back.

Lakeview is, of course, just one of hundreds of Upload options. If you want to "heaven-shop," a big pneumatic tube will suck you into previews of any number of other afterlives, from luxurious (Apple's Cove beach resort, Disney's Eternity) to budget (Kmart Villa Scape). Whether you prefer an eternity of savanna adventure in Nat Geo Instagram Safari or the soul-deadening casino clamor of Panera Facebook Aeon, there's something for every taste. But stay far away from the faux-Tuscany of Tutti Tempo, the Italian-American Upload heaven—unless you *really* like Sinatra, that is.

LARRY'S HEAVEN

Curb Your Enthusiasm

On HBO's *Curb Your Enthusiasm,* comedian Larry David (or at least his fictional alter ego, Larry David) has suffered every embarrassment and indignity known to man and lived to kvetch about it. It stands to reason that, eventually, he would face the ultimate trial: death and its aftermath.

In the 2005 episode "The End," Larry donates a kidney to his friend Richard Lewis but dies of complications in the hospital. As his heart stops, he feels himself floating toward the ceiling, which shatters to reveal a sky of bright clouds and then a tunnel of light.

If you emerge into the same heaven that welcomed Larry David, you'll see a misty white realm of the kind familiar in TV afterlives, with plenty of fog from dry ice machines concealing the soundstage floor. It's not a particularly Jewish heaven. Bits of picturesque marble ruins can be glimpsed through the clouds: mossy cracked colonnades, classical statuary. For some reason, there's one leafless tree.

Most of the spirits wandering and chatting in the clouds are clad in hooded white robes, but as a newcomer, you may find yourself wearing a pale version of your earthly attire. Larry David's spirit wears a white sport coat over a beige polo. If, like Larry, you were bald at death, you'll now be sporting a fine, full head of hair.

Your orientation will be provided by two wise, bearded guides who were your guardian angels in life and know everything you ever saw or did. They'll introduce you around. If you're lucky, you'll meet luminaries from earth who know and admire your work (in Larry's case: Ponce de León, Marilyn Monroe, and golfer Ben Hogan, who wants to shoot a few rounds with him on one of heaven's many fine courses). If you're unlucky, you'll run into people from your past that you've been hoping to avoid. In Larry's case, that's his nagging mother, played by Bea Arthur in her final role.

Much has been written about the joys and glories of heaven, but the first thing Larry notices is a kind of bliss never mentioned in holy scripture: he doesn't need to pee anymore. In fact, he never will again. If you've been an elderly person for any amount of time at this point, that's a pretty big deal.

THE 1928 PORTER

My Mother the Car

"Everybody knows in the second life we all come back sooner or later," began the theme song of TV's *My Mother the Car*, in a bold theological claim, "as anything from a pussycat to a man-eating alligator." But on the short-lived 1965 sitcom, David Crabtree's deceased mother put the "car" back in "reincarnation," reentering her son's life as an antique 1928 Porter touring car. Hijinks ensued.

Why a car? Evidently the increasing complexity of technology makes machines a more plausible "second life" nowadays than they would have seemed to ancient Hindus or Buddhists, who never envisioned souls returning to earth as plows or windmills. Mother tells Dave that the dead don't have any choice over the form of their return, and in fact most don't want to come back at all—"The application bin is usually empty." One acquaintance of hers did have to come back as an Edsel, she says, implying that the automotive sector is a common destiny for rebirth. Does that mean that today's reincarnated souls may choose newer machines like Segways, laser printers, and Roombas? It certainly seems possible.

If you come back to earth as a car, you'll still have many of your human faculties. You can talk to your living charges through the car radio (though *My Mother the Car* never explained why a beat-up jalopy from 1928 had a radio in the first place) and alert them to danger by honking the horn or backfiring. You'll still eat (motor oil, not food) and sleep (in the garage). You'll be able to see 360 degrees, thanks to your mirrors. In fact, you'll have broad powers over every auto part on your chassis: you can open and close doors, put the top up and down, even deflate your tires. You can be driven normally, but you always have the option of overriding your driver and taking control of the wheel. Mother was a self-driving car fifty years before Tesla.

There are some downsides to life as a two-ton metal machine, of course. Your radiator might boil over when you get mad. Too much antifreeze gets you drunk, and if you're an older car, acceleration can be a strain. Even the slightest fender bender can cause you injury or even amnesia. But most of your problems will probably revolve around keeping news of your vehicular return quiet. Your loved one(s) will want to let the world know that the dear departed can come back as cars, and that's generally a bad idea. Dave Crabtree was forever getting weird looks for having long conversations with his car radio, but at least that problem's now been solved by cars with hands-free phone dialing.

My Mother the Car was green-lit in response to the success of outlandish sitcoms like *Mr. Ed* ("A talking horse, why not a talking car?") but its premise was more than a little confusing. Mother died on August 23, 1949, but was somehow reincarnated in a car manufactured twenty years earlier? Then she spent years sitting in a used car lot with a sign reading "Fix'r Upper" in hopes that her son would wander by? It's not exactly an airtight view of the afterlife.

Perhaps it's not surprising that *My Mother the Car* was canceled by NBC after a single season and often tops lists of the worst TV shows ever made. At least 1960s broadcast standards meant we never had to see Dave pumping gas into his mother, which would have been a truly horrifying mental image. Hope you come back as an electric!

World Without End

OCEANSIDE

Forever

Even faithful believers sometimes find themselves wondering if heaven might be stultifyingly boring. You thought Tarantino movies were a little long? Well, welcome to the afterlife. It literally lasts forever.

The 2018 Netflix series *Forever* cleverly explored this theme by making the next world a direct extension of humdrum daily life—and of marriage in particular. Fred Armisen and Maya Rudolph play a couple in a comfortable but dull marriage who are suddenly forced to reckon with the fact that they might be trapped in their passionless relationship for an eternity.

In the afterlife of *Forever*, you'll awake on neatly mown grass in a bland suburban neighborhood. For Oscar and June Hoffman, this is Riverside, California, not far from their earthly stomping grounds. In fact, it's a real neighborhood that's been evacuated and gated due to mold or something. The authorities who have apparently arranged these empty residences for the souls of the deceased are never revealed.

That's because this is an afterlife entirely without God—but there is a shuffleboard court. It's an easy life, if you don't mind the lack of answers. The cupboards and closets of your home will provide clothing and your favorite foods every day, and equipment for peaceful middle-aged hobbies like pottery making and crossword puzzles will appear regularly. Everyone stays the physical age they were when they died, and those who died young tend to be weird and maladjusted, like child actors. Days, months, even years will pass. It's hard to be sure.

Your neighborhood will have some source of water, like a fountain, that powers you. Wander too far away from the water, and you'll feel weaker

> **LEARN THE LANGUAGE**
> The deceased in this afterlife call themselves "formers," while the living are "currents."

and weaker. But it is possible to recharge by absorbing life energy from the living. You can "juice" a current by placing your hand on their neck and focusing all your energy on their pulse and your breath.

The Hoffmans find that all roads from their neighborhood eventually lead to Oceanside, a huge mansion perched on a cliff overlooking the beach. The formers there have each chosen to forget their earthly life, with all its fear and guilt and "negativity," and instead focus on the simple, hedonistic pleasures of eternity. In Oceanside you can spend your evenings dancing to live music among the rococo pillars of its stunning terrace. Then head out to the highway with friends for the simple thrill of letting cars and trucks pass through your incorporeal body. And don't miss "ocean stands," the soothing practice of wandering out onto the seafloor, where you can watch the fish and seaweed swirling silently around you. Once a year, you'll join your neighbors in "the Cleansing," a massive beach bonfire in which they burn all their possessions. It's a "reminder to always forget," they say, but of course your things will reappear in your rooms the next morning.

But what if you find the glamour of Oceanside to be just as claustrophobic and empty as suburbia was? Oscar and June discover that there are destinations beyond Oceanside. Head out into the waves as if for an "ocean stand," but just keep walking. Eventually you'll emerge on a new and distant shore.

THE OTHER SIDE OF THE WORLD

The Leftovers

If you spent your earthly life playing video games, you may be looking for an afterlife with kill quests, side quests, a character creator, and a boss level. If you don't mind a dash of David Lynchian surrealism as well, you may want to check into the ▲ Hotel & Spa from HBO's *The Leftovers.*

Based on Tom Perrotta's 2011 novel, *The Leftovers* takes place in a world where 5 percent of humanity has abruptly disappeared in a Rapture-like "Great Departure." Justin Theroux's character, Kevin Garvey, has a hard time distinguishing reality from fantasy following that trauma, so we aren't sure what to think when, on three separate occasions, he visits a surreal afterlife—each time managing to return to his body intact. *The Leftovers* was a show that always pledged to "let the mystery be," but there's a strong suggestion that Kevin really is visiting the next world in these little adventures. "It was real!" he later insists. "Maybe I was dead but I never felt so alive!"

Visitors to the "other side" will be reborn from water, slithering naked from pounding surf or an overflowing bathtub. When you get dressed, choose your clothing carefully. Kevin's closet contains a police uniform, priestly vestments, cult member robes, and a slim tailored suit. "Know first who you are, and then adorn yourself accordingly," a plaque instructs him. Choosing the suit turns him into an international assassin with the not-very-clever alias of Kevin Harvey.

In Kevin's first two jaunts past death, his milieu is an anonymous business hotel with endless corridors and a sunny atrium lobby. Each time, a guide (one actually named Virgil, in a nod to Dante) gives him a quest or

> **TRAVEL TRIVIA**
> The filming location for this afterlife is actually the Sheraton in downtown Austin, Texas, but it's been redressed with a wordless new logo: a blue triangle on a gold circle.

trial to complete. Your mission might be as simple as singing a song at a karaoke night or as perilous as assassinating a presidential candidate. Complete it, and "you'll be delivered from this place." You may return to the world of the living.

That's right: this is a hotel, with *guests* passing through. Not everyone on the other side is a permanent resident. You'll probably cross paths with some deceased acquaintances who act as non-player characters (NPCs) on your quests, but you'll also pass plenty of folks on crazy missions of their own.

> **TRAVELER BEWARE!**
> Just don't ever drink the water, no matter how thirsty you get. It has Lethe-like properties. A single sip can strip you of all your earthly memories. Then you'll be an NPC forever.

The world to come is bigger than just one hotel—and its geography seems to be much like our world. Kevin drives all night on Interstate 55 to take his assassination target to the Orphan's Well in Jarden, Texas, where he drowns her. And in his third afterlife visit, he wakes up in Australia (literally the other side of the world) and takes on two self-destructive identities: he's playing the game now as two twin brothers (international assassin Kevin Harvey and US president Kevin Garvey) who each want to kill the other.

Keep an eye out for reflective surfaces on your journey—mirrors, eyeglass lenses, and so forth. They have mystical properties. Through a flickering hotel TV screen, Kevin speaks with his still-living father, who seems to be glimpsing the next world on a drug-fueled vision quest of his own. And when Kevin enters the afterlife as twins, he learns he can switch between Player 1 and Player 2 by looking at his own face reflected in glass.

But if you make the mistake of drinking the water, you probably won't remember any of this advice. You might not even know your own name. Long-term residents may recall their own deaths through flashes of déjà vu or mistakenly believe that they're the ones who survived the rest of their families. Your best bet for identifying this afterlife is probably the deafening strains of the "Chorus of the Hebrew Slaves" from Verdi's *Nabucco*, which accompanies all of *The Leftovers'* posthumous fantasies. It's an opera chorus sung by a group of exiles yearning for a home they know they can never return to again.

Best. Afterlife. Ever.

PARA-DIDDLY-DARADISE

The Simpsons

The Simpsons, now in its thirty-somethingth season, may be immortal, but its cast of characters is not. Deceased supporting characters like Maude Flanders and Rabbi Krustofsky have been seen in the afterlife, but so have still-living regulars like Bart and Homer. Don't have a cow, man—these postmortal glimpses are typically presented as dreams, visions, Halloween stories, and other flights of fancy. But sometimes they're a perfectly cromulent part of the show's canon.

In a change-of-pace 2017 episode, we learned that medieval analogs of the Simpsons believed that their souls would move on to the "Fields of Bliss," where the dead wave ribbons and enjoy frolics most joyous. (Dissenting voices include Duffman, who prefers an eternity of slaughtering and being slaughtered by his enemies; a troll version of Milhouse's dad, who plans to spend the afterlife counting his goblin lords' money; and the old sea captain, who just wants seventy-one mermaids—some where the fish is the top half!) But the show's modern-day episodes usually depict the dead in a traditional heaven of blue skies and fluffy clouds, alongside Jesus, St. Peter, and God Himself.

GOD GUIDE
The Judeo-Christian God is a giant robed figure who sports a gray beard and the same yellow skin as *The Simpson*'s Caucasian characters. The main difference: unlike the show's four-fingered characters, God has a freakish *five* fingers on each hand. Homer describes Him as having "perfect teeth, nice smell . . . a class act all the way."

When Homer finds himself entering the afterlife in a 2005 episode about the Rapture, heaven turns out to be a luxury resort complete with nature walks, a pedicure hut, and a state-of-the-art showroom featuring beloved artists like Los Lobos. The café is called Pope of Sandwich Village, a joke that probably could have used a few more minutes in the writers' room. Change into a cozy bathrobe and tune your hotel TV to channel 23 to see what's going on down on earth. Any comfort you desire will be yours just by wishing—except for entry to the water park. That's closed until next summer. (Leprechaun labor troubles.)

CELEBRITY SPOTTING

Every time *The Simpsons* visits heaven, it's fully stocked with famous names: Jimi Hendrix and Ben Franklin playing air hockey, Leonardo painting Dean Martin's portrait, Beethoven and Tupac performing in the "Ultimate Def Jam." Comedian Tracy Morgan is somehow there even though he isn't dead. The allure of dead celebs is so strong that the 2008 *Simpsons* Halloween episode imagined a whole "Celebrity Heaven," separated by a fence from the less fancy "Regular Heaven." There notables from Neil Armstrong to John Lennon to a gay Abraham Lincoln enjoy nightly events like poker tournaments at the rec center. Springfield celebs are there are well, with Krusty the Clown confiding to Homer that the one true religion was "a mix of voodoo and Methodist."

Your chances of getting into *Simpsons* heaven went way up recently. Realizing that the place was populated only by little old ladies and Promise Keepers—and that a whole new mixed-use complex for baby boomers was going empty—God decided to open heaven to good people of all faiths, including deserving atheists. Even Mr. Burns briefly makes it in, as Smithers's plus-one.

This means you have several possible destinations in your *Simpsons* afterlife voyage. You might wind up in Protestant Heaven, full of insufferable preppies playing croquet and badminton. Across the way, Catholic Heaven, festooned with lights and streamers, is a lot more lively: Italians sharing a big pasta dinner, Mexicans playing mariachi music and whacking a piñata, Irish folks fighting and Riverdancing.

In Jewish Heaven, on the other hand, Rodney Dangerfield gets plenty of respect, Einstein and Moshe Dayan invite Gal Gadot up to chat, and even Portnoy has no complaints. Don't-miss highlights include the Kosher Pickle Forest, the Joe Lieberman Presidential Library, a box store called Oys R Us, and a re-creation of the Brooklyn Dodgers' Ebbets Field where everyone in the stands gets free egg creams. Elsewhere in the clouds is an entrance to the templelike Hindu Heaven, where you'll see Vishnu holding a clipboard with two of his four arms. In one alternate future, Homer heads there to be reincarnated and chooses to return as a turtle rather than the lowest possible option, "pharmaceutical CEO."

What about hell? In an early *Simpsons* episode, Bart has a vision of rising to heaven on a golden escalator, passing the angelic spirits of his great-grandfather and the family's original cat, Snowball. "Please hold on to the handrail. Do not spit," says a prerecorded announcement in both English and Spanish. Bart spits over the edge, of course, and the escalator flattens into a ramp and whisks him down to a fiery hell based on Hieronymus Bosch's painting *The Garden of Earthly Delights* (see page 266), where the devil reminds him to "lie, cheat, steal, and listen to heavy metal music!"

If you are unfortunate enough to enter the *Simpsons* version of hell, expect to see the tortures of the damned: conveyor belts where new arrivals are chopped up into hot dog meat, a barbecue serving warm German potato salad and coleslaw with pineapple in it, and an "Ironic Punishment Division" where gluttons are force-fed donuts. (D'oh!) Mr. Burns will be there in a little froglike body; so will historically awful people like Benedict Arnold, Blackbeard, and John Wayne. Take a look at the watchdog Cerberus. He'll be sporting the heads of Springfield Elementary's three bullies: Jimbo, Dolph, and Kearney. Satan himself might be the traditional giant red figure, goat legged and goateed, or he might look like Herman (that one-armed guy from Springfield's army-navy store) or even the Simpsons' genial neighbor Ned Flanders. Weirdly, Ned has also appeared on the show before as God. That's a dilly of a theological pickle!

On the Clock

THE REAPERS

Dead Like Me

The short-lived TV series *Dead Like Me* was Showtime's answer to *Six Feet Under*, but the arch, death-soaked dramedy played more like *My So-Called Afterlife*. A moody teen is killed by a bit of plummeting space debris (a toilet seat from the Mir space station!) and learns what happens after death. Unfortunately for her—and you, if you're chosen for the same fate—the answer is a near-eternity of dull temping.

See, some of the dead stay on earth to become "Grim Reapers," functionaries assigned to collect the souls of the deceased. You won't wear a black robe and wield a scythe. Instead, you'll have a corporeal form that looks mostly like your living body did, though with your face altered enough that nobody recognizes you. Every day, your supervisor will hand you a Post-it bearing a name, a location, and an ETD—estimated time of death. You need to be on the scene in that person's final moments to confirm their identity and touch them purposefully. That will pop out their soul, saving them from the pain of death that awaits them. You can then escort the dead soul into the Great Whatever, a portal of floating light. The Lights will seem to hold a tempting reward personal to the deceased, but it will all stay a complete mystery to you. You'll never see the angels that make up "upper management." You're just a grunt, a bail bondsman for the disembodied.

The stakes for your job performance couldn't be higher: if you miss a soul, it stays trapped in its body, and the deceased can't move on into the Lights. You and your team are just one of countless cells extending all over the globe, and each is assigned to specialize in a certain type of death. There's a Natural Causes Division, a Plague Division for disease, an External Influence Division for murders and accidents, and so forth. As a Reaper, you'll see what the living cannot: these deaths are all being arranged by Gravelings, little porcupine-quilled gremlins who live in cemeteries. Like Reapers, Gravelings are dead souls (nasty ones!) chosen for a new duty, but their work isn't really any better or worse than yours. Their lethal shenanigans keep the universe in balance.

To be perfectly honest, being a Grim Reaper is nobody's dream career. For one thing, you don't get paid. To scrape by, you'll have to either get a day job or leverage the fringe benefits of Reaper life, grabbing cash off the bodies of your "reaps" or squatting in their newly vacant apartments. You now live on the margins of society, aiming to be noticed by no one. You shouldn't have friends among the living, let alone relationships. Definitely don't haunt your old life; you may even start to lose memories of your loved ones if you keep hanging around them. If nothing else, they'll grow old over the decades while you stay the same age.

That's right, this new gig may last a half century or more. There is a set number of "reaps" required for your next promotion, but you have no idea what that quota is. On the plus side, your semi-immortality does make you virtually indestructible. Wounds heal instantly; alcohol won't give you a hangover. Your new faster metabolism means you can eat whatever you want—and, if you're like many Reapers, abuse all the substances you want.

There are a few bright spots punctuating your new job. On Halloween, your team all wears masks, because Reaper legend has it the living can recognize your real identity on that day. Occasionally, you'll get assigned a VIP reap, or "viper," that comes with enough cash to get you access to the soon-to-die celebrity. Every few years, the Gravelings take the day off and nobody dies, so you can kick back and catch up on paperwork. But for the most part, it's a daily grind, and you're on call 24/7. You'll sit around reading the obituaries like sports pages, with a raincoat on hand in case of blood splatter, just waiting for the next Post-it. For decades. It's a living!

ROBOT HELL

Futurama

Human beings are spoiled for choice when it comes to the afterlife, but artificial life seems to have few options. If you're a robot, what happens when you die? Matt Groening's *Futurama*, set in the "New New York" of the year 3000, offers the most definitive cosmology.

When robots die in ignominious ways, such as suicide, their software is exported to the computational cloud. Their limbo is an infinite loop that might last forever. But robots who made even worse choices wind up in Robot Hell. This is a literal underworld located deep beneath Reckless Ted's Funland, an abandoned amusement park in Atlantic City, New Jersey.

Behind a mirror in the park's "Inferno" funhouse, you'll find the entrance to the pit of Robot Hell. It's a fiery maze of sheet-metal smokestacks and ducts and giant saw blades, crisscrossed by slides and mine-cart tracks. Robotic demon torturers dismember the mechanical damned, scourge them with fiery whips, zap them with electric slime, and update the myth of Sisyphus by forcing them to push boulders up treadmills.

Agonizing *and* ironic punishments await you on all sides. On level one, smokers might get wrapped up in a giant cigar and lit on fire. On level two, gamblers are strapped to a giant wheel of fortune and spun to reveal their fate: Bake, Parboil, Fricassee, Sauté, Deep-Fry, or Pleasant Massage. (That last one probably doesn't come up much.) On level five, robots who pirated music have their hard drives removed—and scratched up turntable-style by the severed heads of the Beastie Boys!

Robot Hell is ruled by a Robot Devil, of course. You can call him

Beelzebot if you like. Beware: he's a trickster whose contracts always have catches. He also fronts an exceedingly irritating jazz trio of robot demons—so don't give him any excuse to sing to you! Your one chance of escape might be the Fairness in Hell Act of 2275, which requires Robot Devil to let you go if you can defeat him in a fiddle contest. Your odds aren't great: he's a fiddle virtuoso who can use a third robot arm to bow duets with himself.

SOUVENIR SHOPPING

If you do somehow beat the devil, you'll take home a solid-gold fiddle! If you *lose* the contest, you get a smaller silver fiddle. (And stay in Robot Hell forever.)

Robots who lived virtuous lives and performed selfless acts have a better option: Robot Heaven, behind some steampunk-looking automatic gates up in the clouds. Inside you may see the glowing form of Robot God: a sleek, futuristic white pod with a black viewscreen. Robot God may not be as charismatic as Robot Devil, but at least He won't surprise you with a song-and-dance number.

SAN JUNIPERO

Black Mirror

Billions of people believe that when they die, their soul will move on to be with God in the clouds. But what if, instead, your soul just moved on to the Cloud?

That's the premise of "San Junipero," an Emmy-winning 2016 episode of the *Twilight Zone*–but–with–cell–phones anthology series *Black Mirror*. The story follows Kelly and Yorkie, two "tourists" visiting the titular coastal California town in 1987. They dance, they play video games, they fall in love. But it soon becomes clear that all is not what it appears in San Junipero. Visitors can only stay in town for a few hours every week. Injuries are impossible, and a shattered mirror is repaired in the blink of an eye. Weirdest of all, the characters can apparently choose to visit San Junipero in different eras, showing up there in 1980, 1996, and 2002. What's going on?

It turns out that "San Junipero" isn't a real town at all, but an extraordinarily realistic computer simulation. It was designed in the 2020s as "immersive nostalgia therapy" for dementia patients, who found it comforting to return to the time periods of their youth. The elderly can lie back, place a glowing white bead on their right temple (this being *Black Mirror*, there is always a glowing white brain bead), and be whisked away to a perfect night in a carefree "party town."

But most of these tourists eventually choose to "pass over"—that is, become permanent residents of San Junipero. When they die, their consciousnesses can be uploaded to TCKR Systems, the tech company that created the San Junipero simulation. TCKR data centers are a maze of server-lined corridors, where automated robots plug the uploaded cores of new arrivals into endless banks of thirty circular ports each. Welcome to the afterlife, SJ 521-12 016! The eight-digit numerical code allows room for one hundred million dead "souls" in San Junipero. (It's not clear if there are other prefixes besides SJ, or if everyone experiences heaven as California.) The simulation is so inviting that guests on "trial runs" must be awoken after five hours to avoid addiction and dissociation. Even euthanasia laws have to be tightened up, because so many people discover they prefer the San Junipero afterlife to dreary old age.

San Junipero is a seaside getaway set below dramatic cliffs that look more like Cape Town than Santa Cruz. (The episode's exteriors were filmed in South Africa.) As you enter, you'll be allowed to choose an outfit, an automobile, and other accessories. You'll also choose an initial era, typical reminders of which will be everywhere as you explore. In 1987, a *Lost Boys* movie billboard might loom above the main drag, and Max Headroom will be chattering away on every TV set. In 1996, the songs from Alanis Morissette's *Jagged Little Pill* will be unavoidable.

Physically, you'll appear to be in your late twenties or thereabouts. Check out the scene at a local watering hole like Tucker's (named as an in-joke by clever TCKR programmers). In 1987, the neon-tube lighting is pastel-perfect, the hairsprayed bangs are tall, and the video arcade has fondly remembered classics like *Bubble Bobble*. If you switch to 2002, the bar will still be there, but now the vibe will be all dry ice and laser beams, *Dance Dance Revolution* will have replaced the old-school video games, and Kylie Minogue might be blasting on the dance floor.

> **MEET THE LOCALS**
> Party and hook up with wild abandon—but keep in mind that at least 15 percent of your fellow club goers are trial-membership "tourists," still among the living, and will disappear at midnight like Cinderella.

Does an eternity of 1980s nostalgia seem like heaven to you, or hell? Many of San Junipero's residents do find that the simulation begins to get old after a while. But remember that, just like in *Bubble Bobble*, the two-player version of San Junipero comes with a totally different ending. If you find true love like Yorkie and Kelly, you'll discover that heaven can be, quite literally, a place on earth. Even if that place is a climate-controlled data center.

OFF THE BEATEN PATH

If you never find that special someone, there are other ways to keep boredom at bay in San Junipero. Many novelty seekers head for the Quagmire, a sketchy fetish club located in an old refinery on the outskirts of town.

A computer simulation might seem like an unlikely afterlife, but hey, stranger things have happened. Like a *Black Mirror* episode that actually has a happy ending.

STO-VO-KOR AND GRE'THOR

The Klingon Empire

On our planet, when people talk about death a lot, we think of them as mopey goths. Not so on Kronos, the homeworld of *Star Trek*'s Klingon Empire! Klingons never shut up about death, but it's because they're a proud, aggressive people who can't wait to die honorably on the field of battle. As a great Klingon once said, "*boghtlhInganpu', SuvwI'pu' moj, Hegh.*"[*] Or maybe he was just clearing his throat.

When a Klingon warrior dies, their wrinkly-headed comrades observe the vigil of *ak'voh*, to keep predators from desecrating the body. They may also stare deeply into the eyes of the deceased and then howl heavenward, warning the dead souls in Sto-Vo-Kor that a combative new Klingon arrival is on their way up.

Sto-Vo-Kor is a Valhalla-like realm where the honored dead carouse with Kahless the Unforgettable, the Klingon messiah who gifted his people their warrior philosophy. But your afterlife won't just be endless feasts of bloodwine and those weird live tapeworm things that Klingons are always eating! You'll also keep your martial skills and your *bat'leth* sharpened by joining your forefathers in the Black Fleet, fighting an eternal battle against the worthiest foes.

But even in the most warlike culture, not everybody can die in battle or honorable ritual suicide. Sadly, some Klingons probably choke to death on a tapeworm or get hit by a spaceship on their way to the post office. If that

---

[*] "Klingons are born, live as warriors, and then die."

happens to you, you'll never see Kahless. Instead you'll find yourself on the dragon-prowed Barge of the Dead, a boat steered by Kortar, the mythical first Klingon. (In typical Klingon fashion, Kortar destroyed the very gods who gave him life and was sent down to punishment in the underworld.) Your face will be branded with a mark of dishonor, and no questions are permitted.

> **TRAVELER BEWARE!**
> While navigating the River of Blood on Kortar's barge, watch out for the Kos'Karii, pale serpents who will try to lure you down into the crimson waters by imitating the voices of your loved ones.

This voyage leads to the gates of Gre'thor, a hellish city of stone walls, lit by flashes of lightning and great flaming braziers. An inverted insignia of the Klingon Empire is carved above the gate. Inside, the hideous monster Fek'lhr oversees the tortures of the damned. Your only hope is that your surviving mate or another relative will perform a heroic deed in your memory, proving your example of courage and freeing you to ascend to Sto-Vo-Kor. Eat your heart out, everybody else in Gre'thor!

Actually, if they'd eaten more people's hearts out, like a *good* Klingon, they probably wouldn't be in Gre'thor in the first place.

MUSIC AND THEATER

THE AFTERLIFE

Paul Simon

Paul Simon has been worried about mortality for a long time. From 1968's "Old Friends" right up through the confused middle-aged narrators of "You Can Call Me Al" and "The Obvious Child," Simon's catalog is filled with anxiety about the inescapable fact that, as he put it on his first solo album, everything put together falls apart.

But the man who at age twenty-six once mused "How terribly strange to be seventy," turned seventy himself in 2011, and that year he released *So Beautiful or So What*. It's a record about God, Simon discovered as he recorded it. And its second single gives his first-person tour of the next world.

On "The Afterlife," accompanied by mellow African guitar and zydeco accordion, Simon gives a fictional account of his own death and what came after. The heaven he envisions is a slow and bureaucratic one, a cosmic DMV. You eventually get to meet God, but, as the chorus keeps repeating, "you got to fill out a form first, and then you wait in the line."

After your death, according to Simon, you'll briefly wander the earth as a spirit wondering what comes next. His narrator goes back to his old apartment, before a light hits him from heaven and a "sugarcoated" voice says, "Let us begin."

Then you'll find yourself in the long, slow queue to the Ladder of Time, where supplicants approach God. As you inch forward, you'll see people from all eras and races with you—Buddha, Moses, everybody. Be patient! The wait isn't just a logistical snafu or an inconvenience. It's specifically God's will that you stew and struggle before reaching His presence.

> **LOCAL CUSTOMS**
> As you wait, please observe the rules. No line-cutting is allowed in heaven, and you shouldn't harass your fellow deceased. In the song, the narrator spots a "homecoming queen" type and chats her up with the immortal pickup line "Hey . . . how long you been dead?" It doesn't go over well.

When you finally reach the ladder and begin your climb through the vastness of space, you'll start to sense the Lord's presence—but you may not be able to describe Him later. It's as if you're swimming in an ocean of love, says Simon, "and the current is strong." But when he tries to put the experience into words, all he can think of is the nonsense syllables of old blues and rockabilly songs like "Be-Bop-a-Lula" and "Ooh Poo Pah Doo." Presumably lyrics like these are specific to being a member of Simon's generation, and a millennial soul might instead describe God as "Zigazig-ah" or "Mmmbop, ba duba dop" or even "Bawitdaba-da bang-da-bang-diggy-diggy-diggy." As St. Paul wrote to the Romans about the ineffability of God, "The Spirit himself intercedes for us with groanings too deep for words."

Same as It Ever Was

BAR "HEAVEN"

Talking Heads

Anyone who's ever read medieval visions of the afterlife knows that the authors always spend more words on the suffering of hell and purgatory than they do on the glories of heaven. Hell has conflict: the torturers vs. the damned. Purgatory has an arc: the eventual redemption of souls. But heaven is endless, unchanging bliss. Narratively, it doesn't have much going on.

David Byrne embraced this static version of the afterlife in Talking Heads' 1979 song "Heaven," from their record *Fear of Music*. Byrne's heaven is not a kingdom but a bar—the kind of New York City hotspot that everyone is trying to get into but proves exceedingly underwhelming once you actually wheedle your way through the door.

In Heaven, as this bar is called, you'll enter to hear that the band is playing your favorite song when you walk in. The novelty of this pleasant surprise may not last, however, when they go on playing it all night, on endless repeat. A party is going on and *absolutely everyone* is there, but all the guests will leave at exactly the same time. (Never?) Share a kiss with someone special in a dark corner, and the kiss will begin again as soon as you pull away, always exactly the same.

"Heaven is a place where nothing ever happens," Byrne repeats endlessly. And yet, according to the minimalist Talking Heads aesthetic, that isn't all bad. There's something fun and even exciting about this bar, Byrne assures us, despite the utter lack of novelty. That's a comforting thought, if your plan for heaven is to spend not just one Friday night there, but an eternity.

THE CLOUDY DRAW

"Ghost Riders in the Sky"

Stan Jones's 1948 country and western song "Ghost Riders in the Sky" has been recorded by music stars from Peggy Lee to R.E.M., Johnny Cash to Debbie Harry to Duane Eddy. Its seductive chorus of "yippie-yi-oh"s and "yippie-yi-ay"s might give the impression that the title characters are having a great time in their spooky cowpoke afterlife, but nothing could be further from the truth.

The song describes a vision glimpsed by an old cowhand who happens to be riding the range during a rising storm. In the clouds, he sees a herd of fearsome cattle pass by, each with shiny black horns, steel hooves, red eyes, and still-glowing brand marks on their hindquarters. Their breath is so hot he can feel it. If that's not upsetting enough, he then sees the riders who drive these cattle—and they can see him as well.

If your eternal destiny is to be a ghost rider in the sky, you'll find that this is no dude ranch, no easy gig. You get to ride horses that snort fire, which is pretty cool, but the cattle you're punching will prove impossible to corral. ("Too all-fired ornery," as they might say on the range. It's not too early to start brushing up on your cowboy slang!) The herd will remain tantalizingly out of reach no matter how hard you ride. Soon your face will be gaunt, your vision blurred, and your shirt all soaked with sweat, but you won't be any closer to their thundering hooves. This trail drive is going to last forever.

Your ghost ride may take you "through the ragged sky," but you'll realize pretty quickly that this isn't heaven. In fact, part of your job is to warn the mortals below to change their wicked ways if they want to avoid your awful fate. You see, partner, this fiery livestock is the devil's herd, and you're in hell. Saddle up.

> The enemy is poverty, and the wall keeps out the
> enemy, and we build the wall to keep us free.
>
> —*Hades*

HADESTOWN

Anaïs Mitchell

The toast of Broadway in 2019 was *Hadestown*, Anaïs Mitchell's song cycle–turned–folk opera that updated the Greek myth of Orpheus and Eurydice to a Depression-era, vaguely New Orleans–y setting. *Hadestown* won eight Tonys, announced a national tour, and took sold-out New York audiences straight to hell, eight times a week.

In a bleak world reminiscent of the 1930s Dust Bowl, shantytowns are everywhere and work is scarce, so desperate people hop freight trains to nowhere. One particular railway runs to the underworld—or Hadestown, as people call it. At the last way station on the road to hell, poor souls like yours will meet three all-knowing women—the Fates—and a dapper, feather-footed man with a silver train whistle. That's Mr. Hermes, your conductor to the other world.

But you might want to think twice about this itinerary, even in hard times. Hadestown is effectively a slave labor camp. You might be lured in with the promise of steady work, but don't sign that contract! You'd literally be selling your soul. The big boss will thunder on about your new freedom from poverty, but in reality you'll be swinging a hammer or a pickaxe day and night, shoveling coal into boilers, or scurrying about on the factory floor of Hades's great mill and machinery. So much for resting in peace. Here, everlasting life is everlasting overtime.

TOP ATTRACTIONS

THE ELECTRIC CITY—You might not have much time off to enjoy sight-seeing in Hadestown, but at least this isn't a dim, gloomy underworld. In what was once a simple gold mine, Hades has opened a steel foundry fed by the fossils of dead things to turn out oil drums and automobiles. It's boiling hot, but also "brighter than a carnival" because Hades has installed electricity: not just lights but blinking neon and movie and TV screens.

THE CHROMIUM THRONE—Hades is no longer the lovestruck young god who first spied Persephone picking flowers in her mother's garden so many years ago. If you manage to get away from the factory or ware-house long enough to spot the King of Shadows and Shades, don't be surprised to find a growly baritone brooding on his throne. Time has corrupted him into an underworld plutocrat, obsessed with his own wealth and terrified of losing all the souls and labor he's hoarded.

THE WALL—This monumental landmark is the most impressive sight in the domain of Hades, who is also the King of Mortar, the King of Bricks. The river Styx is now a river of stones and steel: a massive million-ton wall of iron, concrete, and razor wire. Ferocious hounds guard the gates. Why a giant wall on his borders? Mr. Hades claims, in the tones of Trump-like propaganda, that the wall keeps freedom in and poverty out. Even in hell, people need to believe there's someone worse off than they are.

> **TRAVEL TRIVIA**
> The wall has only been breached once. Orpheus got past by singing so beautifully that its stones were literally moved.

EATING AND DRINKING

THE ROAD TO HELL—If Hermes allows, stop in the railway station sa-loon for a last meal before your train leaves for "the underside." You might even brush elbows with some celebrities. Every spring, Persephone steps onto this platform after six months in darkness, finally able to enter the sun and resume her role as Queen of the Green and Growing Earth. She'll spend the summer riotously living it up free as a honeybee and drinking dandelion wine. (She might also turn to the harder stuff, even morphine, as summer draws to a close. Persephone doesn't like herself very much.) If you arrive in the quieter winter months, take a close look at the young-sters waiting tables. One of them might be a young, gifted poet named Orpheus.

OUR LADY OF THE UNDERGROUND—Once you've entered the gates of Hadestown, your refreshment options are a lot more limited. During the winter, see if Persephone's chambers are unlocked. She can supply you with the memories of life "up top" that you miss the most: spring flowers, the wind in a jar, the rain on tap.

GETTING AROUND

Most travelers arrive at Hadestown via the convenient train service. There's another way in that doesn't involve giving up your soul, but it's a long, dark journey along the telephone poles and railway track. That's the road Orpheus traveled in search of his beloved Eurydice, while Hades was busy seducing her in his private office. If you somehow get into Hadestown without signing away your life, don't tell any of the workers your name or even look them in the eye. They'll absorb your breath and essence without even noticing and then you'll be stuck down in the dark forever with that bunch of stiffs.

That's Hadestown, Jake.

THE HEAVISIDE LAYER

Cats

The first thing you have to understand is that the annual Jellicle Ball is where Old Deuteronomy decides which cat will ascend to rebirth in the Heaviside Layer. No, wait. The first thing you have to understand is that Old Deuteronomy is the wise patriarch of the Jellicle cats, who . . . no, hold on. The first thing you have to understand is there is apparently a tribe of small, cheerful cats called Jellicle cats, who can dive through the air like a flying trapeze, turn double somersaults, walk on a wire, and sing at the same time in more than one key. None of this will make any sense to someone who hasn't seen the musical *Cats*. But if it's any consolation, none of this makes any sense to people who *have* seen the musical *Cats* either.

To astronomers, the Heaviside Layer is a zone of ionized gas orbiting the Earth at a distance of about sixty miles. It makes long-distance radio communication possible. But to composer Andrew Lloyd Webber, the Heaviside Layer is a metaphysical realm, the unspecified heaven to which his "Jellicle cats" aspire.

Webber adapted *Cats* from the poetry of T. S. Eliot, who, while finishing a children's anthology called *Old Possum's Book of Practical Cats*, once wrote to a friend that his feline characters might eventually ascend in a balloon "up up up past the Russell Hotel" (the London hotel across from which Eliot's office was located) to the Heaviside Layer.

Lacking a real dramatic arc in Eliot's anthology of nonsense cat poems, Webber pounced on this scribbled notion of a "Heaviside Layer" to create a whole Jellicle mythology. Once a year, when the Jellicle moon shines down, all the Jellicles are invited to the Jellicle Ball, where they introduce themselves through song and dance. Just before dawn, the leader of their tribe, an ancient cat named Old Deuteronomy, announces the "Jellicle choice." One of his company will be chosen to leave this life and ascend to the Heaviside Layer. Onstage, this ascension is often accomplished via a giant tractor tire, which rises to the rafters like a flying saucer.

LEARN THE LANGUAGE

What does "Jellicle" mean exactly? Who knows. Apparently some kind of bipedal cat with a job and a bodysuit.

What awaits that lucky Jellicle in the Heaviside Layer? It's difficult to say. We know that every cat wants to go there and see its wonders—presumably alone, since only one Jellicle ascends every year. But if you are ever lucky enough to glimpse the Heaviside Layer, you might not stay long. The cats believe that the Jellicle choice's destiny is to "come back to a different Jellicle life." Presumably that's on earth, since Old Deuteronomy is said to have lived "many lives in succession." You might be right back in the junkyard arching your back weirdly and singing songs about trains and magicians in no time!

HUIS CLOS

No Exit

In 1944, Jean-Paul Sartre's one-act play *No Exit* (in French, *Huis Clos*, meaning "Behind Closed Doors") opened in Nazi-occupied Paris. The play's short running time was a legal necessity: audiences had to get home before the German curfew. But in just ninety minutes or so, Sartre sketches out a chilling vision of a self-service hell, where the damned are also the torturers.

Sartre's hell is an endless series of drawing rooms, linked by passages and stairs. As you are shown to your room, you will probably ask the not-very-helpful valet the same questions everyone does: Where are the torture chambers? Why no mirrors and windows—in fact, no reflective surfaces at all? Where are my personal effects? (Ladies get to keep their handbags, but without a compact or a toothbrush to be found inside.) There are no beds or light switches, you will discover, because the electric lights stay on all the time. No one, including the valet, ever closes their eyes to sleep—or even blinks.

NO-FRILLS ACCOMMODATIONS

Temper your expectations of a luxury stay here. Each room has a door, but it usually won't open. There is a bellpull, but it often doesn't work. The décor will match your period but not your taste. Sartre's three protagonists, for example, get a room with elaborately upholstered Second Empire furniture (one sofa in blue, one in wine red, and the third in a livid green) and a hideous Ferdinand Barbedienne bronze on the mantelpiece.

The longer you stay, you and the other deceased ("absentees" is the preferred euphemism) will notice that your room is uncomfortably warm. You will be able to "watch" life continuing on earth in your mind's eye, but not for long. Strangely enough, time passes more quickly in hell than it does for the living, so glimpses of your postmortem days and even months (your funeral, your family and colleagues discussing you) whiz by during your first hours in hell. When people on earth stop thinking about you, as they soon will, your video feed ends.

The drawing room in Sartre's play houses three "absentees": Joseph Garcin, a journalist from Rio de Janeiro; Estelle Rigault, a Paris society lady; and Inez Serrano, a poor post office clerk. Though no one is specifically told, upon entering hell, why their soul was damned, it turns out that each of these three utterly deserves their fate. Garcin cruelly paraded his mistress before his sensitive wife for years, and when war broke out he tried to desert the army with a cowardly escape to Mexico. Estelle's lover killed himself when she drowned their illegitimate baby girl in a Swiss lake, and Inez's affair with her own cousin's wife led *both* spouses to commit suicide.

The three realize quickly that their room is effectively a prison where they will learn to despise one another, but their attempts to just leave each other alone are complete failures. Whatever algorithm is used in hell to assign roommates must be the same one university residence halls use, because these three are perfectly wrong for each other. Garcin and Inez each have utter contempt for the moral cowardice of the other, while Estelle's shallow self-absorption annoys everyone. Despite this, Inez is immediately attracted to Estelle, but Estelle only wants Garcin. Things get so heated that Inez tries to stab Estelle with the letter opener from the mantel, but to no avail. There is no death in hell.

"We were told about the torture-chambers, the fire and brimstone," laughs Garcin. "Old wives' tales! There's no need for red-hot pokers. Hell is—other people!"

ROCK AND ROLL HEAVEN
The Righteous Brothers

The possibility of mingling with celebrities is one of the biggest draws of the world to come, but you should bear in mind that most celebrities are awful people and will probably not be assigned to the same eternal destiny you would otherwise choose. The Righteous Brothers didn't agree, however. Their last big hit describes a heaven where the *only* named residents are celebs: the biggest stars in popular music.

"Rock and Roll Heaven" actually began life in 1973 as a song written by Johnny Stevenson and Alan O'Day (whose big hit was "Undercover Angel") and recorded by the band Climax (whose big hit was "Precious and Few"). The original song imagined a combo of 1960s music legends gone too soon—Jimi Hendrix, Janis Joplin, Otis Redding, and Jim Morrison—jamming together in heaven. The second verse resurrected Buddy Holly and Ritchie Valens from the cornfields of their 1959 Iowa plane crash and had them join the band.

When the Righteous Brothers scored a comeback hit in 1974 by turning the song into one of their signature slices of melodramatic blue-eyed soul, they replaced the "Day the Music Died" verse with one about two more recent rock deaths: Jim Croce and Bobby Darin. As a result, the combo you'll hear perform in "Rock and Roll Heaven," though they're described as "a hell of a band," will certainly be a strange live act: six lead singers and/or guitarists of wildly different musical styles, backed by no rhythm section at all. Maybe heaven will provide a house band of angels to accompany them?

Almost two decades later, the Righteous Brothers updated the song as

"Rock and Roll Heaven '92," unveiling a new ten-person band of more recent inductees, including Elvis, John Lennon, Marvin Gaye, and the Beach
Boys' Dennis Wilson. Finally! A drummer!

MEET THE LOCALS
It's not clear who's in the crowd in Rock and Roll Heaven—other, lesser
dead musicians? Angel groupies? Deceased fans who won some kind
of call-in contest? Is Rock and Roll Heaven a subdivision of regular
heaven or its own discrete "artists only" world? The song stubbornly
resists theological inquiry.

It's at least possible that Rock and Roll Heaven is less selective than it
first appears. The bridge of the song suggests that "there's a spotlight waiting" for you there as well, because "everyone's a star," raising the horrifying
possibility that Rock and Roll Heaven is actually some kind of karaoke
stage. If that's true, don't miss the chance to jam with your heroes. Take
over at the mic and make Jim Morrison switch to tambourine or something.

Please note that even the Righteous Brothers themselves don't seem
convinced about their vision of the next world. "*If* there's a rock and roll
heaven," they sing in the conditional mood. They are positing a hypothetical afterlife, not promising one. But half of the Righteous Brothers presumably knows for sure now, tenor Bobby Hatfield having passed away in
2003. If Rock and Roll Heaven is still an all-oldies affair, maybe he's on the
bill now as a solo act.

You'll Never Walk Alone

UP THERE
Carousel

Ferenc Molnár's play *Liliom* was not an immediate hit when it debuted on the Budapest stage in 1909. And maybe that's to be expected of a romantic "comedy" with such an unlikely title character. Liliom is a raffish ex–carnival barker who drinks, gambles, beats his wife, and eventually kills himself after an armed robbery gone wrong. What's even stranger is that *Liliom* is best known today as the basis for the Rodgers and Hammerstein musical *Carousel*. That's right! Those two masters of Broadway sentiment had one of their biggest hits with a play in which a raffish ex–carnival barker drinks, gambles, beats his wife, and eventually kills himself after an armed robbery gone wrong.

But death isn't the end of the story for *Carousel*'s Billy Bigelow. In the afterlife, he's given one final chance at a good deed, as so often happens in fiction. And, unlike his Hungarian counterpart in *Liliom*, Billy takes the chance.

If you venture "Up There," as the afterlife is called in *Liliom* and *Carousel*, you'll be met at the moment of your death by a pair of Heavenly Friends who call each other "Brother," possibly using the annoying New England accent that the whole cast of *Carousel* has. They'll conduct you up into the clouds, and don't be surprised if the first thing you see Up There is a clothesline. You've arrived in heaven's backyard, off the familiar tourist track. Up front are the pearly gates; the back gate is just mother-of-pearl.

This rear gate is staffed by the Starkeeper, a genial fellow with a notebook who may be perched on a shimmering silver stepladder, pinning freshly laundered stars to heaven's infinite clothesline. (Once stars are dry, the Heavenly Friends are charged with hanging them in the night sky.) He'll likely remind you of some benevolent old man you knew in life, like a minister or a country doctor. If you have unfinished business on earth, the Starkeeper will let you return for a day—and maybe accomplish the good deed that can get you inside the mother-of-pearly gates. But don't dawdle! Every minute in heaven is a year on earth, and once everyone who knew you in life passes on, it will be too late to go back.

If you want one last day among the living, look down through the gauzy clouds and wait. The power to see what's happening down there will come to you gradually. Once you've returned to earth, the living can see you whenever you want them to. As you scope out a good deed that needs doing, remember: they're rooting for you Up There, looking for any excuse to let you in. In the case of Billy from *Carousel*, just whispering to someone that they are loved is enough to save his soul. Liliom, on the other hand, can't bring himself to change anything, even after sixteen years of "purification" in heaven. He's just a bum. No wonder Rodgers and Hammerstein changed the ending.

BEST TO AVOID

The Up There of *Carousel* is an American-style backyard—a much better option than the rigid Prussian vibe of the original *Liliom* version. In *Liliom*, Up There is more like a police court, complete with a phalanx of alabaster-skinned guards dressed all in black, with heavy walking sticks. The stern, bearded magistrate might still allow you one more day on earth, to complete "affairs of the soul," but he's a real hard-ass who might sentence you to years of "purification by fire" before you're deemed ready to head back and attempt your good deed.

MISCELLANEOUS

THE BANQUET

The Allegory of the Long Spoons

Some versions of the afterlife are so appealing that they transcend geography or culture. The "allegory of the long spoons," for example, is variously claimed to be a Jewish, Christian, Muslim, Hindu, or Buddhist tale. In 1935, the Jewish folklorist Alter Druyanov attributed the allegory to Rabbi Chaim of Rumshishok, an itinerant preacher who supposedly told the story as he wandered nineteenth-century Lithuania. But Rabbi Chaim probably adapted an even older folktale, about a miserly host outwitted by his hungry guests. The roots of it seem to go all the way back to Aesop.

Today the story may vary slightly depending on where it is being told. If it's presented as a medieval Christian parable, the departed are eating stew. In the Chinese or Vietnamese telling, they are holding chopsticks. But the basic outline is always the same.

In this afterlife, you are taken to hell, where rows and rows of tables are set with magnificent food. But the food is untouched. All the guests, young and old, sit emaciated and groaning with hunger. Why? Check out the spoons. They have such bizarrely long handles that the dead can't lift any food into their mouths. (In some versions, the utensils are normally sized, but the guests have had their arms splinted so they can't bend their elbows toward their lips.)

This, then, is hell: to be tantalized by the most sumptuous luxuries but unable to partake. And what is heaven? you ask. The layout there is the same: the same tables, the same diners, the same dishes, even the same long spoons. But in heaven, no one goes hungry. *They have learned to feed each other.*

The lesson, of course, is that the quality of heaven or hell or any other place depends only on the character of its people. There are no flames or tortures in hell, because the tenants are bad enough. But now that you, a savvy traveler, know the secret, could you outwit Satan's utensil-based torment by borrowing heaven's strategy? Eat all you want in hell with one weird trick! Demons hate him!

Not according to Rabbi Chaim. When, in his vision, he saw how the souls in heaven fed each other, he raced back to hell to try to help the starving. "Use your spoon to feed your neighbor," he pleads with one man, "and he will surely return the favor and feed you."

"You expect me to feed the detestable man sitting across the table?" says the damned man. "I would rather starve than give him the pleasure of eating!"

THE DJALIA

Marvel Comics

When journalist Ta-Nehisi Coates took over writing the *Black Panther* comic book for Marvel in 2016, he inherited a Wakanda where King T'Challa, the Black Panther, had recently returned and retaken the throne. T'Challa's sister, Shuri, however, was dead—killed in battle with the minions of Thanos. Coates promptly reintroduced Shuri, whose spirit was revealed to be wandering a new Wakandan afterlife called the Djalia.

If you journey to the Djalia after your death, you'll find yourself in a lush African landscape of savannas and forests, dotted with abandoned villages and the ruins of great cities. Take some time to gawk at the great pinnacles of red rock curving skyward, like the fingers of some primordial giant.

The only way to see the Djalia is a guided tour. You'll be met upon arrival by a trusted loved one, like your mother, but you'll realize instantly that that's not *really* your mother. She's all your mothers, a collective ancestor of your people. This is a griot spirit, a storyteller and caretaker of African history. On this "plane of Wakandan memory," you'll walk through the centuries together as your guide arms you with the power of memory and ancestral song.

Nightlife here is all about storytelling around the campfire, but by day, the Djalia is an outdoor adventure paradise. Follow your griot's lead and dress for action in a white martial-arts outfit, because things can get intense. Adrenaline junkies can spend their days scaling cliffs, flying through the sky on winged panthers, or even sparring with their quarterstaffwielding spirit guide. This is a superhero universe, after all. Even a talky Ta-Nehisi Coates comic book needs *some* fight scenes.

LOCAL CUSTOMS

Not sure which Wakandan tales to request from your storyteller? You can't go wrong with the classics: the people of Adowa, who refused to be conquered; the people of Nri, who could fly; or the people of Bako with their unbreakable skins of stone. Your griot's stories can cover just about any time period, from the distant past (the prehuman Originators, the first inhabitants of Wakanda) to recent years (your own parents' courtship).

THE EIGHTH UNDERWORLD

Grim Fandango

In video games, the afterlife is typically a perfunctory affair: a brief stop-over after a violent end, followed quickly by a return to gameplay as a sadder-but-wiser player character. But gamers do have a few more elaborate options, ranging from the demon-filled hell of the *Doom* series to the beer-soaked college town of the 2019 indie *Afterparty*. The most memorable video game Land of the Dead is found in LucasArts' 1998 *Grim Fandango*—a commercial flop that helped tank the entire adventure game market for over a decade but is today recognized as a cult classic and a masterpiece of the genre.

Grim Fandango takes place in the Eighth Underworld, a massive continent that separates the newly dead from their eventual destiny, eternal rest. If this is your afterlife, you'll be awoken after death by a black-robed reaper with a scythe. But here, this familiar psychopomp is also a salesman. The Department of Death sends these agents to show the dead their travel options. If you were truly saintly in life, why not splurge? Treat yourself to an upgrade: deluxe direct passage via sports car, zeppelin, or luxury cruise to your final destination. But if you lived a more pedestrian life, you'll begin the afterlife as a literal pedestrian. Your travel agent might hand you a walking stick and tell you to start your journey on foot—or even pack you up in a casket and mail you across the Land of the Dead as freight.

The unaccelerated journey of the soul through this strange land will take you up to four years, but the silver lining is that there's a lot to see along the way. You and the other skeleton-people form a vast society.

Some linger here for pleasure; others stay because they've decided that eternal rest doesn't even exist. Many of these lost souls wash up in Rubacava, a foggy port city on the Sea of Lament. Pause here to enjoy the salty air and the gaming that has poured in with big-city underworld money. It doesn't get any better than the giant cat races at Maximino's track or the plush High Rollers' Lounges at the many casinos.

Outside Rubacava, endless excursions are available, but not all are safe. In the petrified forests nearby, the stone marrow of the ornately tendriled trees is harvested to make cement, but keep an eye out for the nightmarish local fauna, including winged spiders and the fire beavers that build bone dams on the rivers of tar. The city of El Marrow is a gleaming metropolis that mixes pre-Columbian architecture with Art Deco chrome, but it's also controlled by mysterious gangsters. You may cross the Sea of Lament in an ocean liner topped with a massive Mesoamerican pyramid, but beware "the Pearl," a gleaming undersea light that lures unwary passengers into jumping overboard.

Why worry about these menaces if you're already dead? Because an even more dire fate awaits those who die a second death in the Eighth Underworld. They'll be "sprouted," with flowers, grass, and roots writhing through their poor bones. This floral arrangement is as disturbing a spectacle to the dead as any gory corpse was in the land of the living. Some criminal elements here have even learned to package garden seeds into firearms, using a fatal quick-growth concoction called "sproutella."

Your final destination is a stone temple in the snowy mountains of the far north, where a bullet-nosed express train called the Number Nine departs regularly to the Land of Eternal Rest. Settle into your seat on the ol' "Double-N" and enjoy your transit to the *Ninth* Underworld, where neither gangster nor sproutella doth corrupt.

TRAVELER BEWARE!
With all the sexy, noirish crime in this Land of the Dead, you shouldn't be surprised to find a lively black market in underworld travel packages. Make sure your "Double-N" ticket is the genuine article by buying from trusted sellers only. A real ticket will be magically drawn to you, as if wafted on a breeze. Those who accept counterfeit tickets on the Double-N sometimes see their locomotive transform into a monstrous demon and plunge them into a fiery inferno below.

THE HATLO INFERNO

They'll Do It Every Time

Newspaper comics are, by and large, not known for their imaginative settings. Occasionally Prince Valiant will venture as far away as, say, Saxony, but for the most part, these strips have been set in the same dull spots for almost a century: family kitchens, suburban backyards, Apartment 3-G. It's a medium for slices of life, not flights of fancy.

But there was once a comic strip set in the afterlife. San Francisco cartoonist Jimmy Hatlo was a household name for his gag panel *They'll Do It Every Time*, which he drew from 1929 to his death in 1963. *They'll Do It Every Time* was a communal bitch-fest about midcentury life's little frustrations: the lady in front of you at the movies who won't take off her tall hat, the waiter who waits until your mouth is full to ask how your food is. But apart from being called out in the newspaper, none of the pests in *They'll Do It Every Time* ever received any comeuppance. They just went about their day, slowing down supermarket checkouts and failing to use their turn signals. Maddening!

Perhaps that's what inspired Hatlo to create a variation on his hit theme. From 1953 to 1958, the color Sunday version of *They'll Do It Every Time* was occasionally accompanied by the only newspaper comic ever set in hell, *The Hatlo Inferno*. Here Hatlo poked fun at the same familiar human foibles—but this time, he punished the malefactors responsible. "Get set to howl with Hatlo as America's funniest cartoonist roasts the dizzy characters you'd most like to see in Hades!" promised King Features Syndicate.

This Inferno is a familiar waste of volcanoes and sulfurous fumes. Should you wind up there in the next life, you'll be tormented by an army of horned red devils—a burly blue-collar crew with mustaches and cov-eralls. Just like Dante, Hatlo divided his underworld into different levels for various sins. But instead of being tortured for lust or envy, you'll face the music for being a run-of-the-mill "erk-jay," as Hatlo put it, in every-day life. Splashing pedestrians with mud puddles, heckling comedians, smacking sunburned people on the back—each punished at last in its own circle of hell.

Occasionally your punishment will be puzzlingly generic (people who spoiled the ends of mysteries get fried on a big griddle), but in most cases, devils will trot out some Dr. Seussian contraption specially designed to give you an ironic taste of your own medicine. If you were a door-slammer, you're manacled to a wall while doors on giant springs are pulled back and rammed into you. If you dropped gum on the sidewalk, you'll slog through a gooey gum mire for two and a half million miles. If you ever annoyed neighbors by mowing your lawn at six a.m., you and your fellow sinners are crammed into a fissure at ground level so devils can walk over your faces pushing a lawn mower. These horrific tableaux somehow passed as family entertainment in the mid-1950s.

You'll notice immediately that these punishments may fit the crime, but they're hideously disproportionate. Do you really deserve to be chained to a deafening pipe organ for all eternity just for whistling sometimes at the office? Should you really have a compressed-air tube jammed down your throat that inflates you into a spherical balloon just because you liked to open the window on the train? Jimmy Hatlo is not a merciful god.

What a Long, Strange Triptych

HELLSCAPES

Hieronymus Bosch

Renaissance art is an endless museum gallery of pious subjects: prim virgins, Israelites dressed like medieval peasants, baby angels with hands pressed together in prayer, doe-eyed saints being martyred. *Except*, that is, for the work of the Dutch visionary Hieronymus Bosch. He was painting surreal, macabre heavy metal album covers on giant palace triptychs when oil paint was still a brand-new invention.

Bosch's most famous visions of hell are panels from his monumental masterpieces *The Garden of Earthly Delights* and *The Last Judgment*. Both works begin, at left, with a traditional biblical scene: the Garden of Eden. But for Bosch, paradise is clearly just an excuse. He wants to get that out of the way so he can spend weeks lovingly detailing the bizarre agonies of hell.

As you enter Bosch's underworld, you'll immediately notice that it's dark and surprisingly cold, cold enough to ice-skate on its rivers. In the distance, refugees flee from burning cities, and ignorant armies clash by night. But you'll be more concerned with what's going on all around you: countless dead humans, all nude and helpless, being tormented by a menagerie of nightmare creatures.

You're going to see it all. Sinners stewing in cauldrons and grinding other sinners with millstones. A pack of lizard hounds tearing out a knight's entrails. A giant pair of ears brandishing a blade and trampling the damned as it scuttles over the rocks. A black beetle-winged ghoul bending a man over a spiked metal wheel. A platypus-headed archer carrying its impaled victim home upside down. A dragon roasting a man drowning in a barrel of frogs. This hell certainly isn't understaffed—there might be more demons on duty than sinners! Demons must have been more fun to paint, with their mismatched ibis beaks and puppy heads and fish scales and deer hooves. Many seem to be all head and legs, with nothing in between. Apparently Bosch hated torsos.

Any sensual pleasure you enjoyed in life will be turned on you here. You liked music? Well, maybe you'll be strung up on a harp-shaped gallows, or crushed by a giant lute, or imprisoned in a drum, or forced to play the flute with your butt in a hellish orchestra where the sheet music has been tattooed onto a different butt. The butt of a guy who got crushed by a giant lute.

By the same token, gamblers are impaled with knives to their own gaming tables, while gluttons are crammed into frying pans or rotisseried on spits. Drunkards are stuffed into a giant wine barrel and squeezed into liquid that gets lapped up by other drunkards, who defecate still *more* liquid. The lustful are groped by demons while being forced to watch these affronts in another demon's reflective butt-mirror. (Bosch may have hated torsos, but he believed—correctly—that butts are very funny.)

Religious hypocrisy doesn't get off lightly either, which seems like a pretty edgy take for the fifteenth century. Look for the sinner cowering inside a giant lantern, naked except for his bishop's miter. Another man is being seduced by a pig wearing the wimple of a Dominican nun—she's trying to get him to buy his way into heaven by leaving all his worldly goods to the church. Apparently it didn't work.

MEET THE LOCALS

It's worth braving the crowds to catch a glimpse of the prince of this hell, a blue, bird-headed monstrosity with a crooked cauldron for his counterfeit crown and a toilet for a throne. He devours sinners and then excretes them from his nether regions in a weird indigo bubble. Then look for the enigmatic "Tree Man" looming above. He's a pale legless giant with tree stumps for arms, boats for shoes, and a giant phallic bagpipe on his white platter of a hat. Inside his broken-eggshell body is a tavern where the damned sit joylessly. His face, some scholars believe, is a self-portrait of Bosch himself.

The air of invention and whimsy in Bosch's hellscapes is striking, with all its oversized kitchenware and songbird-headed demons and odd things going into or coming out of people's bottoms—though candy-colored touches like these will likely provide little cheer for the damned themselves. The great Spanish poet Quevedo once imagined himself chatting with the devil about the way hell is depicted by writers and artists. "A little while ago," says Satan, "Hieronymus Bosch was here and when asked why he had made such a hotch-potch of us in his dreams, he replied: because I had never believed that devils were real." You, unfortunately, will have no such luxury.

THE INFERNO ROOM

Mr. Toad's Wild Ride

No one boarding a kiddie theme park attraction expects to plunge into a vivid, steamy vision of Hades where they will suffer along with the damned. But that's exactly what has awaited passengers on one disturbing "dark ride" for over sixty years. And what haunted Bradbury-esque carnival midway conceals this horror? Try Disneyland in sunny Anaheim, California. You know, "the Happiest Place on Earth."

Kenneth Grahame's 1908 children's classic *The Wind in the Willows* is a bucolic idyll of disappearing English country life, set in a strange world where anthropomorphized animals and Edwardian humans interact. Subsequent interpreters, from A. A. Milne to Walt Disney to Monty Python, have mostly jettisoned all the gentle nostalgia—Mole and Rat packing picnics and puttering about in boats and so on—to focus more tightly on Grahame's most inspired creation: the irrepressible Mr. Toad. Toad is an amphibian Falstaff, the village squire who's forever blowing his vast wealth on naughty, faddish indulgences like horse-drawn caravans and motorcars.

Disney's 1949 cartoon adaptation of *The Wind in the Willows* is a footnote in the studio's history today, but it was just a few years old when Disneyland opened in 1955, making it an obvious choice for one of the "spook house"–style attractions of Fantasyland. Mr. Toad's Wild Ride is one of the few original rides that survive in the park to this day. Riders play the part of J. Thaddeus Toad by boarding tiny automobiles and recklessly zipping around the corridors of Toad Hall and the English countryside, eventually landing—like Toad in the novel and film—in court and then prison.

In Grahame's book and the Disney cartoon, Toad escapes from his cell, retakes Toad Hall, and lives happily ever after. But not so for the millions of tourists who retrace his steps in Anaheim! In a surprisingly dark twist, the puckish Disney "Imagineers" who designed the ride decided to end it by killing off Toad (that is, you) in a sudden head-on collision with a train.

In this afterlife, you will motor into a place Disney staffers call "the Inferno Room," the word "hell" being verboten at the Happiest Place on Earth. But make no mistake: this is truly hell. The temperature rises abruptly as you pass through the fanged jaws of a grinning stone devil, and your glasses may fog up. You will enter a subterranean cavern complete with all the traditional sights: stalactites, stalagmites, glowing fires, and little bouncing demons.

The ride's jaunty tune, "The Merrily Song," will continue playing while ominous laughter announces the return of the bewigged judge from earlier in the ride, this time with horns, claws, and bat's wings. His pointing finger will sentence you to your doom, and a wheezing green dragon will aim its fiery maw in your direction. That's it; that's the end of the ride. You suffer forever for your bad road etiquette, Mr. Toad. Should have observed posted speed limits and used your turn signal!

GOD GUIDE

The Wind in the Willows' theology is a bit different in the original novel. In chapter 7, the animals do encounter a frightening, horned figure with a beard and goatish hooves, but it's not Satan come to drag them down to hell. It's some kind of pagan woodland god, and they worship him. Musician Syd Barrett liked this chapter so much that he even named the first Pink Floyd album after it: *The Piper at the Gates of Dawn*.

THE LAND OF THE UNLIVING

DC Comics

Ancient Greeks and Egyptians could only aspire to a cosmology as complicated and confusing as the ones in superhero comics. The shared universe of DC Comics has been ordered and reordered countless times since *Action Comics* #1, featuring the debut of Superman, hit the stands in 1938.

With over eighty years of history dreamed up by literally thousands of writers and artists working on tight deadlines, the DC Comics theology doesn't make a *ton* of sense. There's a Judeo-Christian God, of course, sometimes called "the Presence," who rules over creation from the gleaming Silver City, surrounded by concourses of bloodless, sexless angels. One of these angels, Lucifer Morningstar, was exiled to hell, where his demons torture "damned souls" who don't realize they've subconsciously chosen this fate for themselves. At one point, the comic book Lucifer grew bored of hell, abdicated his dark throne, and opened a popular piano bar someplace almost as bad: Los Angeles.

But then there are also the Greek gods in *Wonder Woman* comics, including Hades in his underworld. There are Egyptian gods in *Shazam* and *Hawkman* comics, Hindu gods in *Deadman*, and nature elementals in *Swamp Thing*. There are Kryptonian gods and Atlantis gods and Martian gods and Jack Kirby's cosmic "New Gods."

As a result, when you die in the DC Universe, your journey comes with plenty of options. You will almost certainly be welcomed by an avatar of death. If you die in the "Fourth World" of the New Gods, it will probably be the Black Racer, a bizarre flying herald with a knight's helmet, a bright yellow cape, and red skis. Earthlings are more likely to see Death, one of the

"Endless" from Neil Gaiman's *Sandman* comics. She's a chipper, pale goth girl dressed all in black and wearing an ankh.

If you're less lucky, you might be greeted by Nekron, a cosmic force of evil. (Like a lot of cosmic forces in comics, he's an abstract concept with an oddly specific look: skeletal monster makeup and body armor.) Nekron rules the Land of the Unliving, where souls await judgment committing them to heaven or hell—but be warned that this isn't one of your more pleasant limbo scenarios. Nekron has been known to raise up the denizens of his realm into a zombie space army called the Black Lantern Corps.

What will your eventual destination be? Your fleshly essence will certainly return to "the Red," a surreal meat landscape well known to readers of *Animal Man* comics, and be reabsorbed into the eternal web of all animal life on earth. Your spirit will go on to one of many "neighborhoods, nations, worlds, and universes," to quote the mysterious hero called the Phantom Stranger. "There are, in fact, as many heavens as there are souls," the Stranger once told Batman, "each one tailored to the beliefs the souls held on earth." Reincarnation is an option as well. But your best bet might just be to hang on for a few years. Comic books are like daytime soaps: death is never permanent, and resurrection is always just one new writer away.

THE OUTER PLANES

Dungeons & Dragons

Make no mistake: Dungeons & Dragons characters may not really be alive, but they can certainly die. When your hit point score drops below zero in combat with a bugbear or an ochre jelly, and all your "death saving throws" fail, it's over. If your party has a cleric, bard, or paladin in tow, they can try a spell like Revivify or Resurrection to bring you back—but they're going to need a pretty big diamond. (Necromancy spells use diamonds, for some reason.)

If all else fails, you'll probably grab some dice and roll up a new character. But what happened to the spirit of your old character? Where did poor Klonkh, the half-orc male barbarian, go?

In D & D, your postmortal fate hinges on your "alignment"—your character's ethical outlook on life. This alignment is a combination of two factors. On the axis of rule-following, you can choose to be lawful, neutral, or chaotic, and on the axis of morality, you can choose to be good, neutral, or evil.

Dead souls travel to the Outer Planes, which lie beyond the physical and astral worlds in the Dungeons & Dragons "Great Wheel" cosmology. There they lose their memories and become "petitioners" to the deities they worshipped in life, because the Outer Planes are the province of gods and demons. There are seventeen different realms there. You can imagine them as a great ring surrounding the central Outlands, where characters of "true neutral" alignment wander.

The other sixteen Outer Planes metaphysically border one another. To consider your options, let's begin on the hellish side of the ring. "Chaotic evil" types who were cruel and selfish in life are sent to the demons of the 666 Infinite Layers of the Abyss. Adjacent realms, only slightly less inhospitable, are the vast cavern called the Windswept Depths of Pandemonium and the orbs of the Tarterian Depths of Carceri. "Neutral evil" petitioners wander the Gray Waste of Hades, while "lawful evil" types—your tyrants and mercenaries—will be at home with the endless conflict of the Internal Battlefield of Acheron, the warring devils and fire giants of the Nine Hells of Baator, or the floating volcanoes of the Black Eternity of Gehenna.

The "chaotic neutral" struggle with endless entropy in a shifting realm called the Ever-Changing Chaos of Limbo, while the "lawful neutral" march around the Clockwork Nirvana of Mechanus, home to geometric shapes and regiments of giant ants.

MAPPING YOUR JOURNEY

Note that these sixteen afterlife worlds, even though they border each other in a great wheel, are also somehow *each spatially infinite*. The Clockwork Nirvana of Mechanus, for example, is filled with an infinite number of giant interlocking gears, each over a thousand miles wide, all meshed at right angles and turning slowly in concert. *Gravity* here can be confusing, let alone navigation.

The "chaotic good"—people who did the right thing in life but used unconventional methods—dwell in the tall forests of Arborea, home to the gods of Olympus. Nearby are the wild shores and heroic struggles of Ysgard, as well as the Beastlands, happy hunting grounds where petitioners take on the pelts and traits of animals. It's heaven, but for furries. The "neutral good" enjoy the idyllic and colorful Blessed Fields of Elysium. Saintly souls of "lawful good" alignment may wind up in the bucolic meadows of the Twin Paradises of Bytopia or the tranquil, orderly Peaceable Kingdoms of Arcadia, where the Orb of Light spins between day and night. If you're one of the purest petitioners of all, you should set your sights on climbing Celestia, a mountain of seven layered heavens rising above a sea of holy water.

Dungeons & Dragons offers almost as broad a universe of afterlife options as life itself, with something for every taste. The only difference is that in D & D, your final destiny has nothing to do with morality, devotion, or predestination. As with so much else in life, it's all up to a roll of the dice.

BONUS
AFTERLIFE PLANNER

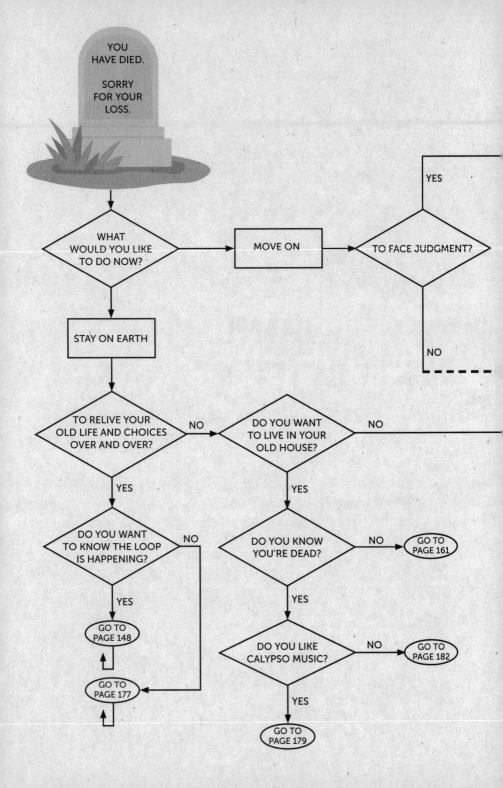

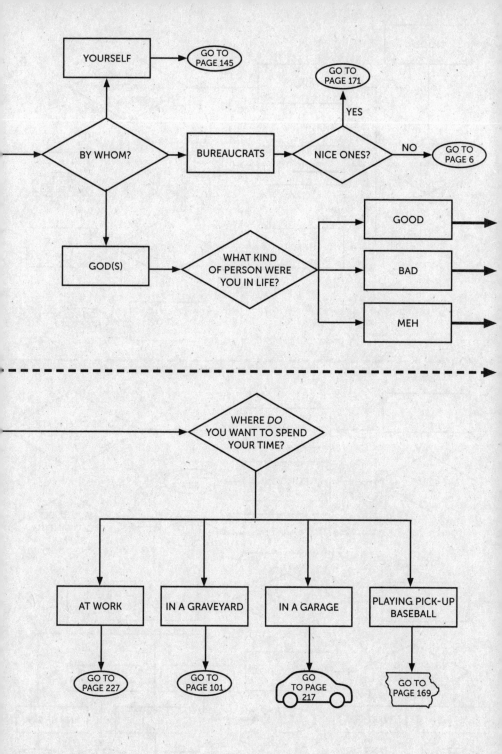

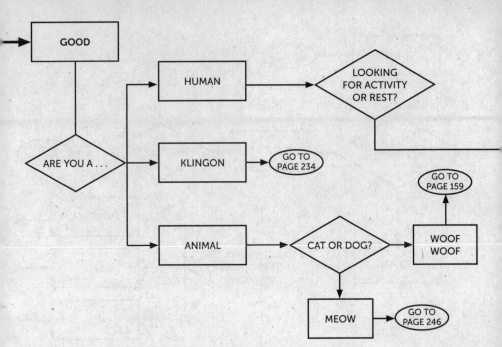

GOOD

ARE YOU A . . .
- HUMAN → LOOKING FOR ACTIVITY OR REST?
- KLINGON → GO TO PAGE 234
- ANIMAL → CAT OR DOG?
  - WOOF WOOF → GO TO PAGE 159
  - MEOW → GO TO PAGE 246

— NO —

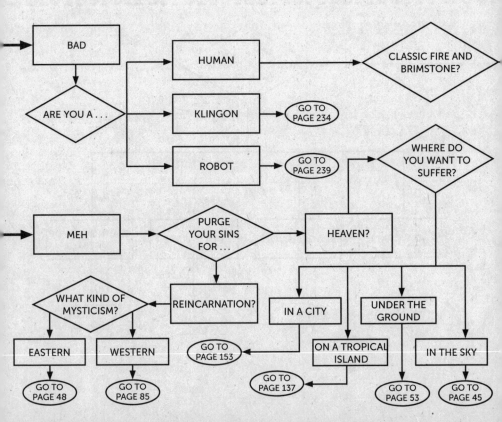

BAD

ARE YOU A . . .
- HUMAN → CLASSIC FIRE AND BRIMSTONE?
- KLINGON → GO TO PAGE 234
- ROBOT → GO TO PAGE 239

WHERE DO YOU WANT TO SUFFER?

MEH → PURGE YOUR SINS FOR . . .
- HEAVEN?
- REINCARNATION?

WHAT KIND OF MYSTICISM?
- EASTERN → GO TO PAGE 48
- WESTERN → GO TO PAGE 85

GO TO PAGE 153

IN A CITY

ON A TROPICAL ISLAND → GO TO PAGE 137

UNDER THE GROUND → GO TO PAGE 53

IN THE SKY → GO TO PAGE 45

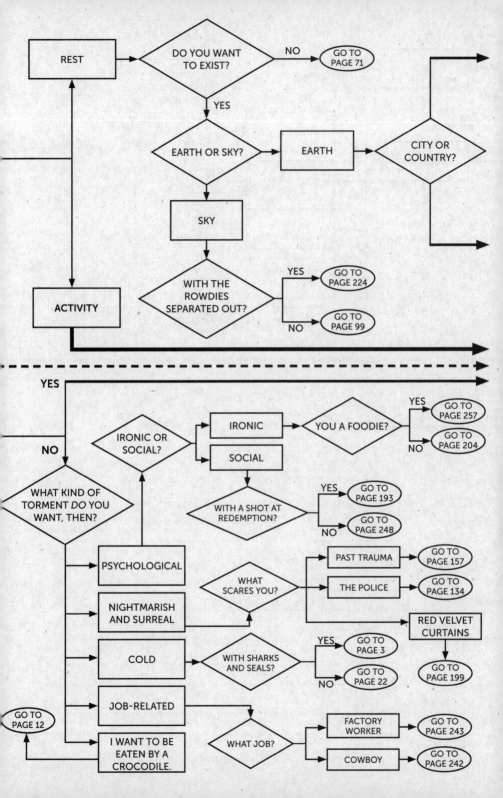

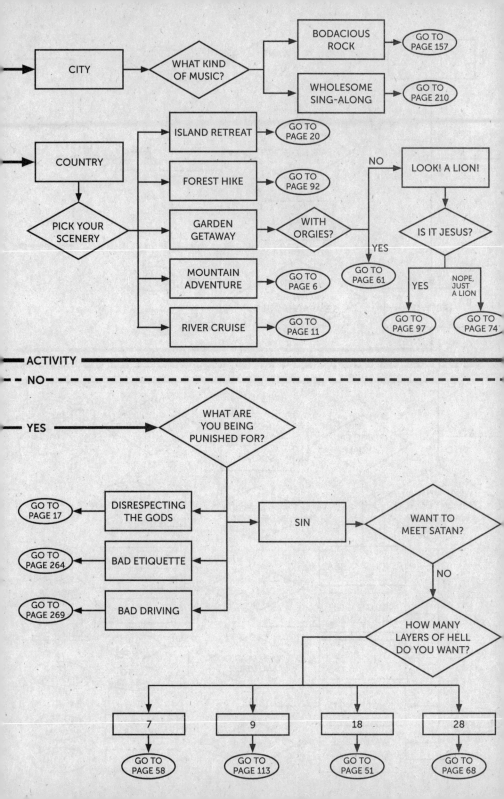

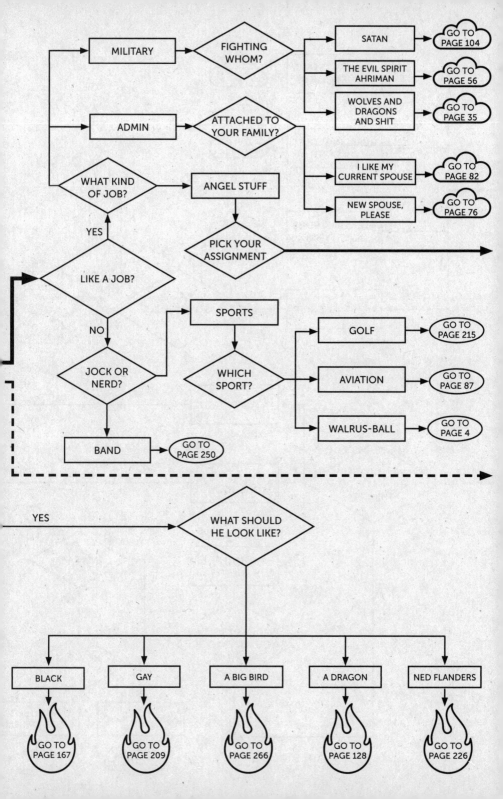

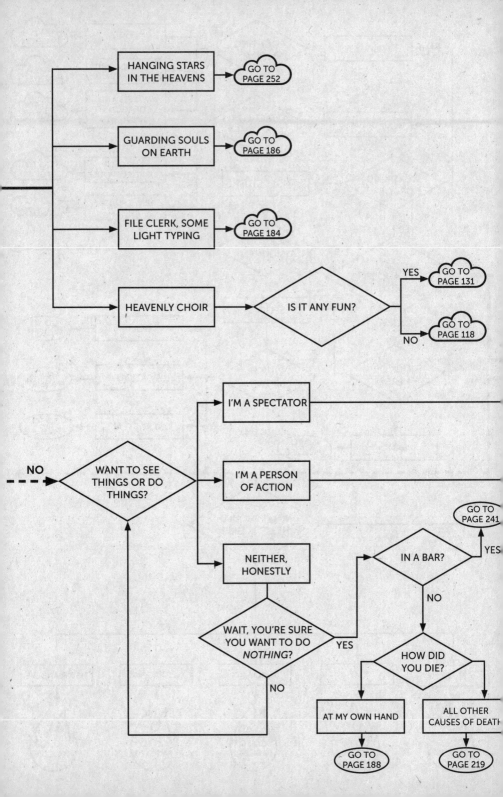

HANGING STARS IN THE HEAVENS → GO TO PAGE 252

GUARDING SOULS ON EARTH → GO TO PAGE 186

FILE CLERK, SOME LIGHT TYPING → GO TO PAGE 184

HEAVENLY CHOIR → IS IT ANY FUN?
- YES → GO TO PAGE 131
- NO → GO TO PAGE 118

NO ⇢ WANT TO SEE THINGS OR DO THINGS?

I'M A SPECTATOR

I'M A PERSON OF ACTION

NEITHER, HONESTLY → WAIT, YOU'RE SURE YOU WANT TO DO *NOTHING*?
- YES
- NO

IN A BAR?
- YES → GO TO PAGE 241
- NO

HOW DID YOU DIE?
- AT MY OWN HAND → GO TO PAGE 188
- ALL OTHER CAUSES OF DEATH → GO TO PAGE 219

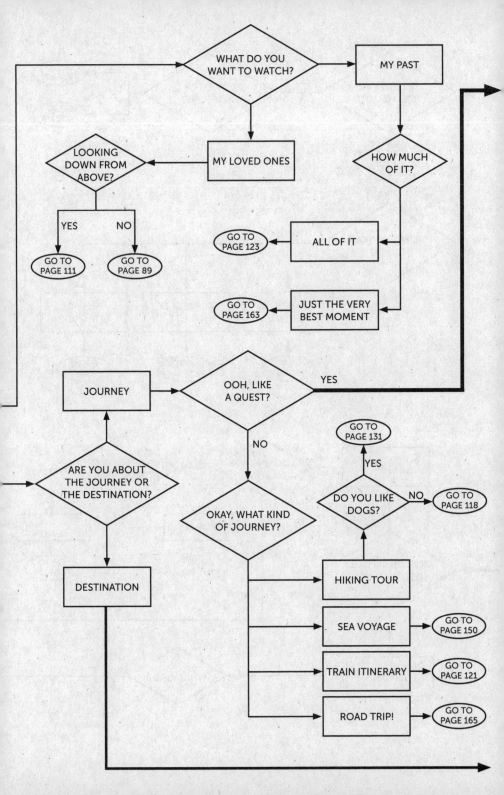

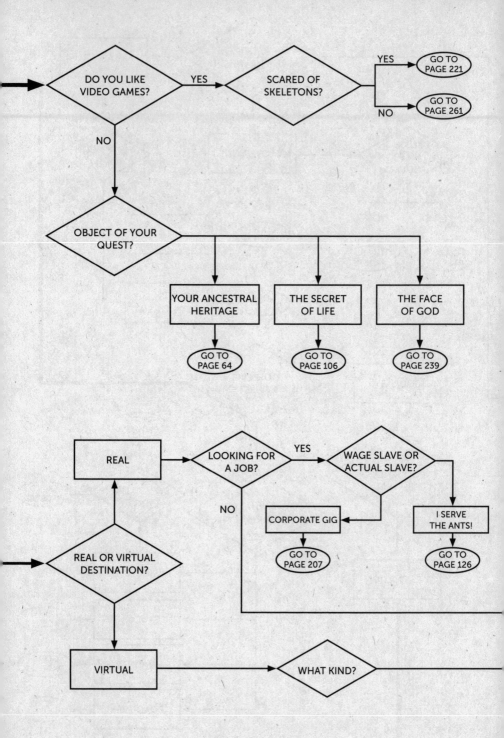

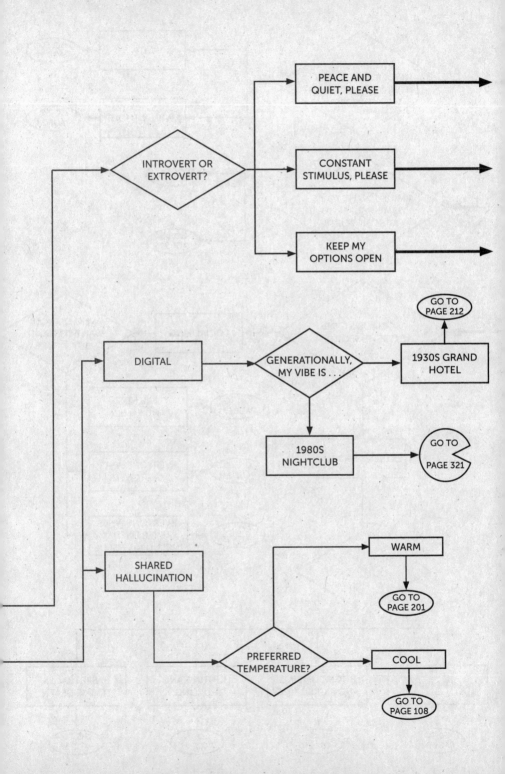

INTROVERT OR EXTROVERT?

PEACE AND QUIET, PLEASE →

CONSTANT STIMULUS, PLEASE →

KEEP MY OPTIONS OPEN →

DIGITAL → GENERATIONALLY, MY VIBE IS . . . → 1930S GRAND HOTEL → GO TO PAGE 212

1980S NIGHTCLUB → GO TO PAGE 321

SHARED HALLUCINATION

WARM → GO TO PAGE 201

PREFERRED TEMPERATURE? → COOL → GO TO PAGE 108

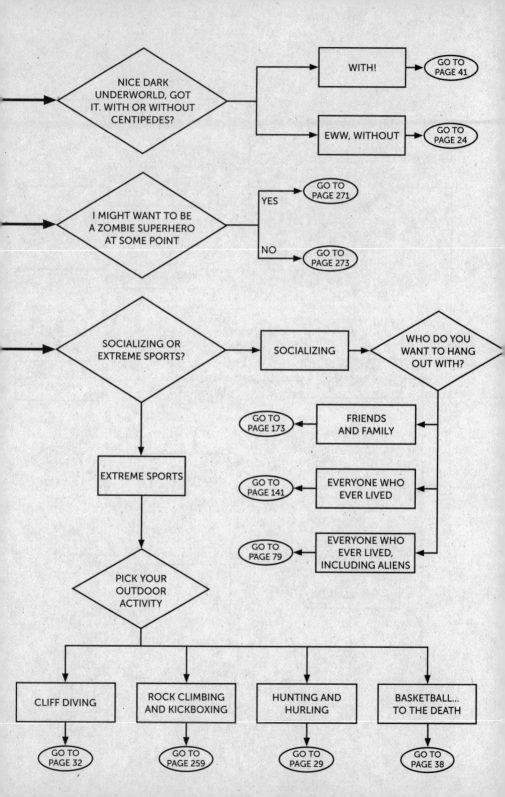

INDEX

Entry titles and their page numbers are in boldface.